DRUNK IN CHINA

DRUNK IN CHINA

Derek Sandhaus

Baijiu and the World's Oldest Drinking Culture

POTOMAC BOOKS | *An imprint of the University of Nebraska Press*

Library of Congress Cataloging-in-Publication Data
Names: Sandhaus, Derek, author.
Title: Drunk in China: Baijiu and the world's
oldest drinking culture / Derek Sandhaus.
Description: Lincoln: Potomac Books, an imprint
of the University of Nebraska Press, [2019] |
Includes bibliographical references and index.
Identifiers: LCCN 2019005300
ISBN 9781640120976 (cloth: alk. paper)
ISBN 9781640122598 (epub)
ISBN 9781640122604 (mobi)
ISBN 9781640122611 (pdf)
Subjects: LCSH: Alcoholic beverages—China. |
Drinking of alcoholic beverages—Social
aspects—China. | Liquors—China.
Classification: LCC TP590.6.C6 S26
2019 | DDC 394.1/30951—dc23
LC record available at
https://lccn.loc.gov/2019005300

Set in New Baskerville ITC by Mikala R. Kolander.
Designed by N. Putens.

To Catherine, for supporting my best and worst habits

O wine, who gave to thee thy subtle power?
A thousand cares in one small goblet drowned!
—*Du Fu, "Setting Sun"*

CONTENTS

ACKNOWLEDGMENTS

A great many people helped bring this book into existence. I owe a supreme debt to my Chinese teacher, friend, and sometimes researcher Duan Li. Your enthusiasm for this project, assistance with translations, and logistical support were invaluable. I hate to think of how this book would have turned out without you.

I would like to thank all the interviewees for taking the time to share their experiences and insights. To those who welcomed me into their businesses and homes or invited me to sit at their *baijiu* table, I am humbled by your kindness. I would also like to thank everyone who helped arrange factory visits and made travel arrangements.

To my fellow travelers—Todd, Alex, and Joel—I thank you and your livers. A hearty *ganbei* also to my friends and drinking companions in Chengdu: Grace, Johan, Walter, Eitan, Dan, Lu Jing, Peter, Will, Pope, Sherry, the other Dan, Daniel, and Soojin. To those who subjected themselves to the Shanghai trials, Jim Boyce and Jeannie Cho Lee in particular, your help was much appreciated.

I leaned heavily on the work of experts who know far more about drinks than I and who pointed me in the right direction when I needed it most. Zhong Jie, Zhong Yuchen, and Yang Chen all deserve a special thanks, as do Peter Kupfer, Patrick McGovern, and David Wondrich. Thanks go to my former Shanghai colleagues, foremost among them Jessica Lee, who shared her thoughts and extended family. Graham Earnshaw, Pete Sweeney, and Andrew Galbraith all shared drinks and ideas that found their way onto these pages. Authors Scott Seligman and David Leffman also provided sage counsel.

Every bartender who contributed a cocktail recipe to this book deserves my thanks and praise. Paul Mathew in particular has gone beyond the call of duty in supporting my work over the years and should be singled out for his commitment to promoting baijiu. Many thanks to earliest readers for their feedback, those already named but also especially Catherine and my mother. Future readers would also thank you if they could see the earliest drafts.

Finally, I want to thank the people who turned this book into a reality. My publisher, Potomac Books, particularly Tom Swanson and Abigail Stryker; my editors, Susan Silver and Ann Baker; and my agent, Peter Bernstein, who made sure my book found the right home. As for those brave souls who shared a baijiu with me along the way, there are too many to name, let alone remember. I am grateful to you all.

NOTES ON LANGUAGE

Jiu, pronounced "j'yo," is the Chinese word for alcoholic beverages. Thousands of years ago there were other Chinese words for alcohol, delineated by their ceremonial function and production techniques, but jiu won out. All Chinese alcohols are today known as jiu: *baijiu* ("white alcohol," for spirits), *huangjiu* ("yellow wine," grain wines), *pijiu* (beer), *putaojiu* (grape wine), and so forth. The imprecise nature of the word—often used casually when describing any alcoholic beverage—makes a literal translation difficult in most cases, so I have opted to assign meaning to it according to the context in which it is used. This allows greater ease of reading while avoiding too much tedious repetition.

Subcategories of baijiu are given as literal translations of the official Chinese *xiang xing* (aroma style) classification system—strong aroma, light aroma, and so on. There are at least a dozen styles of baijiu and, though their names give no indication of it, they are largely divided by regional production techniques. Readers should note that each is a distinct spirit, like whiskey or gin, and most of them bear little in common aside from a shared Chinese origin.

Translations of Chinese-language texts and interviews are my own unless otherwise specified. I have included a list of references to outside translations in the appendix for further reading. In all instances I have attempted to translate in such a way that preserves the intended rather than literal meaning. In transliterating Chinese words in general, I have attempted to use the contemporary pinyin romanization system to write Mandarin words and phrases, but there are notable exceptions. If a brand name is commonly written in an older romanization system—Kweichow Moutai as opposed to Guizhou Maotai—I have left it as it is printed on the bottle.

I have also refrained from rewriting published words of past commentators. In all such cases context should make my meaning clear. All interviews were recorded for accuracy, and informal firsthand anecdotes are related as remembered by the author. Some names have been changed or omitted at the speaker's request or the author's discretion.

TIME LINE OF ALCOHOL IN CHINA

Circa 7000 BCE | The oldest known alcoholic beverage is created at the Jiahu settlement near the Yellow River.

2070–256 BCE | Alcohol plays a prominent role in religious and secular society during the three ancient Chinese dynasties (Xia, Shang, and Zhou). Elaborate bureaucracy guides production and consumption. *Qu*, the microbial basis for most fermented Chinese foods and beverages, is invented.

551 BCE | Confucius is born; he later advocates alcohol's ceremonial use in moderation.

221 BCE | Qin Shihuang defeats final rival kingdoms and unites China under a single ruler.

206 BCE–220 CE | The Han dynasty enjoys a period of relative stability. Successful state monopoly on alcohol spreads huangjiu throughout China.

Third century | The Seven Sages of the Bamboo Grove define the Daoist ideal of enlightenment through drink.

618–907	China enters a golden age of drinking during the cosmopolitan Tang dynasty.
701	Li Bai, China's most revered poet and drinker, is born.
Circa eighth century	Alcohol distillation is likely invented by Middle Eastern chemists.
1127	Jurchen invaders (Jin) force the Song dynasty to flee south of the Yangtze River, where huangjiu finds a new spiritual center.
1271–1368	Mongolian ruler Kublai Khan defeats the Jin and Song, absorbing China into an empire spanning most of Eurasia. Sorghum becomes a popular cereal crop. Distilled alcohol makes its first confirmed appearance.
1300	Marco Polo publishes an account of his travels to the Far East and praises Chinese alcohol.
1368–1644	Distilled spirits proliferate in Ming dynasty China, especially among peasantry. Distillers create regional liquor styles resembling modern-day baijiu.
1644	Qing emperor Chengzong sacks Beijing and establishes Manchu rule in China.
1686	Emperor Kangxi permits maritime trade with Europeans in Canton, modern-day Guangzhou.
1842	The United Kingdom defeats the Qing in the First Opium War. European powers start establishing colonial settlements throughout China.

Late 1840s	An initial wave of Chinese immigration to the United States begins.
1878	Baijiu competes on the international stage at Paris's Exposition Universelle.
1912	Revolution topples the Qing dynasty, ending imperial rule in China. First modern baijiu distilleries are established shortly thereafter.
1949	Chinese Civil War ends with the Communist Party victory, establishing the People's Republic of China. The first state-run distillery, Hong Xing Erguotou, is registered in Beijing.
1950s–1970s	The state consolidates and reorganizes the alcohol industry. Baijiu production techniques are studied, improved on, and codified.
1972	President Richard Nixon becomes the first sitting U.S. president to visit China; he shares a baijiu toast with Premier Zhou Enlai.
1978	Deng Xiaoping assumes leadership of the Chinese Communist Party. Private enterprise returns to China.
2007	Diageo, Louis Vuitton Möet Hennessy, and Vin and Spirit announce strategic partnerships with Chinese distilleries, becoming the first foreign spirits concerns to invest in the baijiu industry.
2012	Xi Jinping assumes leadership and enacts anticorruption measures, barring government officials from excessive alcohol spending with public funds.

DRUNK IN CHINA

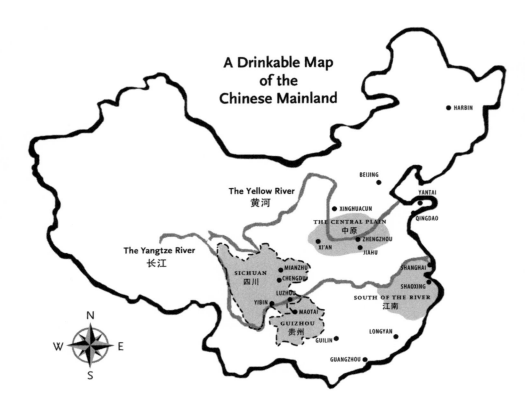

A Drinkable Map
of the
Chinese Mainland

HARBIN

BEIJING

YANTAI

The Yellow River
黄河

XINGHUACUN

QINGDAO

THE CENTRAL PLAIN
中原

XI'AN

ZHENGZHOU

JIAHU

The Yangtze River
长江

SICHUAN
四川

MIANZHU

CHENGDU

SHANGHAI

LUZHOU

SHAOXING

YIBIN

SOUTH OF THE RIVER
江南

MAOTAI

GUIZHOU
贵州

LONGYAN

GUILIN

GUANGZHOU

N
W   E
S

Introduction

THE FIRST SIP

RUNAWAY HORSE

JESSE SHAPELL—*Win Son, Brooklyn*

Combine *three-quarters of an ounce* each of **light-aroma baijiu** and **lime juice**, a *half ounce* each of **Rapa Giovanni Ratafià Cherry Liqueur** and **prickly ash syrup**, and *two dashes* of **Regan's Orange Bitters**. Shake, strain into a coupe, and float a lime wheel on the surface.

The first time I drank baijiu was Thanksgiving Day, 2006. I was at a high-rise apartment in Shanghai with recently arrived English teachers and a handful of our Chinese friends celebrating the holiday for the first time, with varying degrees of enthusiasm, through the great U.S. institution of the potluck. Each of us had come with watery yellow beer or barely drinkable wine, but Avi—a smart-ass kid from Philly with conspicuously cool sneakers—brought something special. He handed me a suspicious green bottle with a red star on it. I turned it over in my hands, and a transparent liquid sloshed around inside. The label was a jumble of indecipherable characters: I could not yet read Chinese.

"What is it?" I asked him. He could have said anything—hair tonic, rat poison, kerosene—and I would have believed him. My suspicions were not far from the mark.

"Give it a sniff," he told me, barely able to contain his glee.

Let's state the obvious: when a grown man asks you to smell something, it's rarely done with noble intent. But this was an odor for which I was entirely unprepared. It smelled as if someone had wrung a garbage bag of soiled gym shorts into a bucket of fish sauce, stirred in an equal measure of Drano, rotten fruit, and blue cheese, and left it to marinate a few days. It was a smell conjured from the pits of hell, the last whiff one senses before waking up in a serial killer's rumpus room. It triggered every alarm my young brain possessed. So of course I tasted it.

My mouth ignited. White hot flames seared every bit of tongue, lips, gums, and throat. The substance singed my esophagus and settled like a lit coal in my stomach. When I regained feeling in my face, and the acid sting subsided, all that was left was a bitter, fruity taste and the urge to consult a war crimes tribunal.

Whatever tricks have been played on me before or since, Avi's was surely the cruelest. But from the moment I first sipped it, I was in on the joke. I passed the bottle to the next rube and perpetuated the cycle of violence. Schadenfreude is a powerful temptation, and I come from Germanic stock. "What do you call this stuff?" I said.

"Baijiu."

"*Bai-j'yoh?*" I repeated, trying the word out. *Bye joe!*

Baijiu—literally "white alcohol"—is the term I later learned signifies all traditional Chinese grain liquor. Chinese spirits have a clear, colorless appearance and a biting, fragrant aroma. Though they are typically distilled from sorghum, they can also be made from rice, wheat, corn, and all sorts of starchy substances. The average strength of baijiu is around 52 percent alcohol by volume, but it can be purchased in eye-watering excess of 140 proof.

It is as ubiquitous as it is potent. Today baijiu is the world's best-selling spirits category, and each year a greater volume of baijiu—almost 2.9 billion gallons—is sold than that of vodka and whiskey combined. A baijiu distillery, Kweichow Moutai, is currently the world's most valuable spirits company, worth more than Diageo, which owns dozens of brands, including Johnnie Walker, Tanqueray, and Captain Morgan. According to research firm Brand Finance in 2018, four of the world's top five spirits brands by value were baijiu producers.

Almost all of it is consumed in China: roughly 99 percent of liquor sold there is baijiu. It is served in every Chinese restaurant and banquet hall, and no traditional festival or holiday would be complete without it. Yet most of the world's drinkers have never heard of it. And of the small sliver that has, many regard it with suspicion, if not scorn. This is an unfamiliar phenomenon in an era when news breaks in seconds, and any gratification short of instant feels excruciating. We have never had more options, in how and where we live, in what we think, and—crucially for our purposes—in what we consume. No meal passes muster until it has been documented in mouthwatering megapixels; no cocktail is too fancy to broadcast on social media. The act of satiation is now a game of one-upsmanship, always looking for the latest hot trend and the next big thing.

It seems impossible that anything could arrive too early in this environment, but this is the curious situation in which we find ourselves with baijiu. We are convinced we can handle any culinary experience, that all the world's cuisines can be easily and rapidly assimilated. We have grown unaccustomed to being challenged by anything. But our collective experience has failed to prepare us for the titan punch baijiu unleashes on the palate.

That first shot of sorghum sauce is a rubber-meets-the-road moment. When the lips purse and the eyes narrow and the head recoils like a slingshot, one gets a rare glimpse at what it really looks like to know about the band before it was cool. This is real-time culture shock turned up to a hundred thousand volts. This is where open minds slam shut. At least that was how I felt that cold Thanksgiving night in Shanghai. If I never tasted baijiu again, it would be too soon.

A battalion of Han Chinese adolescents in Miao minority costumes welcomed us with songs and smiles. They clapped in unison as we stepped from the bus. We had arrived at a monolithic golden cube fringed with neon accents, a sci-fi set with an unwieldy name: the Guiyang Southwest International Business City Convention Center. "Shiny shiny bling bling," explained the bus host, who wore a smile like it was tattooed on her face.

This LED monstrosity had been built solely for the competition. Its construction had taken just a hundred days and cost roughly forty-five million dollars. Shiny shiny bling bling, indeed. The year was 2015, and I was in Guizhou. Some years before I had visited my first Chinese distillery in the remote, backwater province, kicking off what would become my journey of spiritual enlightenment. This was where it would lead me: the Spirits Selection of Concours Mondial de Bruxelles. Over the course of the next three days, I would join fellow jury members to collectively sample some 1,400 spirits from forty-four countries. For baijiu this was to be a coming-out party. Chinese distillers had entered more than five hundred bottles in the competition. They wanted to show that Chinese spirits could compete on a global stage. I could hardly wait.

Though my younger self would never have believed it, I had become one of baijiu's leading foreign advocates in the decade since that Thanksgiving party in Shanghai. And I had returned to China in this capacity. My judging panel comprised five members: an Italian, a Spaniard, a Frenchman, a Chinese, and me. None of us was perfectly fluent in the others' languages. I served as interpreter for the technical manager of Beijing's Red Star distillery, Ai Jinzhong. Whenever English proved untenable we resorted to Spanish, which I then translated mentally into English and verbalized to Ai in my now-rusty Mandarin. We began by calibrating our palates with a crisp, flavorless vodka. We jotted down appraisals and passed them to our Italian captain, Bruno.

"Perfect," he said, looking down at the results. "We are all in a line."

We started with white brandies and moved on to rums before finishing with Guizhou's celebrated baijiu. A disturbing trend had surfaced by the end of the first session, and Bruno wanted to make sure we knew it.

"Your scores," he said, with a look that took in both Ai and me. "They are very much in a line." From the tone of his voice and the Frenchman's arched eyebrow, I could tell this was not a compliment. What he meant was that I was out of line with the European panelists; I had become culturally unstuck. Summing it up, he said, "What is for *us* a defect is for *you* a strength." It was an odd, backhanded affirmation of my work—and a reminder of how much work was left to do.

Ai, a wiry old man with a gentle face, remained oblivious to the exchange. He just smiled and waited for me to translate. I gave him the sanitized version: "You and I, we like the same drinks."

A smile widened across his face, and he clapped me on the shoulder. "Very good," he said, deploying one of his few English phrases.

That afternoon, at the ballroom of a luxury hotel that smelled of fresh paint, there was a forum on baijiu's international development. Aside from Spirits Selection's Belgian chair Baudouin Havaux, I was the lone foreign speaker. I told the audience that I thought baijiu's future lay overseas, and the time to strike was now. I concluded my remarks with a rhetorical question: "Who will launch the first great international baijiu brand?" In truth I was hoping that it would be me. A team of like-minded outsiders and I had been secretly negotiating with one of China's oldest and most esteemed distilleries for months. With any luck we would launch a brand in the coming years.

The mostly Chinese audience listened via simultaneous headphone translation and politely clapped when I finished. I listened with a mixture of amusement and disbelief as my co-panelists laid forth their vision for baijiu's future. Mostly, it was a bland recitation of industry statistics and the latest Communist Party talking points.

For one speaker it was simple. France had Bordeaux, he said; everyone knew they made the best wine there. China just needed to explain to the foreigners that Guizhou is the Bordeaux of China. Another man suggested that if baijiu needed a cocktail culture to succeed abroad the Guizhou provincial government could just build several hundred baijiu cocktail bars around the world. I moved a hand over my mouth to stifle laughter. That's just how things work in China: the government decides to build a thousand miles of highway and it happens. But could baijiu become the darling of the international cocktail scene by Communist Party decree? It seemed unlikely.

When it was the chair's turn to speak, Baudouin said that education was critical. No one would ever drink it if they didn't know what it was. He noted that I had been one of the few people writing about baijiu in English, but with a caveat. "It's not enough," he said.

By the final day of the tasting, our jury had settled into a pleasant rhythm. We were all leaning on one another, translating speech and flavor. The Spaniard, Javier, helped explain the intricacies of rum. Bruno and Olivier covered the brandy. Ai and I consulted on baijiu. "What do you think about the fifth glass?" one of them would ask. We would briefly confer. *Hen xiang*, we would say. How fragrant.

Before the last ballot was submitted we were, as Bruno might say, in a line. When the winners were announced, roughly a third of all Chinese spirits medaled, including eight winners of the prestigious double gold award. "Chinese Liquor Wins International Competition" ran the headline in state-run media the following day. This was not precisely true—liquors had been considered only in their respective categories—but it was a start.

At the competition's outset the foreign judges openly derided baijiu, but now they talked about it with enthusiasm. In the security line at the airport, a Canadian beer aficionado told me he had come dreading baijiu, but after a week he was forced to concede. "Some of the baijius I tasted were pretty damned good."

A few days later my colleague Bill and I met Ai in Beijing's Qianmen District. Just a few blocks from Tiananmen Square, it had centuries earlier been the Chinese capital's distillery row. The driver let us off on one of the city's wide avenues, and Ai led us through a maze of narrow gray alleyways. Walking through them, I found it was impossible not to become nostalgic for a past that I knew only from books: blocks dotted with opera houses and brothels, the intersection of Chinese peasantry and Manchu aristocracy, curios and birdcages, camel trains and mule carts, dust and sand—the papered-over old Peking, of which few traces remain.

Ai came armed with an assortment of his distillery's baijius, though anyone who has spent even a short time living in China well knows Red Star, the Coca-Cola of baijius. He set before me a small glass of his baijiu and one made by his chief competitor, Niulanshan. He nodded with approval as I politely praised his brand's relative merits. Then he poured me a shot of his export-grade blend. It had the characteristic mild floral notes of a northern baijiu but also a pleasing sweetness that reminded me of dried apricots.

A smile spread across his face, and he lifted an upraised thumb at me. "Exactly right," he said, turning to Bill. "His tastes are just like ours."

I had never been prouder. But Baudouin's words still weighed on me. It was not enough. There was still much to do.

The room shook with the force of a hundred rumbling tanks. All morning the streets were deserted. When I had ventured out earlier for a coffee and *jianbing*, Beijing's answer to the breakfast crepe, not a single shop was open. A city of more than twenty billion closed for business. The silence was eerie.

Then the government unleashed the full might of the People's Liberation Army. It was the anniversary of China's victory over Japanese imperial forces in 1945. A grand military parade was planned, the likes of which the world has rarely seen since the end of the Cold War. Foreign dignitaries were in attendance, and President Xi wore his finest Zhongshan suit—the collarless style made popular by Mao. The factories had closed their smokestacks, and Beijing's rarely seen sky was clear. Mountains I had never known existed could be seen in the distance. The crowd had been carefully selected, and the general public was instructed to give the day's proceedings a wide berth. If they wanted to watch, they could do so on television. Only those on the warpath could witness it firsthand.

Mine was a surreal multimedia viewing, watching the action unfold on television until it appeared outside my window. Dozens of fighter jets screamed across the sky, leaving rainbow-colored contrails in their wake. Helicopters, antiaircraft batteries, and armored personnel carriers came next. Finally, a deafening stream of tanks roared past my hotel. The procession took more than an hour to pass, then the barricades came down. A few motorbikes sputtered across the wide intersection outside, and the city jumped back into life as if nothing had happened.

I don't care what anyone says: China is many things, but never boring. And now the nation was mobilizing. From Guizhou to Beijing the Communist Party was rallying its troops, sharpening its propagandistic knives. It wanted to project an image of Chinese greatness out into the world, an effort that depends more on cultural cachet than military prowess, more on liquor bottles than intercontinental missiles.

Baijiu is coming for the world. Whether the world is ready for baijiu, or baijiu ready for the world, remains to be seen. But it's coming, and sooner than you might expect.

This is a book about Chinese alcohol. More accurately, it is a book about alcohol and China. Better still, it is a book just about China. The alcohol is implicit, because without it there would be no China. It was the pursuit of intoxication that led a band of nomadic East Asians to settle along the Yellow River almost ten thousand years ago. Alcohol has since permeated all aspects of China's culture, leaving a soggy stamp on its religion, art, and literature; its politics, philosophy, and warfare. Confucian scholars bureaucratized drink, the Daoist mystics aspired to it, and the Communist Party cadres insist on it. Throughout the life of a people whose history spans the ages, whose territory has extended from Mongolia to the Arabian Peninsula, thirst has been the enduring constant.

So why does China covet baijiu so much, and the rest of the world so little? What caused the rift, and can it be surmounted? These are the principal questions this book seeks to answer. But at its core this is a love story: between a nation and its liquor, a man and a nation, and, ultimately, a man and that nation's liquor, with the tantalizing possibility of a polyamorous relationship between that liquor and the world.

To understand the unlikely circumstances of my conversion from baijiu skeptic to evangelist, I must first relate what happened in the years following my arrival in China. I must also explore how spirits became a dominant feature of contemporary Chinese life, and what this tells us about China's place in the world. It is a tale that crosses millennia and continents in pursuit of a national identity that may never have existed.

I have aimed—so far as my skill and imperfect memory allows—to take readers on a journey round all corners of the Middle Kingdom, past and present, to show a side of Chinese life that is at once essential and overlooked.

Hardened China watchers, a group largely disillusioned and rightly distrustful of China memoirs, will, I hope, find enjoyment in these pages. Much of what I discuss presents familiar themes through a new lens. What I want to do is look at China through beer goggles—or, more precisely, through baijiu goggles—to bring sense to seemingly senseless drinking rituals, to add a little flush to the pale cheeks China so often presents to the outside world.

There is also something here for the sober reader, and not simply the chance to live vicariously through the author. Alcohol has given meaning and form to Chinese lives. Far from engaging in a juvenile celebration of inebriation for its own sake, I have aimed to examine the many ways in which alcohol has shaped Chinese society and its rituals, at times with disastrous consequences.

It should be stressed from the outset that I did not approach my subject as an expert, at least not initially. It is only by strange historical coincidence that I became something resembling one: little to nothing has been written in English on this important subject. Other writers will come after me, and I welcome their contributions. But until they arrive, I feel compelled to share the more interesting features of what I have discovered.

Whoever you are, and whatever poor life choices led you to read about alcohol instead of drinking it, I commend you your decision and shall endeavor to make it worth your while.

Sitting down for a drink is to my mind the easiest way to get to know someone. What better icebreaker exists than the casual conversation over alcohol—letting down one's guard, revealing and uncovering idiosyncrasies a glass at a time, warming up to another as the inhibitions slip away. What better way to know a nation?

PART 1

Climbing the Sky

A sober man will never find friendship.
                    —*Traditional saying*

1

The Wild West

SICHUAN SOUR

SHANNON MUSTIPHER—*Glady's, New York*

Combine *one and a half ounces* of **strong-aroma baijiu** with a *half ounce* of **Rum Fire Jamaican Overproof Rum,** a *half ounce* of **Giffard Passionfruit Liqueur,** and an *ounce* each of **lime juice** and **pineapple juice.** Shake over ice and strain into a coupette.

"The road to Sichuan is hard," wrote the immortal poet Li Bai, "hard as climbing the sky." Sichuan is a world unto itself, cut off from the rest of China by geography, distance, and culture. More than a thousand miles west of where it spills into the East China Sea, the Yangtze River rushes down from the Tibetan Plateau and into southern Sichuan. Its tributaries cut a network of waterways that further isolate the province from the distant eastern coast.

In ancient times the emperor would send wayward officials there as a punishment. Though I would not characterize my time there as burdensome, I ended up there in much the same way.

It started back in 2011. I had just moved back to the United States and married my then longtime girlfriend, Catherine, who had recently accepted a diplomatic position in the United States Foreign Service. And on a mild summer afternoon in Arlington, Virginia, the State Department subjected us to Flag Day, equal parts induction ceremony and hazing ritual.

The auditorium hushed as a short man in his forties, goateed and balding, walked to the podium and introduced a series of distinguished guests. Not a word from their lips registered in a single ear. All eyes were trained not on the lectern but on the rows of tiny flags behind them, each of which represented a country where one of the newly anointed officers might be sent. I sat with Catherine's father and brother in the back of the room, clutching with white knuckles a list of potential landing spots.

Several weeks earlier Catherine brought the list home from training. We spent hours researching and weighing the merits of various potential postings, as if our opinions mattered. A U.S. diplomat's job requires what is euphemistically called "worldwide availability." In reality this means something like, "We'll send you wherever we god-damned please." It's the diplomatic equivalent of being shot from a cannon.

Bangkok would be nice, we thought. So would Tel Aviv or somewhere in Eastern Europe. For reasons that still remain unclear, almost everyone in Catherine's class was pulling for a job in Ouagadougou, Burkina Faso, possibly because it was fun to say aloud. I had a few ground rules. Places with child soldiers, abnormal levels of ethnic violence, or high likelihood of a grenade attack were low priorities. Second-level concerns included electricity, running water, and malaria. Above all, I didn't want to go to China.

Rather, I didn't want to go *back* to China. The People's Republic had seemed like the answer to a range of life's questions when I'd first arrived there. I had recently graduated from college and was working a dead-end job in a miserable suburb of Boston, let's call it Waltham (its name), waiting for Catherine to graduate.

In the first decade of the 2000s, U.S. life had reached what then felt like impressive new lows. The economy was bad and, though nobody realized it at the time, about to get much worse. Unilateral warfare and freedom fries were the politics du jour, indignities that feel quaint in retrospect.

Meanwhile, many worlds away, a beacon of hope emanated from an unlikely source. Every day newspapers ran front-page spreads heralding China's "economic miracle" and its seemingly inevitable rise to global supremacy. The twenty-first was to be China's century, they said.

Two of my co-workers had already broken free of their capitalist fetters and bought one-way tickets to the mysterious Communist stronghold. They set sail with a single suitcase and vague promises of English-teaching opportunities. "You should come over," they told me after they arrived. "Get here and the job finds you." It sounded like a dream. Granted, the sum total of my life experience was an impractical philosophy degree buffeted by a cloud of bong smoke, but it still seemed better than staying. So, after she graduated, Catherine and I packed our suitcases and moved to Shanghai.

We had come planning to teach for a year, learn the language, and return to the United States conquering heroes with "international experience." A year later we were haggard from performing—educating feels too strong a word for what we did daily to adorable but inexhaustible Chinese schoolchildren. We were living on a steady diet of the world's best fried noodles and worst beer, rotting ourselves from the inside out. We barely spoke Mandarin and had no better prospects than when we had arrived, but we had fallen in love with the sprawling cosmopolitan metropolis we then called home.

Before our arrival I hadn't known what to expect. My childhood exposure to China consisted largely of "Big Bird Goes to China," visits to Chinese restaurants with my extended Jewish family, and an elementary school art teacher with a fondness for Chinese watercolors. It is from the signature on a piece that I did in her class, an ink-on–paper towel study of monkeys clutching bananas, that I obtained my Mandarin name, De Li, or Righteous Power. I also recall my father's sustained amusement whenever he heard the name of Chairman Deng (pronounced "Dung") mentioned on early nineties National Public Radio.

Life in Shanghai was hectic, cramped, and crazy but indescribably vibrant. I assumed, as was common in those days, that China was a colorless authoritarian hellscape—North Korea on a grander scale. What we found instead was an enchanting blend of colonial charm and aggressive Chinese futurism: quiet strolls down the leafy lanes of the former French Concession and neon-flooded rooftop parties a thousand feet in the sky.

That first day, driving into the city from remote Pudong Airport, I saw more high-rises than I had in my entire life up to that point. In the years that followed I watched the city build more than a dozen subway lines, host a World Expo, and bulldoze and replace entire neighborhoods more or less overnight. Every day was a blur of unfamiliar sights, smells, and tastes, a cacophony of new words and accents, a sensory shot to the cerebral cortex.

It was too much to process all at once. One year stretched into five. The opportunities came, as did the Mandarin, in fitful bursts. Catherine's gift for language landed her an unlikely gig hosting an Italian podcast at an internet start-up. I got into tourism, then public relations, and finally publishing. I started wearing shirts with buttons and collars, and then jackets and ties. We settled into the comfortable doldrums of long-term expatriate life in a country with gross pay disparities and a revolving door of trendy restaurants, cocktail bars, and massage parlors. The novelty wore off when we realized our existence in China had begun feeling predictable, boring even.

The country has a way of grinding people down. Over time the minor annoyances of life in a developing country—pollution, construction, congestion—built to a crescendo. The daily challenges that I once savored became tiresome. I grew nostalgic for home. The shortcomings of U.S. life faded from memory, and I began to miss the friends whose lives were drifting further and further from my orbit. Even if it meant giving up the relative comfort to which we had grown accustomed, it was time for a change. Leaving China would be bittersweet, but if we didn't leave after five years, we might never tear ourselves away.

When Catherine was accepted into the Foreign Service, it felt as if a prayer had been answered. Here was a life that would satisfy our wanderlust but keep us firmly tethered to home. We could have it both ways, or so I thought.

Three months after our repatriation, I was starting to understand the full gravity of being a diplomatic spouse. They could send us anywhere in the world. *Anywhere.*

I was already sweating through the armpits of my shirt when the first flag lit up the screen behind the podium. Young, smartly dressed professionals rose to polite applause as they collected their flags. Some people were luckier than others. You could see it in their eyes and smiles, genuine and forced. Whenever a desirable posting was crossed off of my list, the audience shed its genial preceremony camaraderie. The better the posting, the graver the ill-defined injury we wished on the recipient.

"San José, Costa Rica." We clapped merrily, willing him prolonged tropical illness.

"Rome, Italy." People choke on biscotti all the time.

"Oslo, Norway." I hope she freezes.

Our sympathies extended only to those unfortunate souls sent to the rougher corners of the globe, for their misfortune precluded ours. Every time the speaker announced a war zone, an unuttered sigh of relief swept the room, presumably minus one officer's family. A particularly dire Mexican border posting went to a small husk of a woman, who returned to her seat wiping tears from her eyes. "Poor thing," we said to ourselves. "Better her than us."

Finally, the screen turned fire engine red as a familiar flag appeared. "Chengdu, People's Republic of China," the speaker announced. And then he called Catherine's name. A month later we were headed to Sichuan.

The so-called Land of Plenty is roughly the same size as California, but home to more than eighty-seven million people. If it were a country, it would be the fourteenth most populous in the world. It is home to panda bears and holy mountains, but an unhurried pace is its chief asset. Sichuanese, to make the first of what will be many overgeneralizations, are outgoing and exceedingly warm folk with a well-deserved reputation for mellowness. They like their conversation lively and their food hot. "Szechwan" cuisine is famous the world over for bold flavors, particularly the numbingly spicy *huajiao*, or Sichuan peppercorn, which exists somewhere on the culinary spectrum between cumin and cocaine. They love nothing more than a discussion about philosophy or classical literature over a bubbling hot pot and a round of drinks.

Chengdu, Sichuan's capital, sits in a basin crisscrossed with slow-moving brackish rivers. It is a cloudy place in the best of times. Mountains on all sides form a natural barrier that traps in clouds of dust from the cease-less construction, which mix with car exhaust and industrial pollution, coagulating into a white haze so dense it is sometimes difficult to see across the street. In Sichuan, it is said, dogs bark at the sun.

I had visited Chengdu years earlier. It was the first place I traveled after arriving in Shanghai. My friend Eric, a fellow midwesterner teacher, had started dating Johanna, the Chinese woman who recruited us to work for a shady-verging-on-criminal teaching outfit. Johanna invited a small group of us to celebrate the Mid-Autumn Festival with her family in Wutongqiao, just outside of Leshan, a small city in southern Sichuan that possesses the world's largest (seated) Buddha, carved from a cliff face where three rivers meet.

As our plane descended toward Chengdu, the cloud cover seemed endless. I could feel we were losing altitude, but still the mist enveloped us. I wondered how our pilot could see through it, how he would avoid slamming into the mountains, then thought better of such musings. Within seconds of the ground materializing we were on it.

Much of the trip was spent hiking Emei Mountain, a harrowingly steep site of Buddhist pilgrimage whose ascent involved countless narrow steps and fighting monkeys off with bamboo poles. You know, China shit.

A romantic quadrangle emerged when one of Johanna's old class-mates, Jeremy, attempted to woo Johanna away from Eric, while Jeremy's girlfriend fought through sickness and humiliation to keep between Jeremy and Johanna. (I am happy to report that Eric and Johanna survived the test and are happily married with two adorable children. I cannot speak to Jeremy's fortunes.)

That first trip to Chengdu supplied a peaceful reprieve from the mountainside drama. It was an idyllic hamlet that felt stuck in an earlier, simpler time. I remember walking down streets beneath swaying canopies of leafy green trees, bicycles drifting past in no particular rush to get anywhere. In the parks and plazas, people sat around tables, drawing sips of tea and nibbling on pumpkin and sunflower seeds, accompanied by the clacking shuffle of mahjong tiles. I recall watching with bemused admiration as my companions ordered dumplings and emptied spoonful upon spoonful of molten hot pepper into the dipping vinegar. For them there was no such thing as too spicy.

I would often think about Chengdu in the years that followed. When Shanghai's pressure cooker dissolved my patience, I would wonder why I had not just moved to that lush oasis on the other side of the country.

As our plane turned its nose down toward the city years later, I was struck again by the endless sky. Outside the window was nothing but impenetrable grayness. Lower and lower, there was nothing but mist. The city waiting for us below—the city we would call home for two years—was not the Chengdu I remembered. There were sleek residential high-rises and luxury car dealerships. What materialized from the haze was a city in flux. It was becoming something else, though it was too early to say exactly what.

Half the city had been torn apart to make way for new superhighways and subway lines. Pipes and wires stuck out of gaping holes in streets and sidewalks, while an army of workers in blue coveralls rushed to staunch the wounds. It was difficult to get from one end of the city to the other in less than an hour, night or day—for all intents and purposes Chengdu was closed for renovation. Even the city's legendary street food had all but disappeared, sacrificed on the altar of Chinese modernity.

It was a city of fourteen million people, but it felt more like a way station than a settlement. Every other foreigner I met had either just arrived or would soon depart. People came here for all sorts of reasons, but the ground shifted too often to plant roots. But you don't move to Chengdu for life, you move for the lifestyle.

Whereas the Shanghainese always seemed aloof, too busy for conversation, a stranger in Chengdu was content to pour a cup of tea and consider any subject for an indefinite interval. In Shanghai we slaved behind desks late into the night. In Sichuan it could seem as if nobody was ever working, and by nine at night restaurants were already dimming their lights. Shanghai had been fashionable, a city of designer dresses and bespoke suits. In Chengdu someone was as likely to don a Buddhist's crimson robe as a silk tie. Even buried beneath tons of rubble and rebar, Chengdu had undeniable charm. Shanghai was a jungle of steel skyscrapers transposed atop a colonial spearhead, but Chengdu retained hints of old China's allure.

Our apartment overlooked a tranquil bend in the Jin River near the Bridge of Nine Eyes, so named because on a clear day its arches reflected in the water to form nine perfect ovals. Looking down from our twentieth-floor bedroom, we could see the magnificent Qing dynasty pagoda shooting up from the leafy bamboo of Wangjiang Park.

In Chengdu they did not use the titles "miss" or "mister," but instead "beautiful" and "handsome" (e.g., "How you doing, handsome?"). Instead of parting ways with the customary *zai jian*, "see you later," they always said, *man zou*, "Go slowly. Take it easy."

There was much about the city's transformation to frustrate and confound, but there was also a refreshing rawness. Call it demolition or reinvention. Whatever it was, it was a departure from the China I thought I knew. It challenged every preconception I held about my adopted country, a process that began with baijiu.

I met Johan my first week in Sichuan. One of Catherine's new colleagues, an energetic and gregarious young diplomat I'll call Tony, invited us to a Halloween party at an Irish pub. The bar itself was unremarkable, the type of third-rate, smoke-filled watering hole you can find in any remote East Asian city. The beer was bad and the cover band worse, but I repeat myself.

Tony, who was wearing the vest and helmet of a Chinese construction worker, leaned in so I could hear him over the music. "There's someone I want you to meet," he said, gesturing toward a tall, lanky man in horn-rimmed glasses, with shaggy hair, frilly white shirt, and plaid trousers. "This is Johan," Tony shouted over a tortured rendition of "Hotel California," or some such garbage. "He runs a baijiu factory."

"Baijiu?" I said, not sure I had heard correctly. "Do you have a card?"

He produced a business card emblazoned in gold with the Mars zodiac symbol and a name: Austin Danger Powers. It was Halloween, he had spared no detail on his costume, and the pop cultural reference was presumably still fresh in Sweden.

"You don't actually like drinking that stuff, do you?"

"Of course," he said, still grinning. "It's fantastic. What do you think about it?"

I told him I had never met a baijiu I liked. Too strong for my tastes, too biting.

"We make weaker stuff too. For the women," he said. "Perhaps you'd like that?"

Meeting a baijiu producer right off the plane is not as remarkable as it might seem. Sichuan is one of China's breadbaskets, and wherever you find Chinese farmers, it is a safe bet there are distilleries nearby. The province produces more baijiu than any other: more than two-thirds of all baijiu originates in Sichuan. So wherever you go in Chengdu, there's a fair chance someone with connections to the industry is nearby.

What is less common is meeting a Scandinavian baijiu magnate. To the best of my knowledge, Johan Simonsson is the only one, and I was dying to know how it happened. I found out a couple of weeks later in the lobby of a luxury hotel downtown—vaulted ceilings, white porcelain, servers in bowties, that sort of thing. Out of costume, Johan was the kind of lanky, eternally youthful Nordic type that instantly makes a short Jewish kid from Kansas feel like he's not going to win this particular game of dodgeball.

Johan's Chinese adventure began in 2004, when he was tasked with exploring business development opportunities for Swedish spirits producer Vin and Spirit, of Absolut Vodka fame. Like his Viking ancestors, he set off to far-flung corners of the globe in search of spoils. He traveled to twenty countries to learn more about foreign brands and spirits that had not received enough attention overseas.

He "discovered" baijiu. It was the largest, best-selling liquor category in the world, and it was virtually unknown outside of China. Its high-sticker price for superpremium brands, which in some cases sold for hundreds, even thousands, of dollars per bottle, proved irresistible. His team studied more than sixty different producers and in 2007 Vin and Spirit struck a deal with one of Sichuan's leading distilleries, Jiannanchun, to create a new joint-venture brand called Tianchengxiang, or TCX.

Johan was supposed to stay only a short time to get the company off the ground, but on May 12, 2008, just four days before TCX was scheduled to begin production, Sichuan was rocked with a massive 8.0-magnitude earthquake. The ground there shook with such force that I felt it over a thousand miles away in Shanghai. Almost seventy thousand people were killed in the quake and its immediate aftermath. Many more were left injured or homeless. Mianzhu, where the Jiannanchun distillery is located, was the second-worst-hit city.

"It was awful," Johan said. "No one was killed at the factory, but in Mianzhu and its surroundings over twelve thousand people died. When I went there a few weeks after for the first time, people would not go there because of the smell from the bodies."

And the smell of the baijiu: the earthquake destroyed an aging facility that contained more than 2.5 million gallons of it, roughly four Olympic-sized swimming pools' worth. The smell was asphyxiating, but also dangerous. Imagine a flood of 144-proof liquid pouring into city streets in the wake of widespread destruction. Smoking was forbidden until the city had been thoroughly hosed down.

According to officials at Jiannanchun, the estimated financial loss to the company exceeded a billion yuan, then about $125 million. Johan agreed to stay in Chengdu to oversee TCX's recovery, and the reconstruction was swift. Within months Jiannanchun had rebuilt its bottling plant from scratch. A year and a half later TCX launched its initial product line.

We tried a sample at his office, a cubicle forest tucked into a Chengdu high-rise. I had still not yet developed a taste for baijiu, but from the first sip it was clear I was dealing with something more palatable than my previous experience led me to expect. He had another for me to try, a low-proof spirit modeled after Korean *soju*—the one he was marketing to female consumers—which had most of baijiu's bark, but none of its bite.

Johan ducked his head into a minifridge and retrieved a few plastic bottles with handwritten labels. Experiments, he explained. They were baijius infused with berries and tropical fruit additives—Johan's answer to flavored vodka drawn from the Absolut playbook. They were still working on the ratios, and he hoped to have something stable soon. It was eye-opening stuff, much of which foreshadowed what would arrive on the baijiu scene a few years later.

In the end TCX never really took off. Shortly before the earthquake French spirits conglomerate Pernod Ricard purchased Vin and Spirit, and the new parent company had little interest in Chinese spirits or Johan's project. Of the many cutting-edge baijius we sampled that day, only one survived, and it was quietly sold back to Jiannanchun around 2013. Pernod Ricard redeployed Johan to its Western spirits division in Shanghai. Not long after that he returned to Sweden.

If Johan had made a mistake, it was arriving at the party too early, though he can hardly be faulted for trying. Baijiu was still too new, too strange, for outsiders to wrap their heads around. But he was onto something. He had seen something in China that the rest of the world had thus far missed.

I left my conversation with Johan with a sense of purpose. I had to know more about baijiu. I had to know everything. If I still didn't trust it, I wanted to at least understand it. If nothing else, it would be a window into my new home, an introduction to living in a second-tier Chinese city, if you can consider a city "second-tier" when it has a population the size of Norway, Ireland, and Costa Rica combined.

The bigger coastal cities like Beijing and Shanghai have dense concentrations of wealth and a cosmopolitan sheen. More foreigners go there to live and visit, and a great many locals have worked, studied, or traveled abroad. As a result, the lifestyle differences between foreigner and local are less obvious. When one goes out to eat and drink, it is typically in mixed company. This happens in the interior too, but to a lesser extent and at sadder venues.

In Shanghai I had virtually unlimited dining and drinking options, many of which would not appear out of place in Paris or London. In Chengdu I found only rough approximations of home, and the bars were generally only a couple of degrees removed from the nightlife options I associated with college dormitories. This is not because the

Sichuanese do not drink. They are prodigious drinkers. It is because they do not generally drink what their foreign counterparts do, or in the same manner. It is very easy to drink in style in Chengdu, but only if you are willing to do so on the locals' terms.

If I was to make a proper go of it, I needed to get into their drinks. I had to get into baijiu.

To my surprise and dismay I soon discovered there was precious little information about Chinese spirits available for the casual English reader. Worse still, much of what had been written was contradictory or demonstrably false. Many commentators simply referred to baijiu as "Chinese rice wine," despite the fact that it is not a wine and is seldom made from rice. To get a subject so wrong was all the more remarkable, given the outsized role of alcohol in Chinese life.

The subject begged for a corrective, but where to begin? Where else but Sichuan? Sichuan has thousands of distilleries and has been an alcoholic innovator since ancient times. It is the buckle of the baijiu belt, the center of what the local government unironically calls the "Golden Triangle of Baijiu." Spirits were such big business there that baijiu had caught the attention of not only Johan but also his competitors. At roughly the same time Johan started TCX with Vin and Spirit, liquor giants Diageo (of Johnny Walker and Guinness fame) and LVMH (Hennessey) both purchased controlling stakes in Sichuanese distilleries.

The world's attention was trained on Chinese spirits. Baijiu appeared on the cusp of an international breakthrough. And cosmic coincidence had brought me to the center of it all to bear witness.

There was only one problem: I hated baijiu.

2 Three Hundred Shots

A journey of a thousand drinks begins with a single sip.

"What do you think?" he asked, swirling the transparent liquid in his snifter. Tony, who the consulate assigned as our social sponsor—kind of a glorified babysitter for newcomers—was fast becoming my secret weapon. He was one of those rarest of creatures: a foreigner with an inborn taste for Chinese firewater.

"It's pretty smooth," I said, gasping slightly. It was just the taste, something akin to a banana soaked in turpentine, that was giving me pause. Also the smell: Jolly Ranchers melted in paint thinner. Jesus, what a smell. And this was the *good* stuff.

Only 269 shots to go. We were kicking off an experiment that night, and I was the guinea pig. I had decided that not only would I learn to enjoy drinking baijiu, but I was going to quantify it. My Kiwi friend Tim put the idea in my head. He was an engineer I had befriended in Shanghai who approached my drinking problem with mathematical precision. He posited the existence of a so-called taste threshold, a theoretical line between love and hate. "Every food or drink has one," he told me.

Think back to your first taste of coffee. More likely than not it repulsed you. Perhaps it was too bitter or too acidic. Some people never advance past this stage, but for whatever reason—the caffeine rush or, more likely, the desire to appear sophisticated—most people go back for a second and third cup, and then a fourth or fifth. Before long you discover that you actually enjoy the taste of the very thing that you initially thought undrinkable. You crossed the line, the taste threshold. Your needle flipped from negative to positive.

With coffee the taste threshold is quite low, usually no more than 5 or 6 cups over the course of a lifetime, Tim continued. With beer the number is slightly higher, somewhere in the neighborhood of 10 glasses. "They've studied baijiu's taste threshold too," he said. "Guess how many glasses it takes?"

"I don't know, 30?" I ventured.

"Three hundred."

Dear God. It seemed an impossibly high number. Then I mulled it over. After five years in China, I had attended my share of weddings and business dinners where baijiu flowed freely. Surely, I already had 50 shots under my belt. Even a conservative estimate would put me 30 shots in the black, and one could get in 15 to 20 more from China's diminutive shot glasses in a single meal. So 270 shots? Manageable.

I was relating the admittedly suspect theory to Tony one night when he cut me off. "Hold on," he said. "I've got something you *have* to try."

He walked out of the room and returned with a bottle of Wuliangye and two snifters. Wuliangye, literally "Five-Grain Liquid," is China's biggest distillery by production volume (second by brand value), and its flagship baijiu is something the average Chinese drinker might compare to Johnnie Walker Blue Label—a readily available drink that signifies taste and wealth. The distillery traces its origins back several hundred years, and its name is something of an allusion to the "five grains" celebrated in ancient Chinese cuisine. This particular baijiu was distilled from sorghum, wheat, corn, and two kinds of rice.

"A friend gave it to me as a gift," he said. "I think it sells for around two hundred dollars."

It was deeply complex, warm, abrasive, and entirely unforgiving. In a word: Chinese. If this baijiu went on the top shelf, my little experiment was going to require a considerable effort. A single glass took me thirty minutes to work my way through. When I'd finished, Tony lifted the bottle. "Another?"

At least he gave me the option. How very American.

At this point in my life, I would like to be able to tell you that my initial foray into Chinese spirits was conducted with the same high-mindedness and academic precision as that of H. T. Huang, protégé of British science historian Joseph Needham. A research student in Hong Kong, H. T. left for his family's ancestral village in Guangdong shortly after the Japanese invaded in 1941. There he made an informal study of Chinese fermentation while waiting for a job appointment in Chengdu. "What intrigued me most were the fermentations of grains into wine and soybeans into soy sauce. They were rather complicated processes that required a high level of understanding and technical skill," he writes in *Science and Civilisation in China*. "What is the scientific basis of these processes? How did they come about? What were their origins? How long ago were they discovered?"

In 1943 he arrived at the University of Chengdu, just a short walk from where I later lived. Not long after he was hired as Needham's assistant. Together the two would travel overland by car and train, uncovering the mysteries of Chinese scientific endeavor like a multiethnic Sherlock and Holmes, as evidenced in Needham's diary: "Lunch in compartment very nice. . . . Read Borrow, H. T. read Tang poems."

Their steps retraced my initial journey to Sichuan exactly, from Chengdu to Leshan and then Wutongqiao, hometown village of my friend Johanna, who had recruited me to China. There they met Shih Shêng-Han, a plant physiologist who had isolated the naturally harvested aspergillus mold used in the fermentation of almost every Chinese alcoholic drink. Shih shared his deep knowledge of Chinese fermentation with H. T., who later in life kept two scrolls of the former's calligraphy in his study. Needham and H. T. next went to Lizhuang near Yibin, today home to the Wuliangye distillery, and continued on to the wartime Chinese capital in Chungking.

Huang later earned his doctorate at Oxford and rose to director of the National Science Foundation in Washington DC. In 1984 he penned the fortieth installment in Needham's *Science and Civilisation* series, *Fermentation and Food Science*, quite possibly the finest study ever written on fermentation methods in China.

Unfortunately, my induction into Chinese alcohol often more closely resembled the story of another writer who found himself in Sichuan during the height of World War II, and whose prodigious drinking has landed him in surveys of many alcoholic beverages. Naturally, I refer to Ernest Hemingway.

Attempting to rally the U.S. public, *Collier's* sent Hemingway and writer Martha Gellhorn (then his wife) to report from the Chinese front in 1941. Meeting with the couple and their interpreter, Mr. Ma, Kuomintang general Yu Hanmou attempted to engage Hemingway in baijiu battle. He had no idea what he was up against.

As Gellhorn, who was allowed to sip tea at a separate table, recounts, "The general began to sweat profusely and two staff officers turned a beautiful mulberry color. . . . The interpreter stammered and swayed and found it hard to translate a toast about glorious armies and final victory, which Ernest happily invented." Mr. Ma got too drunk to continue translating, and the drinking ceased when the general announced that he had run out of liquor. The episode ended in a swirl of guffaws without any real business having been accomplished.

Another battle near the front lines went down much the same. Hemingway suffered more damage, but he soldiered on until the military brass were red or green in the face, or had lost consciousness.

So, though I aspired to replicate Huang, I more often found myself in Hemingway territory. This underlying tension between the intellectual and the corporeal defines the Chinese drinking experience, and it confuses any attempt to describe it. The central problem with baijiu is that one goes from spoonful to tsunami in an instant. My first experience had been among expatriates, where the stakes were low. In the years that followed, I was introduced to the more exacting local custom.

A particularly excruciating example came from my short-lived stint as a public relations executive. It was my first *real job*, for which I sold a part of my soul for a visa during the dark days of the 2008 Beijing Olympics, when foreign "troublemakers" were driven out in the name of internationalism. Every day brought with it a fresh moral compromise. Some days it was sending Chinese journalists on "media trips" to Europe in exchange for writing thinly veiled advertisements disguised as think pieces. Often the same article, copied word for word from our press release, would appear in a dozen Chinese papers with a dozen unique bylines.

On a good day I would get to write a speech about protecting the environment for an oil executive. This was the part of our work filed under corporate social responsibility. It made me long for public relations' good old days, when a person could still do an honest day's work promoting smooth and healthful U.S. tobacco.

What is relevant to the present study is the time my company went on a team-building retreat to Huang Shan. This is the fabled Yellow Mountain in Anhui Province, and its craggy peaks cresting the clouds are unparalleled for their beauty. It took us seven hours to reach its base by bus, and we had to endure a five-hour strategy meeting before we were allowed a glimpse of its summit. Our boss gave us thirty minutes to take pictures before shoving us back on the bus for the next corporate struggle session.

The drinking was similarly joyless. "Derek, we are going to show you how to drink in the Chinese way," said our lieutenant-manager, whom I'll call Big Lu. He filled my stemmed thimble-sized glass to the brim with fragrant baijiu and raised his own glass high in the air. He motioned for me to do the same. "Now make a toast to General Manager Cao. Clink glasses and drink together."

"Cheers, Cao," I said. *Ganbei*—drain the glass—China's customary drinking refrain. I met his glass with mine and downed the fiery liquid.

"No, no, no, no," said Lu, in his high-pitched lilt. He grabbed the carafe and refilled my glass to its starting position. "You need to say it with feeling. Let him know how much you appreciated this beautiful meal and the opportunity to work for him."

"Thank you, Mr. Cao. Truly, this is a wonderful meal." I met his glass and the sorghum juice screamed down my esophagus. I grimaced involuntarily.

Big Lu looked back at me with his predatory gaze, shaking his head and clicking his teeth. "That won't do," he said, filling my glass yet again. Cao nodded in agreement. A good toast, Lu explained, needs to be a heartfelt expression of profound respect. You need to tell Cao how grateful you are for this job (I wasn't), how much you admire him as a person (I didn't), and how happy you are to be on this retreat (those fuckers stole my three-day weekend).

But these were days of self-abnegation and dubious ethical choices, so I raised my glass and said, in as servile a voice as I could muster, "Mr. Cao, I'd like to take a moment to recognize the invaluable contribution to my professional development. I feel that in these past four months I have learned more than in the rest of my professional life put together. I know you are my boss, but also I've come to think of you as a mentor and something of a father figure. If I were to die tomorrow, I would do so without regrets, knowing that I had the opportunity to work for Damon Cao (not his real name). Every day you inspire us to greatness, and I toast your health in the hopes that you might be with us for many decades to come." Or something like that.

We clinked crystal a third time, and I winced through another shot. This time I was granted a reprieve until the next round of shots, and the one after that. They just kept coming. By the time we finished the meal, my head was spinning. I was told we would be leaving soon for karaoke and more drinking. I had done something very wrong, and this was my hell.

Needless to say, I didn't last long in public relations. But I lasted long enough to realize the truth of an oft-repeated observation about baijiu: it's the context in which it is consumed as much as the drink itself that makes it hard for the outsider to stomach. At your average

Chinese banquet, it is standard practice to crack open a half-liter bottle of hundred-plus proof baijiu and throw away the cap. The expectation is that everyone at the table, whether there are five or ten persons, will polish off the entire bottle in one sitting. The further requirement that one may drink only when toasted by another ensures that all drink in equal measure. It is not uncommon for the host to open a second bottle when the first is emptied, starting the morbid ritual anew.

At the risk of meandering deeper down the path of cultural chauvinism, I must say, this is completely insane. A few shots of baijiu are enough to send the most level heads reeling, but a quarter bottle, a half bottle? That way lies deep, irreversible, stumbling drunkenness, with all the inevitable complications and consequences. I suspect that there would be far fewer whiskey drinkers if newcomers were initiated with peaty Islay scotch by the bottle. But this comparison is misleading: baijiu is typically bottled at much higher strengths than whiskey, a full 25 percent stronger in most cases.

So past experience was my first clue. Taking baijiu out of its natural habitat, the dreaded ganbei banquet, seemed a promising avenue for unlocking the drink's mysteries. If I could sip and savor it absent the toasting imperative, perhaps I could learn to understand just why the Chinese were so taken with the stuff.

I mean, if hundreds of millions of people drank the stuff every day, how bad could it be? There had to be something to it that I was missing. There just *had* to be.

Rounding out the Chengdu baijiu auxiliary was my Chinese tutor, de facto research assistant and friend, Duan Li. She was a vivacious Sichuanese woman who instructed half the consular community, from the consul general down to us lowly "trailing spouses," as we are known with all due condescension. Duan was uncommonly forthright about her culture and patient with my frequent lapses in tone and pronunciation. More than anyone else, she made sure I never wandered too far afield in my investigations. Every day we met at a cafe called Bingo Bagel, down the block from my apartment. It was never open during breakfast hours and frequently out of bagels—more accurately, dense bagel facsimiles—but it had passable coffee, and in Chengdu that is enough.

My compatriots were seldom charitable when discussing my project. "How's the *research* coming along?" they asked, laughing and making a tipping-the-bottle-back gesture. But Duan was always supportive, enthusiastic even. I think she found the idea of an aspiring U.S. baijiu aficionado hilarious, or at least a pleasant change of pace from teaching homemakers how to haggle for silk dresses. Every day she would bring in new bits of alcohol miscellanea for me to study, or she would help me transcribe the bits of interviews with baijiu distillers that had sailed over my head.

"Me? Oh, no. I don't drink baijiu," she said, when I asked her about it. Upon prodding I learned that this statement carries less literal weight in China than it does where I'm from. Saying you abstain means something more akin to "I don't drink often" or "I do drink, but I don't enjoy it much" or "I drink a great deal when custom dictates." She was, after all, Sichuanese. For example, she told me that her father gave her a first taste of baijiu when she was just seven years old. When it comes time to celebrating the Chinese New Year at the Li household, the family regularly downs four or five bottles between as many people. This isn't negotiable.

"Perhaps it's because my family is traditional," she told me. She and her brother must always toast their elders and accept their toasts in return. This usually means that they, as the youngest members of her extended family, have to kick off any holiday with fifteen to twenty shots before the casual drinking begins. She might not enjoy it, but it would be impolite to do otherwise. "It'd be really strange celebrating without liquor," she said. "It just wouldn't feel like the holidays."

Duan provided my first glimpses of the cultural dimensions of Chinese drinking that had previously escaped me. There were unspoken rules and an intricate web of obligations that dictate when one should and should not pick up the glass. I learned that everything about the drinking ritual, from the selection of the bottle to the seating arrangement, carried significance. And my education was only beginning.

So, with Tony and Johan as lab assistants and Duan as chief counsel, it was time to get down to the serious business of drinking. I started by bringing two bottles from a local convenience store to a small dinner. One of the baijius, a fruity Sichuanese blend, was tolerable. The other, a sour-tasting bit of nastiness from Guizhou, was deemed a biological hazard and set aside after three shots. We finished the better bottle and concluded with beers at a bar down the street inexplicably run by a teetotaling devout Buddhist.

The night's lesson: not all baijius are created equal. Of greater significance was the realization that there are distinct subcategories of baijiu, and that these drinks are wildly dissimilar. Baijiu is not a specific drink but a category of drinks. The word *baijiu* literally means "white spirits," but it actually signifies any of a range of spirits made in a traditional Chinese style. There are more than a dozen unique varieties, and they can be as different to one another as vodka is to tequila.

I returned home twelve shots to the good, with a growing sense of accomplishment. The next morning I awoke feeling fantastic in mind and body. If I kept up the current pace, three hundred shots would be a cakewalk.

Reality provided a compelling rejoinder as I opened the bathroom door. Why, in the middle of the night, I had opted for the bathtub instead of the toilet, I'll never know, but I spent all morning with a mop pondering this decision. Again, I was forced to confront the fact that this might not be as easy as I would like it to be.

Whereas a smarter man would have called it quits, this one kept hitting the town, chasing that white lightning. I still wasn't sold on baijiu, but the peppery sweetness of the local blend was becoming more palatable, particularly in conjunction with the fiery delights of Sichuan cuisine. A bottle of Ronghe over hot pot: 254 shots to go. Yunnanese mint beef, goat cheese, and Niulanshan Erguotou: 249 to go. Fiery braised pig's feet with Quanxing: 240.

I tried everything I could think up to round out baijiu's rougher edges. One night I threw a baijiu cocktail party. Unmitigated disaster. Back then I was a lousy bartender, and in Chengdu mixers were in short supply. Erguotou and Sprite? Ick.

Another night I acquired extract of *synsepalum dulcificum,* better known as miracle berry, which scrambles your taste buds and renders sour tastes sweet. Sadly, it too was no match for the flavor juggernaut hiding in a bottle of baijiu. There are no shortcuts where baijiu is concerned.

Tony left Chengdu—everyone does sooner or later—but I was well on my way. Johan and a growing cast of the curious picked up the slack. Meanwhile, I began blogging my baijiu trials on a website I called *300 Shots at Greatness*. To my surprise I learned I was not alone: there was a small but devoted contingent of foreigners who delighted in sorghum sauce.

Yet for all my efforts to tame the baijiu beast, I was still coming up short. A few months in and sixty shots deep, I was beginning to lose heart. I had learned to tolerate baijiu, but I had yet to develop anything resembling affection. You just can't force an epiphany. I repeat: there are no shortcuts. Then one day inspiration struck where least expected.

3   The Way

The breakthrough came on the cusp of Spring Festival, which would usher in the Year of the Dragon and the corresponding eruption of pyrotechnics. The provincial Foreign Affairs Office had invited diplomats and their families for a day of entertainment to celebrate the auspicious occasion. Catherine had accepted on our behalf, telling me something vague about a countryside picnic with her colleagues, which sounded pleasant enough.

My heart sank as I boarded a minibus and received a typed itinerary. As a rule, I despise organized tours, or really any activity that involves being carted from place to place in a bus full of strangers with no hope of escape. The paper I was holding outlined twelve hours of activities. By any measure, it would be a long slog.

We started the day at a private international school, where a Party official detailed government schemes to attract foreign investment. It was a recitation of mind-numbing development statistics punctuated by bursts of polite applause. Upon our minders' prompting, we were placed atop bicycles and told to ride around an asphalt loop for approximately five minutes while local media snapped our pictures, presumably for propaganda purposes: Chengdu! Cosmopolitan metropolis of the future! Happy foreign cyclists! Build a production plant! Build a hotel! Cheap labor! Give us your money! Excruciatingly dull, and we were already running behind schedule.

A lavish luncheon followed. Catherine and I sat front and center at the table of honor. A number of consuls general from France, Germany, and elsewhere were seated with us, presumably because Catherine was the highest-ranking American in the room. None of the other U.S. officers had been foolish enough to show.

Then I saw something that piqued my interest. At the center of each table were bottles of an extravagantly expensive Sichuanese baijiu called National Cellar 1573. I'd read about it in my research and seen ads for it on the side of buses. The baritone jingle announcer's *yi wu qi san*, "1573," was burned in my mind. Luzhou Laojiao, its producer, was the one of the oldest distilleries in the nation. It traced its history back almost a thousand years and enjoyed a reputation as the prototypical Sichuanese distiller. (By happy coincidence I later ended up working with the Luzhou Laojiao distillery. This in no way colors my telling of this story—I wrote a similar account on my old blog years before any money changed hands.)

Before me was its flagship top-shelf spirit, fermented in a workshop that had been in continuous operation since 1573. At the time a single bottle of it retailed for hundreds of dollars. And it was just sitting there in the center of the table, ignored and untouched. Did they not realize what they had served us? I did the only sensible thing when good booze is being wasted. I drank it.

It was a revelation. It hit my tongue with a rush of pineapple and apricot, leaving an expanding mélange of white pepper and licorice in its wake. It was smooth and rich and refreshing. This was not simply a magnificent baijiu. It was a magnificent drink. Period.

Protocol be damned, I poured myself another shot. And another after that. It was a good thing I did, too, because the next bit of entertainment involved models in chintzy ethnic-minority costumes performing dances, acrobatics, and torch juggling wholly unsuitable for an indoor venue. Did I rush for a fire extinguisher or despair over the remaining nine hours of the ordeal? I did not. I embraced the absurdity and had another drink.

The rest of the day should have been a soul-crushing succession of rote Party speeches and propaganda photo ops showing cooperation between the provincial government and its "foreign friends." It was exactly what I enjoyed least about life in China. But for a change I found myself bemused.

An hour after lunch I was in Pujiang, a "small" Chinese city of about a quarter-million people, most of whom were there to watch me dance. I was in the middle of a cordoned-off intersection in the city center, surrounded by a battalion of a hundred adorable, pink-cheeked girls in red silk costumes. I also wore silk, a royal blue traditional jacket that my minders provided me after lunch. The girls were armed with drums. I had one too. One of them had tied it to me before dragging me from my seat. The girls were performing an intricate drum and dance routine, which try as they might to teach me, I had no prayer of following. The onlookers pointed and laughed. I laughed along with them.

This was pure, undiluted joy. This was the precise moment when I realized I had fallen hard. I was hopelessly, irreversibly in love with baijiu.

That day I stumbled onto the missing piece of the puzzle. I had always feared traditional Chinese celebrations, because of the tedium and the obligatory baijiu shots. I had thought that to enjoy baijiu it needed to be modified in some way, taken out of its natural context. But now I understood that the baijiu was what transformed the tedium into something else, something far better. What's more, I had found a baijiu I actually enjoyed drinking.

I beat on a drum with children. Later I picked oranges in a field, danced a Chinese circle dance with villagers, and watched a fireworks display, holding hands with my wife and a plush elephant that I acquired at some point. I loved it, loved every minute of the day-long ordeal, and I had my fiery new friend to thank for it.

Lest my memory of these events be called into question, I have photographic proof. The next day I appeared in newspapers and websites across China—traditional costume, drum, ear-to-ear smile, the works. For a time, perhaps even still, my happy face featured prominently in the promotional brochures for the Sichuan Foreign Affairs Office. I'm cool with this. They earned my acquiescence.

It had taken less than three months and no more than seventy shots. I had crossed over. There was no turning back.

After that everything fell into place. My fear morphed into eager anticipation. There were baijius I now savored, particularly the spicy-sweet blends of Sichuan. Even the styles I had earlier considered difficult to stomach were now at least tolerable, if not enjoyable. Once I had experienced baijiu at its best, it was possible to understand what lesser iterations were trying to accomplish.

In this one respect, the idea of a taste threshold has merit. There was a certain similarity with how I had come to appreciate drinking inferior beer only after tasting the good stuff on a trip through Germany as a teenager. It was not about flipping a switch from bad to good, it was about finding what was good and looking for echoes of it in lesser products. It's not so much about crossing thresholds as establishing baselines.

In Sichuan I had learned to enjoy baijiu, and for that I will always cherish it. But it was time to broaden the scope of my investigation. I had my foot lodged in the door to Chinese alcohol connoisseurship, and it was time to throw it wide open. Chengdu had shown me the way, but it could only ever be a starting point. I had once mistaken Shanghai for China. I was not going to repeat this mistake.

China is vast. From a distance the world's most populous nation can appear monolithic, but there exists within it tremendous diversity. China has more than twenty provinces, sharply bound by culture and language, geography, and ethnicity. In each province, city, and village are new worlds to discover, stories to be heard, drinks to be drunk. I would experience as much of it as I could.

Perhaps the average Chinese has little more initial fondness for whiskey than I had for baijiu. But I was on their turf: the onus to respect the traditions of this magnificent if frustrating place surely fell on me. Could

I say I made an honest effort to understand China if I was unwilling to make the easiest of concessions, drinking in a new context? What I sought was the means to achieve common ground, or at least a sloppy medium. It felt like I owed my adopted home this much.

So two months after my epiphany, I was back at Chengdu's Shuangliu International Airport, waiting for my flight to be announced. There was a path to be charted, and it would take me across the country and thousands of years into its past. I approached my subject with my mind open and my glass full.

I would move beyond the fierce baijius of Sichuan, seeking out drinks from all corners of the Middle Kingdom. I would sip the mellow rice baijius of the southeast, the pungent fungal brews of Guizhou, the icy daggers of the north, and everything in between. I would not confuse baijiu with the panoply of Chinese alcohol. I would seek out Yangtze Delta huangjiu, fermented grain wines popular for millennia, as well as sweet rice *mijiu*, medicinal tonic, beer, and fruit wine. If China fermented or distilled it, I would drink it.

Armed with a box of business cards and a notepad full of contacts, most of whom I had never met, I was wading out into the great alcohol-producing hotbeds of China. I wanted to learn the art of Chinese alcohol and the consumption rituals that surround it.

On the long journey that followed, I would talk my way into massive state-run megadistilleries and smaller, family-owned outfits. I would seek out the company of historians and blenders, Party members, snake oil salespeople, and casual drinkers. My quest would take me deep into the nation's dynastic past and reveal glimpses of its future. I would be gone a month, maybe longer. However long it took. After winging it in China for years, this was to be my greatest test.

If, as Li Bai suggested, the road to Sichuan is tantamount to ascending the heavens, where would the road out lead? Would my journey into the heart of Chinese alcohol bring me back down to earth or cast me into the depths of dipsomania?

Three electronic chimes sounded. "Ladies and gentlemen, we will now begin boarding."

PART 2

Jiu's Story

How many great men were forgotten through the ages?
Great drinkers are better known than sober sages.
                    —*Li Bai, "Invitation to Wine"*

4 Drink of the Dead

In 1983 Chinese archaeologists led by Zhang Juzhong found the Holy Grail. They were excavating a site called Jiahu in central China's Henan Province, the heart of the Central Plain along the Yellow River and its tributaries. Nomadic tribes began settling in this region almost ten thousand years ago, creating the wellspring of Chinese civilization. Almost everything we associate with today's China, from bureaucracy to fried noodles, traces its roots to this place. It was where ancient shamans began etching characters on tortoise shells. It was where craftspeople sculpted clay into jars and cups. It was where the Chinese first got drunk.

The settlement unearthed at Jiahu dated from about 7000 to 5800 BCE, and it possessed a culture of striking sophistication. The people who lived at Jiahu had the rudimentary beginnings of a symbolic language, with characters uncannily similar to those found in the so-called oracle bone script, China's earliest unified language. Their primitive tools included percussive instruments and flutes made from the wing bones of cranes, still usable today and designed to play the pentatonic scale, later used in traditional Chinese music. Among the Jiahu relics were clay goblets, though it was impossible to say what they had once contained at the time of their discovery.

"They had special pools for raising fish, and they had the early rice, and they had the first domesticated pigs and dogs," Dr. Patrick E. McGovern explained to me. "Jiahu is really a very broad-based view of what Neolithic life might have been like." McGovern, a pioneer in the field of biomolecular archaeology, specializes in prehistoric alcohol. Sometimes called "The Indiana Jones of Ancient Ales," he applies the latest scientific analytic tools to historical findings—forensic science for the world's coldest cases.

I met McGovern on a snowy morning in January 2018 at the University of Pennsylvania Museum in Philadelphia. A genial man, tall with a long white beard, he showed me to his office in the Archaeology Department. It was the typical monastic cube of the academic, crowded with books and the faint hum of public radio classical music, but with a few eccentric flourishes. There was the odd bottle of Chinese liquor on the shelf, alongside an award he won at the 2009 Great American Beer Festival—he calls it his "shrine." There were also the file cabinets with large handwritten labels reading, "Beer," "Wine," and so forth.

In 1999 a colleague invited him to Shandong Province to join one of the first international archaeological excavations allowed in the People's Republic. The conditions were spartan—no heat, terrible beds, and a concrete trench for a bathroom—or, as McGovern relates it, "very exciting." Knowing that he would be in China for six weeks, he wanted to make the most of his time and arranged his travels to meet with several of China's leading archaeological scientists. "I began to see that China really had a long tradition of technology, cultural development that was sometimes even earlier than the Middle East," his principal field of study. "Pottery goes back to 16,000 BC in China, but the earliest pottery in the Middle East is 6000 BC. So China had ten thousand years on the Middle East, and I was just amazed."

Wherever he went he was treated like visiting royalty. Every day brought a fresh banquet. "We'd be out in Anyang," he said. "They'd take me to the restaurant, which is out on a boat in the Yellow River, and they'd serve up the big fish, and I'd use my chopsticks to take the first bite, and everyone applauds." And inevitably came the baijiu, which he quickly learned to eschew in favor of milder rice wines.

Eventually, he made his way to Zhengzhou, Henan's capital, where Zhang Juzhong presented him with pottery samples from the Jiahu site. Working with an international team of analysts and researchers, he subjected the Stone Age pottery to a variety of tests to extract trace residue. The team's findings rewrote the history of alcohol.

Up to that point, the long-standing assumption had been that intoxicating beverages originated in the Near East or the Caucasus, but the Jiahu samples contained the remains of the oldest alcohol ever documented—and not just a little older, thousands of years older than anything hitherto discovered. (At the time of this writing, the Jiahu sample remains the world's oldest known alcohol, though McGovern hinted this may soon change with new findings from the Near East. There also remain several still-untested Chinese pottery samples much older than those found in Henan.)

What Jiahu proved beyond a doubt is that China's love affair with alcohol predates its recorded history, perhaps even its civilization. As long as there has been a Chinese identity, there has also been a Chinese drinking culture. Just how far back this tradition goes may be suggested by the term ancient Chinese scholars used to describe the country's earliest quaffs: *yuanjiu*, literally "ape wine." This is no exaggeration. And though the reader may wonder where these drunken primates procured their booze, the explanation is simple.

It all begins with fermentation, the process by which yeast gobbles down sugar and converts it into carbon dioxide and alcohol. Fermented fruit becomes wine. Honey—the most saccharine substance in the natural world—ferments to become mead. Fermentation can happen naturally without human intervention, when a fruit falls from a tree and comes into contact with airborne yeast. It's so simple a monkey could do it, and, according to seventeenth-century scholar Li Rihua, they do: "There are many monkeys in Huangshan. In the spring and summer they collect miscellaneous flowers and fruits and store them in a rocky crevice. In time they ferment into wine. The fragrant aroma would be detectable hundreds of steps away. A woodcutter venturing deep into the woods may come upon it. But he should not drink too much of the wine lest the monkeys discover the reduction in the amount of fluid left. If so, they would lie in wait for the thief and playfully torture him to death." Other ancient sources indicate that monkeys were up to a similar mischief in southwest China, intentionally fermenting fruit for love of drink.

But beer is not monkey business. Grains contain little sugar, so starches must first be converted to sugar—a process called saccharification—before they will yield forth frothy ale. Early humans likely first fermented grains by chewing on them and spitting them out, utilizing enzymes in our saliva to break down starches. The first alcoholic beverages consumed in China were thus almost certainly created by accident, when some early human or protohuman consumed something sugary that had crossed paths with airborne yeast and fermented naturally.

Whatever it was that this protohuman first ate or sipped, it didn't kill him. He must have liked the taste and, more important, the pleasant way it made him feel. Perhaps the drink made protoman bolder in the presence of protowoman, made his protojokes seem funnier, protodancing less awkward, and the harsh struggle for survival less brutish. Whatever that first intoxicated biped—Drunk Zero—did or did not feel, he unknowingly took the first step in the long, slippery road to mass inebriation.

Central to the question of alcohol's origins is its role in the development of agriculture. Yeast's second greatest gift to humanity is the way in which it makes dough rise and thereby gives us our daily bread. With the similarity of ingredients, beer has often been called "liquid bread," a label that implies bread came first. This may not be the case.

Traces of protohuman life have been discovered all across the landmass that became China. Early Chinese lived nomadic, foraging lifestyles for hundreds of thousands of years. Then about ten thousand years ago, for reasons unknown, humankind decided to settle down en masse. During this so-called Neolithic revolution, people around the world began forming communities and turning to agriculture as the principal means of subsistence.

Anthropologists initially believed that the decision to adopt a sedentary lifestyle was motivated by a desire to secure a healthier diet while expending less energy. But we now know that sedentary life, at least initially, was much more difficult than what had preceded it. Most modern hunter-gatherers put in *less* time and energy than their farming counterparts. As Jared Diamond writes in *Guns, Germs, and Steel*, "only for today's affluent First World citizens . . . does food production (by remote agribusinesses) mean less physical work, more comfort, freedom from starvation, and a longer expected lifetime." The situation for ancient farmers who had to invent the technologies needed to procure grain was decidedly grimmer—more work, more exposure to disease, and a shorter lifespan for a less abundant and diverse food supply.

And this is where Drunk Zero comes back into play. If the switch to agriculture was not motivated by hunger, it may have been by thirst. As early twentieth-century archaeologist Wu Qichang suggests, "Our ancestors first planted rice and millet with the goal of brewing alcohol not making food. . . . Eating rice actually arose out of alcohol."

The theory goes something like this. Drunk Zero eventually sobered up and decided he had to get his hands on more booze. Ethanol releases dopamine, endorphins, and serotonin into the brain—pleasantly addictive. He found the fruit or honey that got him drunk, and he experimented with it until re-creating the conditions that first got him tipsy. This could have happened days or years later, and it must have been an exceedingly tedious process, but remember: there was no internet back then. When Drunk Zero, or whoever, had unlocked the secrets of fermentation, he or she could replicate the process at will. Other protodrinkers tried it and also liked the intoxicating effects. Alcohol became a sought-after commodity, a thing to be coveted and worshipped. The more prestigious alcohol became, the greater the pressure to find reliable sources of fruits and cereals. And this demand, the thinking goes, prompted groups of people to band together and undertake plant domestication.

This so-called "beer-before-bread" theory started gaining traction in the late twentieth century, and the scientific evidence to support it was not far behind. The nine-thousand-year-old alcohol discovered at Jiahu provided a compelling exemplar. The "Neolithic grog," as McGovern calls it, was neither wine, beer, nor mead but a combination of all three. Made from an amalgam of grapes, hawthorn fruit, honey, and rice, it would have been a sweet, aromatic blend. So much was going on inside of the grog that one likely had to drink it with a straw to avoid getting a mouthful of thick sediment.

China is the counterintuitive home for the world's oldest known grape wine. Though the modern country contains over half of the world's wild species of grapes, no local varietal has ever been domesticated, and wine never enjoyed lasting popularity in ancient or medieval China. Yet the earliest libations there contained grapes.

What was even more surprising about the grog was that it contained rice. It is impossible to say at this remove whether the rice was wild or domesticated, but it was one of the earliest known instances of rice cultivation anywhere in China. It suggests that rice was used to make alcohol long before it became a staple in Chinese cooking.

Not content to have merely discovered the world's oldest alcoholic beverage, McGovern also wanted to taste it. In 2005 Sam Calagione, owner of Delaware's Dogfish Head Brewery, with whom McGovern has collaborated to re-create several ancient ales, began experimenting with the known ingredients of the Jiahu grog. With only minor substitutions—Dogfish Head did not, for example, break down rice starch with human saliva—they created what is called Chateau Jiahu the following year. It is a crisp amber brew with an astonishingly rich flavor. It has the syrupy sweetness of a mead with the fruity tartness of a Lambic. If it is a fair approximation of the original, it foreshadowed the millennia-long Chinese preference for tangy tipples.

Almost ten thousand years have passed since the last time anyone sipped Neolithic grog, but humankind still knows a good drink when it tastes it. Chateau Jiahu netted a gold medal in a blind tasting at the

Great American Beer Festival, and it remains McGovern's favorite collaboration with Calagione, hence the shrine.

Back in his office McGovern had just returned the medal to its place when he reached for a small baggie tucked away on his bookshelf and asked, almost as an afterthought, if I would like to see one of the clay samples from Jiahu. I was not allowed to remove it from the plastic, but it was still remarkable to touch something so ancient. It was a little shard of beige pottery, incised with thin lines on the inside ("very unusual," McGovern noted, "possibly to collect sediment"), a piece of a wine jug fabricated nine thousand years ago.

But the decision to upturn an entire way of life, to give up the open plain for the farmhouse, forever changed humanity. It seems unlikely that a beverage, even a very good one, could inspire such a revolution.

Jiahu tells a different story. Much of the ancient alcoholic paraphernalia discovered there, and at other archaeological sites in China, lay sealed within burial tombs. These cups and carafes were found buried alongside handcrafted tools, totems, and other domestic treasures. We can infer that alcohol was something highly prized in the Stone Age. We will never know why exactly they drank—they lacked the language to leave any record behind. Yet there are clues in what was written much later that suggest drink was central to prehistoric life, and no less so the afterlife.

"Of the various kinds of ceremonies (both religious and civil)," writes Qing-era scholar Pu Qilong, "there is none to be put before sacrifice." Sacrifices were many and varied, ranging from gruesome, sometimes cannibalistic, offerings of enemy captives to more palatable offerings of food and drink. A sacrifice was a commercial exchange between the human and spirit realms. The Confucian *Book of Rites* warns subjects not to provoke the gods' wrath through being stingy or by making the same request twice. The spirits were fickle, and the purpose of sacrifice was not only to curry favor but to reemphasize humanity's lowly position in the divine hierarchy. The gravity of the occasion was reflected in the amount of alcohol offered, and the spirits were thirsty.

In the ancestral sacrifice ceremonies practiced during the first millennium BCE, possibly earlier, a human stand-in, or "corpse," represented the departed spirit. Leading up to the ceremony, the impersonator, usually a relative of the deceased, prepared for one week by fasting and meditating on the spirit he was meant to embody.

With a sprinkle of wine on the ground, a ruler or shaman called the "spirit" to earth to begin the ceremony. The ruler took a sip from the cup, reserving the remainder for the spirit, who would sip thrice. The ruler's wife and ministers would repeat the offering with more wine and food; occasionally they slaughtered an animal. All the while a strict three-to-one spirit-to-human consumption ratio remained in effect. The "corpse," half-starved and likely already hallucinating, must have been irredeemably smashed after only a few glasses.

Seeing the spirit inebriated, the assembly commended themselves on a job well done and moved on to the more animated part of the rite. Confucius explains that the impersonator was merely consuming the food and drinks the spirits had left him, so when he rose, presumably to vomit and pass out in the corner, "the ruler and his three ministers partook of what he had left." And the ministers took what the ruler left, and so on and so forth in a debauched cascade. That's when the party really got going. The humans continued toasting the spirit, the spirit started toasting the humans, and then everyone started toasting one another until the solemn occasion devolved into a rip-roaring hootenanny.

For one who has drunk baijiu with the Chinese, it is impossible not to recognize in this ancient ceremony the origins of today's notorious ganbei slugfests. And this is likely no coincidence. Most of the wine jugs recovered from Jiahu tombs sat alongside the skulls of the deceased. "It's almost like they're drinking in the afterlife," McGovern noted.

A contemporaneous poem from the *Book of Odes*, "The Great Summons," captures the mood:

Roast crane is next served, steamed duck and boiled quails,
Fried bream, stewed magpies, and green goose, broiled.
O soul, come back! Choice things are spread before you.

The four kinds of wine have been subtly blended, not rasping to the throat:
Clear, fragrant, ice-cooled liquor, not for base men to drink;
And white yeast is mixed with must of Wu to make the clear Chhu wine.
O soul, come back and do not be afraid.

All aspects of China's early drinking culture were ordered. Whether you drank a little or a lot, every gesture was rigidly prescribed. Foremost among ancient Chinese drinking mores was the idea that you never drank to satisfy a craving. You drank always with a nobler intent. It's like what a Chengdu baijiu trader once told me, "When someone is born we drink. When someone dies we drink. When someone gets married we drink. You never drink without a purpose."

It was the same in antiquity. People drank to celebrate life as well as death. People drank for courage before battle, and they drank again when returning victorious. Both oaths of fealty and matrimony required drink. Even executions required a stiff drink. Most important, then and now, was the banquet. Far from being a trivial diversion for the wealthy, the banquet was an important tool by which leaders consolidated power. Feasting ensured the continued survival of the community: a proper stuffing and sousing could win over enemies and cement an ally's loyalty. Lavish dining required surplus, which required more grain cultivation and larger concentrations of humans, which in turn created villages and cities.

The drinks spread, whether by independent inspiration or from village to village along what McGovern posits was a prehistoric "Silk Road." From Jiahu, or wherever the Chinese first drank, alcohol proliferated from the East China Sea to the Caucasus, where grape wines appeared a thousand years later. After another thousand years people brewed beer in the Middle East and fermented mare's milk in the Asian Steppe.

And the drinks flowed in both directions. Two additional unearthed alcohols that date four thousand years after Jiahu—the Liangchengzhen grog in Shandong and a protobeer from Mijiaya in Shaanxi—both contain traces of barley, suggesting ingredients and techniques imported from Mesopotamia or the Mediterranean. Along similar routes ideas borrowed from Persian Zoroastrianism and Greek Hellenism would later enter China.

Not only did alcohol give gave rise to civilization; it nurtured it to maturity. The earliest examples of written Chinese are carved into tortoiseshells or ox bones in the form of questions to the gods. A shaman heated these so-called oracle bones until they cracked, and the fissures revealed divine will. Among the characters etched into these oracle bones is *jiu*, composed of the symbol for water next to the symbol for jug. Today jiu is the Chinese word for any and all alcoholic beverages. Chinese spirits are *baijiu* (white alcohol), grain wine is *huangjiu* (yellow alcohol), grape wine is *hongjiu* (red alcohol), and so on. But thousands of years ago, when the oracle bones were used, jiu referred to a specific drink: a sweet, filtered wine probably made from rice or millet. It was one of the strongest drinks the world would know prior to the invention of distilled spirits.

Jiu was by no means the only alcoholic beverage popular in ancient times, and surviving records indicate the ancients drank at least four other beverages. Jiu's chief competitor was *li*, a thick but weak sweet wine fermented from rice or millet with sprouted grains. There was also a wine made from pulverized fruit and water called *luo*, a grain wine mixed with its sediment called *lao*, and a ritual drink called *chang* fermented from herbs, flowers, and resins.

The great explosion of alcohols may be attributable to the rise of the semimythical Xia and Shang dynasties, who ruled the Central Plain from 2070 to 1046 BCE. With them came bureaucracy, and with bureaucracy came state-sponsored wine making that elevated the craft to a profession. By the first millennium BCE the royal court had a superintendent of jiu, a master of jiu, a preparer of *chang*, and a keeper of the ritual herbs. The master of vinegar alone had a staff of more than sixty. Chinese governance and drinking have been inseparable ever since—the administrator of sacrifices, the *jijiu*, or "superintendent of alcohol," morphed into the title held by the head of China's Imperial Academy until the nineteenth century.

"In China, mankind's most complex alcohol culture evolved in accordance with an extremely elaborate ceremonial system and an enormous bronze vessel fabrication system with an unmatched variety of forms and names for each type of vessel," writes leading Chinese wine scholar Peter

Kupfer of the University of Mainz in "Amber Shine and Black Dragon Pearls." The production of countless intricately worked bronze cups, goblets, and carafes, which peaked during the Shang dynasty, created a distinctly Chinese aesthetic, which may have given rise to the region's distinct artistic style.

The effect on language was no less profound. As Kupfer notes, there are more than four hundred Chinese characters containing the component *you*, which signifies a wine jug. Just as the Inuits have over fifty words for snow, a Chinese culture suffused with alcohol developed innumerable ways to express the concepts of drinking and libations.

Of the ancient court winemakers we know precious little. The earliest record attributes the "invention" of alcohol to Yi Di. We know nothing about her for certain, save that she served the court of Yu the Great, legendary founder of China's first dynasty, the Xia.

Though Yi Di's gender has long been a matter of dispute, most historians refer to her using feminine pronouns. This reflects the prominent role of women in early Chinese wine making. "In almost all civilizations," writes Kupfer, "females were/are mainly responsible for the production and the supply of alcoholic beverages, as manifested in the goddesses Ninkasi in Sumer and [Yi Di] in China."

The fullest account of her story says that Yu's daughter ordered Yi Di to make wine as a tonic for her overburdened father. When the wine was presented to Yu, he found it sweet and refreshing. Yet, in his wisdom, he proclaimed that alcohol would lead future rulers to ruin. He promptly banned wine making. Some versions of the story say he banished Yi Di from the realm.

Others credit Shao "Du" Kang with producing China's first grain wine. His identity is unclear: he may have been grandson of a later Xia king. In any case, the court tasked Du with overseeing the palace kitchen. The absentminded Du stored imperial millet in the hollow of a tree and promptly forgot about it. One day he strolled past the tree and smelled something sweet. Pleased by the aroma of rotten grain, Du intuited it would make a smashing libation.

Women always get short shrift in Chinese history. Yi Di was run out of town for making wine to order, and Du Kang flubbed his job to universal acclaim. Today Yi Di is all but forgotten, while Du Kang is revered as an immortal. Later generations would boast, "A round of Du Kang's wine can make you drunk for three years." Or, as the warlord Cao Cao wrote, "What can dispel the sorrow? Only Du Kang." Yi Di first unlocked the secrets of wine but receives blame for the intemperance of male leaders.

The problem is where one draws the line between history and myth. The oldest Shang oracle bones date from the fourteenth century BCE— five thousand years after Jiahu—and it would be another thousand years before the first recorded mention of alcohol's origins. "None of the [stories] are supported by textual evidence," explains the Song dynasty *Record of Alcohol*, with a hint of exasperation. "It's mostly just empty talk."

This does not mean nothing can be gleaned from these tales. In Du Kang's tale we see the possible origins of traditional Chinese grain alcohol, which depends on an interaction between steamed grains and the surrounding environment. And Yu the Great's warning on the destabilizing abilities of alcohol was likely a later historian's embellishment with the benefit of hindsight.

Both the Xia and Shang dynasties supposedly met their end in the bottom of a glass. King Jie of Xia was a legendary drinker whose name became synonymous with tyranny. The philosopher Xunzi compared his rule to Yu the Great's, saying, "Yu used government; Jie used disorder." Together with his favorite lover, Mo Xi, who shared Jie's penchant for cruelty and debauchery, he held nightly orgies with a coterie of concubines, musicians, actors, fools, and dwarves. "They were reckless, arrogant, and profligate," recounts the *Classic of Poetry*.

King Jie ordered construction of a tower that reached into the heavens and a lake of wine large enough to float a barge on. He commanded groups of up to three thousand to drink from it naked like cattle, and he took special pleasure in watching his subjects drown in it. When his minister Guan Longfeng urged a lighter touch, Jie put him to death. He imprisoned his rival Tang of Shang in the tower but later set him free—his one regret. Tang overthrew the dissolute Jie, founding the Shang dynasty. He set Jie and Mo Xi adrift at sea, and they died in exile.

The legend of the final Shang king's story is better fleshed out but is functionally identical to Jie's. King Zhou, or Di Xin, was in his youth an intelligent, capable administrator, but his fondness for drink led him down a path worthy of the most salacious tabloid. Perpetually drunk, he ignored the basic affairs of state and quashed any dissent with horrific violence. When the king's uncle Bi Gan urged him to reform his ways, the king ordered his kinsman's heart cut out.

Only the king's debauchery outshined his cruelty. According to China's Herodotus, Sima Qian, Di Xin constructed "a pool of wine and a forest of hanging meats. He'd force men and women to chase each other through the forest in the nude, drinking away the night." For the drunken, naked aristocrats, slathered in animal grease, every carnal desire was within arm's reach. Later generations use the expression "pools of wine, forests of meat" to describe a lifestyle of wanton depravity, which it undoubtedly was.

King Wu of Zhou led a revolt, vanquishing the Shang armies in a battle of such gratuitous violence that witnesses recalled the soldiers' wooden spears floating in a literal torrent of blood. The mad king Di Xin retreated to his palace, where he poured himself a drink and self-immolated. He was not missed, but his wine was. After founding the Zhou dynasty, King Wu banned on pain of death the consumption of alcohol for all but sacrificial purposes.

The swift transition of power was ensured by a concept called the mandate of heaven. It states that a leader's authority derives from right actions, pleasing to the heavens, and provides a justification by which Chinese reconciled the transfer of authority to a new imperial line without undermining the dynastic system's legitimacy.

It is diabolically clever. The former dynasty had the moral authority to rule right up to the point that it lost power, when the usurper asserted *his* authority by seizing the throne. It explains the downfall of Jie and Di Xin without questioning cosmic wisdom. Not only does it mean that anyone could theoretically rule China, it means Chinese rulers are never wrong. If they were, they would lose power. It reduces political philosophy to tautology.

This was revolutionary in ancient China. The Shang king had been seen as semidivine, deriving power from his exclusive access to the spiritual realm. During sacrifices he was the representative of humanity who could enter negotiations with the gods and spirits, and thus he acted with godly purpose. With the mandate of heaven, the authority to rule was externalized, and the government became in essence secular.

Drinking culture also began to come down to earth. As had been the case in earlier dynasties, the Zhou employed a large retinue of winemakers specializing in a variety of drinks for public and private use. Sacrificial rites continued, but the human "impersonators" were replaced by idols. People no longer drank solely for the gods and spirits but also to exult one another. And in a secular world, the government could limit the production and sale of alcohol without offending the heavens.

King Wu of Zhou's alcohol prohibition, the first in Chinese history, was short-lived and ultimately ineffective. By this point the role of alcohol in daily life had become far too ingrained at all levels of society. The Confucian *Book of Documents* records the opinion of an official writing around 650 BCE, who notes that stopping the flow of alcohol is "beyond the power of even the sages. . . . The people would not do without." This was as true in China as it was elsewhere in the ancient world.

Clean water is so ubiquitous today that we often forget that humankind built cities long before it figured out plumbing. Pollution and waterborne illnesses rendered urban water supplies unfit for drinking, so many societies turned to wine and beer. Yeast is antimicrobial, killing off competing pathogens and making drinks healthier. The Egyptian laborers who built the pyramids at Giza were given a daily allotment of slightly more than a gallon of beer. Europeans continued to drink a comparable quantity until the arrival of more stimulating alternatives, namely coffee and tea.

In China tea and its predecessor, boiled water, were what allowed the Zhou to even consider banning alcohol. Alcohol contains toxins that can, after just a few drinks, cause flushing of the skin, headaches, nausea, and nastier chronic illnesses. To compensate for this is an enzyme called alcohol dehydrogenase, which metabolizes the toxins before they inflict damage. Cultures like those in the Middle East and Europe that relied on alcohol for hydration developed these enzymes through natural selection: if you couldn't drink alcohol, you didn't survive.

But in Asia people adapted to water pollution by boiling water, and as a result many of them never developed an alcohol tolerance. This enzyme deficiency—known informally as "Asian flush" for the way it reddens faces—affects more than one in ten Chinese, and as much as half of the population in the Pacific Rim, and provides a strong biological incentive against overindulgence in alcohol. It also meant that alcohol prohibitions were never challenged on the grounds of public health.

Over the course of the dynastic system, Chinese monarchs would attempt to outlaw intoxicating beverages more than forty times. The reasons were usually sound—grain shortages, philandering officials, and so forth—but drinkers and brewers always found ways to skirt the laws. That the government repeatedly reinstated prohibition should give some indication of their effectiveness.

What had emerged in the earliest chapters of Chinese history was an uneasy relationship between alcohol and the state. Alcohol had helped create a civilization and provided its people with a rich spiritual life. The people in turn worshipped alcohol, even after it had been stripped of its religious connotations. But alcohol also gave rise to mischief, disorder, and all manners of bad behavior—hardly the stuff of good governance.

The questions of when one should drink, how much one should drink, and to what purpose one should drink loomed large. The answers, and the colorful characters who espoused them, would define the golden era of Chinese drinking culture, the age of huangjiu.

5 Drink of the Immortals

Everything changed in 221 BCE. Soon after Alexander the Great conquered the world from the Mediterranean to the west of India, Qin Shihuang conquered most everything to its east. Smashing through the kingdoms that splintered off the Zhou dynasty, the Qin war machine crushed its rivals and established Chinese rule far beyond the Central Plain. The Yangtze River Delta became part of Qin's empire, as did far-flung regions along the South China Sea and to the west in Sichuan. The nation's boundaries began to resemble those of modern China, and thus the Qin—pronounced like the *chin* in chino—is considered the first proper Chinese dynasty.

Though a brilliant militarist, Qin Shihuang was a tyrannical and exceptionally unpopular leader. It was he who ordered the construction of the Great Wall and the legions of terra-cotta warriors that guard his tomb, both built on the blood and bones of countless conscripted laborers. He suppressed competing ideas and buried his critics alive. His dynasty barely outlived him, but it laid the groundwork for four centuries of growth and relative stability under the Han dynasty. Tellingly, ethnic Chinese refer to themselves as the Han people rather than the Qin.

China's political unity coincided with a subtler revolution in wine making: the rise of *qu*. Together with the compass, gunpowder, paper, and printing, qu (pronounced "chew") is one of the all-time great Chinese innovations. The Chinese sometimes refer to it as the "fifth invention." On its surface qu is just a dried-out clump of mashed grain, but within it lurks a diverse ecosystem of microorganic life. And that's the point.

Grain alcohol is more complex than fruit wine. Grains are high in starch and low in sugar. Yeast eats sugar and spits out alcohol and carbon dioxide (fermentation), so brewers working with grains need to first convert the starch to sugar (saccharification). With Western grain alcohol like whiskey and beer, this process is often accomplished through malting or the help of enzymes. With the ancient Chinese beer *li*, brewers sprouted grains by soaking them in water to achieve the same effect and waited for airborne yeast to convert the malt into beer. In both cases it was a two-step process: saccharification, then fermentation. What made qu revolutionary was that it reduces the process to a single step. The yeasts and other microorganisms within qu break down the starches and sugars simultaneously, turning grain directly into alcohol.

It works like this. One takes grains—steamed, roasted, raw, or a combination of these preparations—mixes them with water, forms them into a cake or brick, and lets that slowly dry out in a relatively airtight room over several days or weeks. While the qu is incubating, molds, yeasts, and bacteria from the surrounding environment form within and without the grains. The compound is then removed from the room and dried out in the sun to halt further growth. If properly stored the life within qu will survive for several years.

Chinese brewers take qu and grind it into a powder before mixing it with steamed grains. The fungal enzymes convert the starches to sugar, while the molds germinate and grow in the grains. The yeasts proliferate and ferment the sugar into an alcoholic liquid. And the bacteria impart the drink with much of its typically fruity flavor.

Not only is this process highly efficient, producing alcohol yields three to four times more potent than ancient Western ales, but it is also highly specific. Whatever life happens to reside in the air determines the character of the drink, so every drink is a reflection of the place it was produced: the notion of *terroir* taken to the next level. This was no mean feat in the ancient world. Their Western counterparts never figured it out, though in fairness the ancient Chinese didn't seem to fully grasp the biochemical underpinning of the process.

The earliest written instructions for making qu come from *Essential Techniques for the Welfare of the People*, written in the sixth century. It states that a boy wearing dark clothing must fetch the water, which no one else may touch. If there is any water left over, it must be discarded without being used by others. Only young boys may make the qu cakes, and they must all face west while working. From the qu mixture the workers must sculpt five figurines, called the "Qu Kings." Workers present offerings of dried meat and wine to the kings before the incubation process, which kicks off when a master of ceremonies reads the sacrificial incantation three times. All present kneel twice to the kings. Much to the credit of the manual's author, Jia Sixie, he notes no apparent change occurs in wine making when one omits the more eccentric steps of the process.

Qu was likely the unintended consequence of ancient Chinese culinary practices. In the Middle East and Mediterranean, the principal cereal grains were wheat and barley, which have hard exteriors and must be ground into flour before they can be worked into food. In China they worked with much softer grains that could simply be boiled in water or, as of about 6000 BCE, steamed. Once a batch of steamed grains spoils, it will eventually begin to ferment. All that is needed is minor human intervention—drying the spoiled grains midprocess—to create qu.

By around the first or second millennium BCE, under the Shang or Zhou, China for the first time encountered grain surpluses, and new qu-based concoctions emerged. They called the drink jiu.

Li couldn't compete. Jiu had a more robust and pleasing flavor, and it was much stronger. It is also possible that, as li depends on natural fermentation, it became increasingly weak over time as sanitary conditions in China improved. As Ming encyclopedist Song Yingxing writes,

"Later generations disliked the lightness of li. When it became obsolete, the sprouted grain brewing method was forgotten." Beer all but disappeared from the Chinese drinkscape for two millennia.

Dozens, possibly hundreds, of different varieties of qu appeared in the centuries that followed its invention, but today there are two basic divisions: big qu and small qu. Big qu is typically made of wheat or barley formed into largish bricks, and it is used in the production of most baijius. Small qu consists of dried-out rice balls and is more commonly used to make grain wines. (I employ the term *grain wine* rather than the Western words for fermented grain beverages, *beer* or *ale*. No English translation properly suits qu-brewed beverages, which are fermented from grain but have a taste and consistency more reminiscent of sweet wines. Certainly the cultural significance of jiu is closer to that of wine in Indo-European cultures. Mentally translate this term into whatever makes you happiest.) Qu formed the foundation of Chinese alcohol and, by extension, of East Asian alcohol.

Qu also made a profound impact on Chinese cooking. By the Han dynasty qu was used to produce vinegar, pickled meats and vegetables, and pastes of meat, fish, and fermented bean. Later it became the foundation of steamed bread, soy sauce, fish sauce, and tofu. Many, if not most, of the flavors we associate with Chinese cuisine derive from this remarkable wine-making innovation.

All grain wines that followed qu's conquest were called jiu, insofar as they were variations on a fundamental theme. Today we call qu-fermented grain wines huangjiu—yellow wine—not simply because most have an amber hue but also, one suspects, because yellow was the imperial color, and huangjiu was the drink of emperors.

Indeed, huangjiu's ability to diversify and conquer China with such rapidity owes everything to the centralized governments of the Han dynasty. The Han started their reign with the de rigueur prohibition on alcohol but quickly reversed course. Pushed into a financial corner by a series of expansionist military campaigns, Emperor Han Wudi (156–87 BCE) replaced the unpopular ban with a state alcohol monopoly. The move was an instant success, and all dynasties that followed copied it in some form. The tax revenue from alcohol became a source, in many cases the main source, of Chinese government revenue. The fate of the nation depended on drink.

With the monopoly in place and a clear financial incentive, the state used its considerable bureaucratic apparatus to spread the latest recipes and brewing techniques to all corners of the empire. Local crops, tastes, and traditions spurred regional variation, but the brewing fundamentals were more or less the same in the capital as in the remotest country hamlet. Huangjiu thrived, and the newly unified China had a national drink.

While China coalesced around a nascent national identity, a quiet revolution in thought was also underway. The specter of lawless and unruly behavior, which had led so many of China's early monarchs to fear drink, gave rise to a moderating voice. If the nation must drink, let them do so with ceremony and respect—so sayeth China's sober sage, Master Kong, or Confucius.

Confucius was born in the sixth century BCE, a moment of supreme political upheaval. The Zhou dynasty had lost its grip on power, and the Central Plain fractured into numerous competing states, a power vacuum that would take centuries and hundreds of thousands of lives to fill. China's ancient dynastic period was in its death throes, yet still had one last gasp of brilliance. Radical thinking was needed to bring order to chaos, and an outpouring of great thinkers, forming the so-called Hundred Schools of Thought, emerged. None left more lasting a mark than Confucius.

A mythology has grown out of the life and teachings of Confucius, but historians generally agree that he was a real man, a minor noble of the Lu Kingdom in modern-day Shandong Province. A scholarly bureaucrat who bounced from court to court, he retired from public life in his late sixties and founded an academy. There he taught poetry, history, and morality, among other subjects intended to create well-rounded individuals.

The idea of self-cultivation, that humans can be molded into useful members of society, was his core teaching. His philosophy was essentially secular, advocating education, moral cultivation, and humane treatment of others. In practical terms this meant the creation of a society in which everyone plays a part for the smooth functioning of the whole. The ruler is responsible for his subjects, parents for their children, teachers for their students, and so on. Relationships are reciprocal: the subject is obliged to follow the ruler, but the ruler is obliged to wield power ethically to cultivate a virtuous society. Confucianism relies on a strict code of conduct to govern private and public interactions.

Confucians acknowledged alcohol's central role in Chinese society but preached mild restraint when drinking. When imbibing, drinkers must respect the cosmic and social hierarchy, each drinking according to status. Gods and spirits always came first, then elders and distinguished tipplers. Drink became the vehicle for demonstrating respect to one's ancestors, superiors, and guests. Alcohol also played an important role in gift giving: when a ruler from Confucius's homeland paid tribute to his rival with a gift of cheap wine, it caused the outbreak of multiple wars.

In his attitudes Confucius was strongly influenced by the drinking mainstream of his era, particularly as put forth by Duke Dan of Zhou, the intellectual brother of the dynasty's first ruler. In the *Classic of History* the Duke of Zhou presents an "Edict of Alcohol," declaring that alcohol's purpose is for sacrifices. With rare exceptions for the sick and elderly, the public should abstain from drinking. He sets forth a notion of principled drinking that prohibits group drinking, in some cases on pain of death. And though an official's duties might require him to drink, he must not succumb to drunkenness.

To the Zhou, alcohol had a special cosmological significance. In the duality of heaven and earth, fermentation revealed a universe in constant flux. As Peter Kupfer writes in "Amber Shine and Black Dragon Pearls," alcohol was seen as a "cosmic and universal natural phenomenon, with its origin in heaven, and . . . man has been given the decision how to make use of it." Heaven would reward virtuous drinking, and alcohol abuse would be punished severely.

Though Confucius was somewhat more relaxed in his attitude, he still believed one should drink only during appropriate occasions, when making a sacrifice or attending an official banquet. One must never drink to excess. Specifically, one should never drink more than three large cups. Why three? Perhaps it goes back to the three drinks of the corpse ritual, though it has also been suggested that the three glasses represent the respective cosmological elements of the universe: heaven, earth, and humanity. In an ironic turn latecomers to a contemporary Chinese banquet are now forced to drink a three-cup penalty upon arrival.

Crucially, a Confucian may drink only at another's prompting. This requirement was enforced in ancient times by a bureaucrat whose sole function was to instruct people when to drink. Failure to heed the shot caller's mandate was seen as an act of rebellion that could result in decapitation. Over time this tradition grew more relaxed, and the shot caller's role became symbolic, more akin to a master of ceremonies than a drill sergeant. It is from this ancient custom that we get the Chinese word for drinking games: *jiuling,* or "drinking orders."

Alcohol is mentioned eighty-eight times in the *Classic of Rites.* Familiarity with proper drinking etiquette was essential to maintaining harmony in the realms of heaven and of humans. Perhaps the best enunciation of the Confucian drinking etiquette comes to us from the Confucian *Classic of Poetry:*

> If when a guest has drunk too much
> He courteously depart,
> His host and he would happy be,
> Each having done his part.
>
> But to remain when one is drunk
> Is not a virtuous thing.
> To drinking, though a custom good,
> One must deportment bring.

The Sage cast a long shadow. Though the Qin dynasty outlawed his teachings, they were resurgent under the Han, becoming the predominant social and political philosophy of classical China. Save moderation, the basic Confucian elements of the Chinese drinking ritual endure to this day.

Had Confucius's voice been the only one at the table, drinking would have become a sedate, humorless affair in the Middle Kingdom. Thankfully, a playful devil sat on China's other shoulder. For every Confucian killjoy frowning at a bottle, there was a Daoist rascal to pour the next glass.

The Han dynasty fell in 220 CE, and, as before, a new wave of thinkers emerged to fill the political void. Unlike their predecessors, who had sought to bring order to chaos, the Seven Sages of the Bamboo Grove tuned it out, drowning their sorrows in a perpetual stream of wine. The Seven Sages were scholar-officials, bureaucrats who lacked a credible government to serve. Rather than align themselves with a corrupt court, they gathered in a bamboo forest in Henan, where they composed subversive poetry and drank like longshoremen.

Philosophically, the sages were devout Daoists who sought truth through harmony with the natural order, the so-called *Dao*, or the Way. Drinking was for them a means of achieving a more carefree, effortless state of being. By washing away their inhibitions, they could forget who they were supposed to be and become what they actually were, a belief akin to the Roman maxim in vino veritas. In huangjiu, truth.

According to legend, Bamboo Sage Ruan Xian convened drinking sessions with his relations around a washbasin filled to the brim with huangjiu. Without concern for decorum, they foreswore utensils and slurped it dry using only their hands and mouths. One day a pack of hogs trudged in and began drinking from the communal pot. Whereas a lesser drinker might have shooed them away, Xian knelt down with the swine and joined them.

Then there was Ruan Ji, whose story provides an illustrative example of the Seven Sages' passive-aggressive approach to political entanglement. When the king of Wei came to Ruan Ji's home to arrange a marriage alliance between their children, Ruan Ji drank himself into a stupor. The king said he would wait for the other man to sober up before hearing his reply but left infuriated after Ruan's binge continued for sixty days.

Liu Ling, the most prodigious drinker of the lot, eulogized himself thus: "The Heavens created Liu Ling, alcohol made him famous." Liu liked to walk around stark naked, even while entertaining guests. When questioned about the habit, he responded that the heaven and earth were his home, and his home his cloak and pants. "So can you explain," Liu asked, in a (Groucho) Marxist turn of phrase, "just what it is you're doing in my pants?"

Liu always kept a bottle of wine on his person and a shovel-bearing servant at his side. When driving his mule cart he would take a swig, proceed a few steps, then stop for another drink. The servant followed close behind, ready to inter Liu at a moment's notice when the drinking finally did him in.

One tale has Liu Ling crossing paths with Du Kang, China's greatest drinker versus its greatest winemaker. (Chronologically, this doesn't pass muster—the two men lived several thousand years apart—but never mind.) Placards outside Du Kang's wine shop claimed that one cup of the master's wine could put a tiger to sleep, and two cups could knock out a dragon. Customers whose intoxication lasted less than three years, another sign read, drank for free.

Liu called Du's bluff and, despite the winemaker's protestations, drank three glasses of wine in one sitting. When it came time to pay, Liu realized he didn't have any silver on him—perhaps he'd forgotten to wear clothes that afternoon—and ran home to gather funds.

Hours passed. Then days, months, and years. No sign of Liu. Du's patience ran out, and he headed to Liu's house to collect. A distraught woman met him at the threshold. Three years prior, said Liu's wife, Liu had returned from Du's shop and dropped dead.

"My dear lady," replied Du. "Your husband isn't dead. He's *dead drunk*."

Subsequent exhumation of the "corpse" revealed the poet alive and just then shaking off his hangover. Turning to Du, Liu exclaimed, "That's some damned good wine!"

Though later writers sometimes portrayed Liu as a bumbling fool, his poetry soars. Rejecting accepted notions of property and propriety, his verse turns drinking into a spiritual act:

He travels without wheels or tracks,
Sojourns without house or hearth.
He makes Heaven his curtain and Earth his seat,
Indulges in what he pleases.
Stopping, he grasps his wine-cup and maintains his goblet;
Moving, he carries a casket and holds a jar in his hand.
His only obligation is toward wine,
And of this he knows abundance.

Later poet Tao Yuanming (365–427) internalized the duality of Chinese drinking culture. An official born into a down-on-its-luck aristocratic family in southeastern China's Jiangxi Province, Tao retired to the countryside at age forty. Some believe Tao was a Daoist, others that he was Confucian; some say he was a patriot, others that he ran from his duties. He embraced the contradictions. In one poem he likens the ongoing war between sobriety and drunkenness to two houseguests always at his side: "They laugh at one another, drunk and sober, and neither understands the other's words."

Tao rarely wrote about alcohol, but his "Twenty Poems about Wine" is one of the finest collections ever composed on the topic. In its preface, he notes alcohol's influence on his work: "Living in retirement here I have few pleasures, and now the nights are growing longer; so, as I happen to have some excellent wine, not an evening passes without a drink. All alone with my shadow I empty a bottle until suddenly I find myself drunk. And once I am drunk I write a few verses for my own amusement." His is a conflicted, sometimes apologetic, drunkenness. Yet through drinking he finds inspiration and release:

Sympathetic friends who know my tastes
Bring a wine jug when they come to visit.
Sitting on the ground beneath the pine tree
A few cups of wine make us drunk
Venerable elders gabbing all at once
And pouring from the bottle out of turn.

Aware no more that our own "I" exists
How are we to value other things?
So rapt we are not sure of where we are—
In wine there is a taste of profundity.

Tao Yuanming and the Seven Sages were not the first Chinese poets to revel in wine, but their rejection of Chinese society and their search for truth in cups transformed alcoholic excess into a rebellious, even heroic, act. But this was only the start. The Tang poets made drinking immortal.

Under the Tang dynasty (609–907) a newly reunified China became the most cosmopolitan empire the world had ever known. Its early emperors expanded Chinese rule in all directions, absorbing modern-day Vietnam and Korea along with much of Mongolia and central Asia. The capital, Chang'an, modern-day Xi'an, had more than a million inhabitants who lived a globally integrated lifestyle hard to imagine existing in its time. As sinologist David McCraw writes in *Du Fu's Laments from the South,* "Vendors brought wine, spices, and gems from Persia and Syria. Minstrels sang psalms of India and strummed lutes of Kucha. Along the [Yangtze] and up the Grand Canal flowed tax rice from the fertile southeast and overseas tribute from Canton and Yangzhou. From Vietnam came tea, via Turkestan Chinese met the chair. And so in a Chang'an tavern you could see blue-eyed Uighurs seated, sipping tea!"

More striking was the profusion of foreign ideas. Buddhism, Islam, Judaism, and Christianity all took root in Tang China, reshaping the way its people viewed their world. Buddhism had a particularly strong influence on Daoist beliefs, and vice versa—in China the Buddhist prohibition on drinking was all but forgotten, at least initially.

Against this backdrop emerged Li Bai, China's most celebrated poet and drinker. Historians believe Li Bai was born in 701 in central Asia near Afghanistan but relocated to Sichuan as a child. He may have been ethnically Turkic, and Chinese may not have been his first language, but under the Tang a man of his talents was welcomed into the kingdom with open arms.

He was a genius. Some even considered him a Daoist immortal, which is to say one who has achieved spiritual enlightenment. He reveled in the role, spending most of his life as a wandering mystic. In his youth he was a swordsman for hire. As an adult, he turned to the more refined pursuits of poetry and science. He served in the courts of the emperor and other high-ranking officials as a translator. Through it all, he drank and drank and drank.

While serving the imperial court at Chang'an, Li Bai often arrived at the palace so drunk he could hardly stand. He performed admirable service nonetheless, so the emperor kept him well lubricated. On one occasion Li was so tanked that the emperor had to clean the sick from his mouth, a gross violation of propriety. When Li left the capital, the emperor sent him off with lavish gifts, none more valuable than a decree granting him free wine for life (hitherto the poet had been haunted by unpaid bar tabs). He spent the rest of his days in a drunken cross-country amble.

It is said that Li Bai could write only when drunk: "a hundred poems per gallon of wine," to paraphrase his contemporary Du Fu. Renowned twentieth-century Chinese writer Guo Moruo once surveyed the works of Li Bai and discovered that as many as 17 percent of his poems involve drinking. His most famous work is "Drinking Alone by Moonlight," in which Li transforms a taboo—drinking alone—into a celebration:

A cup of wine, under the flowering trees;
I drink alone, for no friend is near.
Raising my cup I beckon the bright moon,
For he, with my shadow, will make three men.
The moon, alas, is no drinker of wine;
Listless, my shadow creeps about at my side.
Yet with the moon as friend and the shadow as slave
I must make merry before the Spring is spent.
To the songs I sing the moon flickers her beams;
In the dance I weave my shadow tangles and breaks.
While we were sober, three shared the fun;

Now we are drunk, each goes his way.
May we long share our odd, inanimate feast,
And meet at last on the Cloudy River of the Sky.

According to an apocryphal story, after writing this poem Li Bai drowned in the Yangtze River while trying to embrace the moon's reflection.

Today Li Bai seems eccentric, if not alcoholic, but his drinking was of a piece with his contemporaries. In Tang China, as translator Arthur Cooper notes, "drunkenness was universally recognized as a state of perfect, untrammeled receptivity to divine inspiration."

Tang poet Du Fu literally immortalized the great poetic drinkers of the Tang, many of whom were his friends, in "The Eight Immortals of the Wine Cup." The concept of the Daoist immortal originated during the Qin dynasty, when court alchemists began searching for the legendary potion of eternal life. It became an honorary title bestowed on Daoism's leading figures. In the alcoholic context it suggests drinkers' temporal displacement, their achievement of a state in which life and death no longer direct their actions.

Aside from Li Bai, there was also He Zhizhang (who "tossed in his saddle like a ship at sea"); Li Jin ("drank three gallons before meeting the emperor"); Li Shizhi ("drank as much wine as a whale drinks of the ocean"); Cui Zongzhi ("looked at the blue skies with disdain and shined brighter than a jade tree in the wind"); Su Jin (a devout Buddhist who "cared nothing for his prayers when drunk"); Zhang Xu ("drank three cups, took up his calligraphy brush, and forgot his manners"); and Jiao Sui ("came alive after drinking fifty liters").

The Eight Immortals' drunkenness was a reversal of the Seven Sages' escapism. Rather than avoid official responsibility through drink, the immortals chose to serve the state *while* drunk. The Tang model has proved more enduring.

This liberal attitude toward drink reflected the relative prosperity and relaxed government regulation in this era. Alcohol was voraciously consumed at all levels of society. The streets and alleys of Chang'an were flush with wine shops and taverns, some of which were towering multistory affairs visible from blocks away. The upper classes bought the finer libations, and peasants brewed rough huangjiu at home. Tang drinking retained rules and rituals from earlier times, though largely divorced of their original meaning. Drinking had become a social activity, undertaken among friends with no nobler goal than intoxication. "Drinking orders" had evolved into diverting games.

The game *huaquan* originated during the Han dynasty and is still played today. It involves two players throwing out a random number of fingers on one hand and shouting a number. The player who guesses the correct number of total fingers wins; his opponent must drink. I have never fully mastered the shouted lingo that accompanies this one, as it always results in staggering drunkenness before the point of retention.

In a more highbrow Tang drinking game, players pour glasses of wine into wooden cups and float them down a stream of water, natural or manufactured. Whoever was closest to the cup when it came to rest was forced to ad lib a verse of poetry. If the lyric was adequate, the poet could send the cup farther downstream, but if it failed to achieve artistic grace, he had to drain the cup's contents.

"Our drinking is different," said writer Liu Zongyuan (773–819). "It is decorous without formality, unconstrained without noise, informal without nakedness, harmonious without music, convivial without a crowd. Simple yet sociable, free and easy yet polite, leisurely yet dignified, it is an excellent accompaniment for the enjoyment of nature and fit relaxation for gentlemen. So I record this for those who come after us."

Those who came after were the Song (960–1279). Though the Song had hard-drinking poets like Ouyang Xiu and enthusiastic literary champions like Su Dongpo, the era was characterized by scientific innovation. It was during the Song that China developed gunpowder for war and the compass for navigation. The Song created movable type and printed paper currency.

Where the Song failed to excel was in strategy. Emperor Taizu founded the dynasty in a military coup, so knew firsthand the danger of placing too much power in the hands of generals. Shortly after ascending the Dragon Throne, he summoned his generals for a sumptuous feast and explained to them that, though he valued their loyalty, they threatened his job security. He ordered them to relinquish their armies in exchange for cushy official appointments in distant provinces and arranged marriages that would bring their children into the imperial family. For their trouble Taizu also plied them with enough money and booze to last many lifetimes. Everyone satisfied, Taizu rested easy.

His successors discovered that the threat was not from within but from without. In 1127, less than seventy years into the dynasty, northern Jurchen invaders overran the dissolute Song armies, capturing the capital and emperor. A fragmented Song dynasty fled south to the Yangtze Delta and reestablished the capital in modern-day Hangzhou.

Song's loss was huangjiu's gain. Pushed into the south, the Song lost dominion over the eastern portion of the Silk Road and the great variety of alcohol that had been carried across it. They were forced instead to focus on maritime trading routes, but since most of their trading partners were Muslim, little alcohol flowed in or out of China via these channels. This turned attention inward and led to a wine-making renaissance. The fertile southern region around the new capital flourished as a wine-making center. Song brewers crafted hundreds of new styles of huangjiu and, building on scientific advancement, brought Chinese wine-making techniques near to full maturity. Shaoxing, a city not far from the new capital, became the Chinese grain wine equivalent of Bordeaux or Napa Valley.

Many of the most instructive works on grain alcohol production were written during the Northern and Southern Song periods, notably Zhu Yizhong's *North Mountain Wine Classic*, a comprehensive history of Chinese alcohol with detailed instructions for producing various types of wines and qus, along with a detailed explanation of fermentation. Scholar H. T. Huang calls it the most significant work ever produced on Chinese wine making, because it shows that the Song understood the difference between fermentation and saccharification and explains the process of pasteurization almost a thousand years before it was "invented" in the West.

A century and a half after moving south, the Song were overrun by another northern invader, the Mongolian hordes of Kublai Khan. The Mongols moved China's capital to Beijing, where it has more or less remained ever since. And as for huangjiu? It never looked back, finding an enduring home in the Yangtze Delta. The geographic center of Chinese wine making had forever shifted southward.

The intellectual soul of the country also remained in the south. The authors of China's "four great" novels—*The Romance of the Three Kingdoms, The Dream of the Red Chamber, The Journey to the West,* and *The Water Margin*—all have ties to the Yangtze Delta. Much of the poetry composed during the subsequent Ming and Qing dynasties was also written by huangjiu-sipping southern intellectuals.

A refined drinking culture had emerged alongside huangjiu, perfectly suited to the scholarly elite who sung its praises. Despite Confucius's best efforts, drinking alcohol, even to excess, had obtained an air of sophistication. It had lost its primitive Neolithic trappings and become a polite activity for gentlemen.

The poles of Confucianism and Daoism had long since begun to bend toward a harmonious center. As much as the Confucian scholar began to indulge, the Daoist intellectual began to moderate. Drinking could still be a path to enlightenment, but only in the right hands. As Liu Ci (891–955) writes in *The Dao of Drinking*, "When the wise man drinks he remains wise, when the foolish man drinks he remains foolish."

But there was trouble brewing. Something was charging toward China with all the fury of a Mongolian raiding party. A new drink was coming to flip tables and shatter windows, to burn the entire drinking edifice down to its foundation. I speak, of course, of baijiu.

6 Firewater

Distilled spirits attacked China like a virus. A radical new element injected into a closed system, it was initially contained and unnoticed. Later it adapted to its host, spread with great rapidity, and mutated. It kept mutating, over and over, until it was no longer recognizable. It had become was something new altogether. Baijiu is not an Eastern drink, nor is it a Western drink. Baijiu is fusion. It is what happens when more than seven thousand years of wine-making tradition gets a technological kick in the ass.

Fermentation occurs naturally: all one needs is sugar and yeast. A monkey could, and very likely did, do it. As a consequence, alcoholic beverages cropped up in every corner of the globe with plant life. Distillation, the process by which we get hard liquor, is more challenging. Spirits have been warming bellies and clouding minds only for about a thousand years. And since they arrived long after the development of intercontinental trade routes, there was likely a single point of origin from which all the world's liquor flowed.

The technological prerequisite for making spirits is a device called the still, which raises a substance's temperature to boiling and collects the resultant vapors. Stills had many applications in the ancient world, such as manufacturing perfume, cosmetics, and medicine. The Chinese developed stills thousands of years ago, as did the ancient Greeks, but both groups largely missed their most important function: stills can get you stinking drunk.

Alcohol has a lower boiling temperature than water, so when wine or beer is gradually heated, the first bit to vaporize will be more alcoholic than what follows. A still takes alcoholic vapor and runs it into a low-temperature chamber, or condenser, where the vapor is cooled back into liquid. That liquid—what we call a liquor or distilled spirit—has a much higher concentration of alcohol than the original liquid.

(Annoying readers will note that it is also possible to freeze distill—repeatedly icing a beer or wine and discarding the watery slush to raise strength. That is true, and the ancients of China's far northwestern reaches in Xinjiang made ice wine this way. But it was an uncommon and impractical method of production before artificial refrigeration's invention and never really caught on.)

Supposedly, Jabir ibn Hayyan (712–815) pioneered alcohol distillation. He was a Renaissance man from the golden age of Islam who dabbled in philosophy, science, and alchemy. Today he is considered the father of chemistry. He wrote his findings in a nearly indecipherable symbolic code—it is from his romanized name "Geber" that we that we get the word *gibberish*. Jabir also refined the Greek alembic still and used it to perform experiments on wine. Jabir believed alcoholic vapor had little practical use outside of scientific inquiry.

Thankfully, less rational minds prevailed, and the technique spread. A contemporary, the poet Abu Nuwas, mentions drinking a new wine "the color of rainwater but as hot inside the ribs as a firebrand." The genie was out of the bottle.

Persian physician Mohammed ibn Zakariya al-Razi (865–925) picked up where Jabir left off, coining the term *al-koh'l* "(mascara) of wine" to describe the liquid created from wine vapors, a nod to the still's primary purpose at the time: producing cosmetics. *Al-koh'l*, anglicized "alcohol," became the slang term for a wine's essence, or spirit, isolated during the distillation process.

When the Norman armies sacked then Arab-controlled Sicily in the eleventh century, distillation fell into the clutches of Christendom. Medieval alchemists in Europe began experimenting with *aqua vitae* (water of life), first as a medicine and then for casual consumption. By the fifteenth century drinkers across the continent were imbibing *gebrannt Wein* (burned wine), or brandy. In Chinese *shaojiu* (burned wine) was also the original term for distilled spirits.

The earliest-known Chinese description of alcohol distillation appears in a medical encyclopedia from the fifteenth century by Li Shizhen, who states, "Spirits were not made in ancient times, but were created during the Yuan Dynasty. The method uses strong wine and flavoring. Steam rises and its liquefied droplets are collected using a device."

Intuitively, it makes sense that spirits would arrive in China during the Mongolian Yuan dynasty. At the height of their conquests, the hordes of Genghis Khan and his successors ruled a territory of over nine million square miles, an empire that stretched from the Pacific Ocean to Central Europe and contained nearly a quarter of the world's population. When Genghis's grandson Kublai founded the Yuan dynasty in 1271, the Chinese Empire had never been so vast, nor would it be again. For a brief moment in history, intrepid merchants could travel from Baghdad to Beijing without ever crossing a border.

The most famous European to make the trek was Venetian trader Marco Polo, who provides one of the first-known Western commentary on Chinese alcohol: "The greater part of the inhabitants of the province of Cathay [China] drink a sort of wine made from rice mixed with a variety of spices and drugs. This beverage, or wine as it may be termed, is so good and well flavoured that they do not wish for better. It is clear, bright, and pleasant to the taste, and being (made) very hot, has the quality of inebriating sooner than any other."

While he was probably describing common rice wine—huangjiu can be served piping hot—the tantalizing possibility exists that he tasted one of China's earliest spirits. In Polo's travels we also see the other means by which liquor could have arrived in China: the Silk Road and other trade routes.

Most of China's ancient international trade routes predated the Yuan—remarkably, there are even records suggesting that the Han dynasty received emissaries from the court of Marcus Aurelius—prompting some historians to suggest that distillation arrived much earlier. Song dynasty scholars write of a "steamed wine," and Tang dynasty records mention of drinks called both "baijiu" and "burnt wine." The poet Yong Tao (789–873), for example, wrote of a trip to Sichuan: "After acquainting myself with the burnt wine of Chengdu, I no longer wish to return to Chang'an."

Some scholars of Chinese alcohol, like the peerless H. T. Huang, have also argued that spirits were a domestic innovation, basing their argument around the anecdotal accounts of Daoist alchemists and a two-thousand-year-old still from the Han dynasty. The device, in the Shanghai Museum's collection, has been tested and found capable of distilling alcohol. But aside from the odd literary reference to the strength of a wine, there is nothing that leads us to believe it was ever used for this purpose, and, in a country where many food products are steamed, one can easily surmise another use.

By the Song dynasty there first appears persuasive evidence of distilled spirits, particularly a comment from 980 CE by one of the era's most celebrated drinkers, Su Dongpo: "When the wine catches fire, smother it with a piece of blue cloth." Only a distilled spirit has enough alcohol to ignite. Moreover, Song chemists had begun distilling flowers into perfume, so the technique was known to them.

Unfortunately, none of the Song wine-making manuals—and there were many—describe a technique consistent with distillation. Concrete evidence first appears in 1330, when Yuan court dietician Hu Sihui writes of a drink called *aliji*: "Sweet and pungent in flavour, strongly heating and toxic. Relieves cold obstructions and counteracts chilling vapors. Heat superior wine to boiling point and collect the dew."

Soon after, the Mongolian hordes conquered the Middle East, and spirits began to invade China, though they were unlikely anything that resembles modern-day baijiu. The Mongols' *aliji* may have been a transliteration of the Arabic word for spirits, *arak*, meaning sweat, or the Turkish equivalent, *raki* (sometimes styled *ariki*), both of which are anise-flavored alcohols. The Mongols, for their part, were notoriously prolific drinkers who traditionally consumed a drink called *koumiss*, made from fermented mare's milk. Their appetites grew with the size of the empire.

Flemish missionary William of Rubruck journeyed to the Mongol Empire in the mid-thirteenth century. In the camp of Batu Khan of the Golden Horde, he notes two drinks: "In winter they make a capital drink of rice, of millet, and of honey; it is clear as wine: and wine is carried to them from remote parts. In summer they care only for [*koumiss*]."

In the court of the Great Khan Möngke in Karakorum, William discovered four styles of drink served in an ingenious fashion: "Master William of Paris has constructed for [Möngke] a large tree made of silver, with four silver lions at its roots, each one containing a conduit-pipe and spewing forth white mare's milk. There are four conduits leading into the tree, right to the top, with their ends curving downwards, and over each of them lies a gilded serpent with its tail twined around the trunk of the tree. One of the pipes discharges wine, a second *caracomos* (refined mare's milk), a third *boal* (a drink made from honey), and a fourth rice ale, known as *terracina*."

Rubruck had nothing but praise for the Mongol's rice wine, likely of Chinese origin: "I could not discern any difference between it and the best Auxerre wine, save that it had not the perfume of wine." Yet he fails to make any mention of a distilled spirit.

The spirits the Mongols drank may have been distilled koumiss or, in starker terms, essence of horse lactate. I have tried a Mongolian milk baijiu, and while it is far better than one might expect, it is hardly typical of contemporary Chinese spirits. More likely, it was a flavored brandy or roughly distilled rice wine.

Though liquor likely entered the Middle Kingdom as a foreign drink, it became thoroughly domesticated in the hands of China's experienced craftspeople. By the thirteenth century China had a sophisticated alcohol industry, with distinctive regional tipples and production techniques unlike anything practiced in Europe or the Middle East. It did not take winemakers long to incorporate the still into their workshops, creating the earliest Chinese spirits, which were probably little more than distilled huangjiu.

Then and now there are two primary distinctions between baijiu and Western spirits: ingredients and production methods. By ingredients, I mean not just the use of qu to induce fermentation but also the raw ingredients. Unlike earlier Chinese drinks, the grain of choice for baijiu was sorghum, a stalky drought-resistant cereal from Africa. It likely entered China a few thousand years ago by way of Sichuan, but it first became popular around the period that distillation arrived. The first conclusive Chinese mention of sorghum comes from Yuan dynasty agronomist Wang Zhen, who writes, "The grain can be hulled and eaten and anything left over fed to livestock. It is a famine food. . . . No part of the plant need be thrown away."

The Chinese also employed a novel method, called solid-state distillation. Unlike whisky or gin, which are distilled as a liquid, baijiu is distilled directly from solid fermented grains, using a still that resembles a giant vegetable or dim sum steamer. Chinese distillers take a basket with a slotted bottom, fill it with fermented grain, and put it over a cauldron of boiling water. Once the heat of the grains rises to ethanol's burning temperature, the alcoholic steam travels through the mash, continually condensing back into liquid and revaporizing as it rises. Finally, the vapor begins peeling off the top, and the distiller collects it and cools it back into a potent liquid. This process creates a drink that captures much of the grain's original character and has tremendous depth of flavor.

This design evolved out of the Chinese kitchen, which by the Song dynasty had started employing bamboo steamer baskets set atop a wok filled with boiling water. A second wok full of cold water was placed atop the basket so that when the steam touched it would condense back into liquid and drip from the bottom of the wok. Two variations emerged, one in which the liquid was collected in a bowl set within the pot (the Mongolian still) and one in which the liquid was funneled to an urn outside the pot (the Chinese still).

French Jesuit missionary Évariste Huc, who in the mid-nineteenth century became the first Westerner to describe Chinese alcohol production, tells us that the first Chinese hooch was "invented" in Shandong, along the northeastern Chinese seaboard. A peasant winemaker was trying to find a use for grains that had grown moldy and unusable, so he fermented the grains and ran them through a still to filter the liquid. By this haphazard method he inadvertently created baijiu.

Big qu, a larger mass-produced offshoot of wheat-based qu that is used to ferment most contemporary mass-produced baijiu, appeared soon thereafter in Jiangsu or Henan, along Shandong's border. Sichuan—two thousand–odd miles upstream along the Yangtze—makes a competing claim to big qu's origin point.

In any case, by the early Ming dynasty (1368–1644), China had a drink that resembled what we call baijiu (white spirits), though this name would not become popular until the twentieth century. Shaojiu distilleries started around this time in Guangxi, Shaanxi, Sichuan, and elsewhere are still operational today.

Zhu Yuanzhang, who founded the Ming, was a devout follower of a Buddhist sect influenced by Persian Manichaeism, or *mingjiao* (Religion of Light). He saw his role as bringing light to a land darkened by foreign rule and thus instituted a more inward-looking xenophobic regime. Domestic harvests of grain and production of grain-alcohol flourished. During the remainder of the Ming and the Qing (1644–1912), China's last two imperial dynasties, China's elaborate bureaucracy facilitated baijiu's precipitous spread throughout other parts of the empire.

As had been the case with huangjiu before it, wherever baijiu went the local craftspeople added their own wrinkles to the process. They worked with different grains and concocted ingenious fermentation schemes. In the north they fermented grains in stone jars buried beneath floorboards. Southwestern distillers used enormous subterranean pits of mud or brick as fermentation chambers. In most places they worked with sorghum, but they also experimented with liquors made from rice, wheat, corn, millet, and other starches. Styles mixed and merged and became new styles. Almost every town and village had its own baijiu, and if you asked any of the locals, they would tell you the local baijiu was the best in China.

But invasion was once more on the horizon. Late imperial China was a stable if unromantic period of widespread prosperity and gradual decline. By the late eighteenth century, strange red-faced, blond-haired barbarians began to appear at China's doorstep, demanding trade concessions and threatening violence. These "foreign devils," as they were called, regarded local spirits with trepidation, unaware that liquor had made the same long journey eastward centuries earlier. And who could blame them? Baijiu had long since shed its foreign trappings.

Early baijiu was rough stuff, not for the faint of heart. Before the industrial age, stills lacked the technical precision to filter out all the foul-tasting impurities. Spirits clawed at larynxes and made people's eyes water. Distillers tried to mask these deficiencies with botanicals, like cinnamon or ginseng, but often the cure was just as bad as the sickness: nineteenth-century liquor sellers in Beijing were notorious for cutting their products with arsenic and pigeon dung.

This was deadly strong stuff, and that was the point. The story of Wu Song and the tiger, from the classic Ming novel *The Water Margin,* is a revealing episode about alcohol, written roughly the same time as baijiu's emergence.

According to the story, the outlaw Wu Song was a hell of a mean drunk. In a rage he beat an official unconscious and fled town. He spent most of his exile in a drunken stupor punctuated by bouts of savage violence. But when he got word the official had survived, he decided to return home.

On the road he came to an inn with a sign hanging outside: "Three bowls won't clear the ridge." He went inside and ordered a bowl of wine and a towering plate of beef. When he had drained his third bowl of wine, he ordered another.

"No more wine," the innkeeper said. "Didn't you see the sign out front? You'll be too drunk to navigate the pass."

"But I'm not drunk," Wu said.

The innkeeper, perhaps sensing Wu's temper, poured him another.

Wu drank the tavern dry and, after eighteen bowls, got up to leave. The proprietor barred his path, saying, "You mustn't cross the ridge. A tiger prowls at night. He's already killed thirty men."

Wu was no fool. He saw that the innkeeper was playing games, trying to steal his coin purse while he slept.

"The tiger is real, sir," the innkeeper insisted. "Read the official warning if you don't believe me."

Wu brushed him aside: "You won't get another copper out of me." Trudging up the mountain with unsteady steps, Wu vomited as he walked. He passed a placard warning of a tiger, then another soon after. It was too late to turn back.

Soon after the sun set, a beast sprang at Wu from above. Wu dodged to one side and swung his cudgel. He missed the tiger, and his weapon shattered against a tree trunk. Once more the tiger pounced, and once more Wu dodged its murderous claws. Taking the tiger by its scruff, Wu forced it to the ground and thrust a boot in its face. He pummeled the tiger's head again and again. After seventy blows it went slack.

The moral: Drink three cups and you can't walk straight. Drink eighteen cups and you can beat a tiger to death with your bare hands. Such is the power of a stiff drink.

The story of Wu Song and the tiger shows a side of Chinese drinking culture that would become central to baijiu's enduring legacy: machismo. The testosterone-fueled show of strength has a way of seeping out when someone cracks open a bottle of baijiu. Regrettable though it may be, drinking has always been part of the great pissing contest that defines male interpersonal relationships in China, and one's liquor tolerance—*jiuliang*—is one of the ways in which males attempt to demonstrate whose is bigger. It is much the same elsewhere, whether this dark impulse manifests itself in vodka shots or keg stands.

Placards such as "three bowls won't clear the ridge" were common in dynastic times. They were at once an invitation and a challenge. As Luzhou-based drinks historian Yang Chen explained to me, "In ancient China, you advertised the quality of your wine by bragging about how strong it was. In those days the strength of wine dictated its quality. The stronger the better!"

And if strength was everything, baijiu must have been a welcome addition to the Chinese drinking table. At its most potent, huangjiu clocks in at around thirty proof. Baijiu starts at around seventy and is commonly sold in excess of a hundred. With hard liquor the means to total intoxication, the inhibition-smashing depths of depravity that inspired the Daoist drinking project and lines of verse without end was now within China's grasp.

But baijiu was not a drink for poets. It was too unrefined: an inexpensive, harsh, and debilitating potion. China's scholarly elite continued to compose panegyrics on the virtues of rice wine, preferring its delicate flavors to the searing burn of firewater. Several books on drinking and drinking etiquette for gentlemen were published in late imperial China, such as Yuan Hongdao's *Rules of the Goblet*, whose author claimed he wrote it on account of the low quality of his drinking companions. It contained not only a history of alcohol but rules for drinking games and suggested topics of conversation. When the upper classes finally began to develop a taste for spirits in the late Qing dynasty, they went instead for French brandy.

The Chinese peasantry had no such pretensions. They were laborers who worked with their hands, who had never been able to afford much more than home-brewed huangjiu. Delicacy did not move them.

China is a populous, historically famine-prone country. Its cuisine, particularly in the towns and villages, is adapted to a culture of scarcity and poverty. It relies heavily on pickling and using fermented preservatives to maximize flavor and spread every ounce of nourishment as far as it will go.

The people wanted more bang for their buck, and this is where baijiu excelled. It was strong enough to halt a bull in its tracks and could be made cheaply from almost any starchy substance. It didn't matter whether a distiller used damaged grains or even sorghum, largely ignored in Chinese cuisine before baijiu. Better still, they could ferment and distill the same grains repeatedly and feed the mash to the pigs afterward. It was the every part of the buffalo drink and a potent spirit that took the edge off the grueling work of the day.

"High-alcohol drinks stimulate your taste buds and make you more comfortable, so that's what the people wanted," historian Yang Chen explained. "It dulled the senses, and that's the kind of feeling common laborers wanted."

With baijiu ordinary Chinese at last had a drink to call their own.

7 The People's Choice

On October 1, 1949, Chairman Mao Zedong looked down on the masses from the Forbidden City's Gate of Heavenly Peace, Tiananmen. Ten days earlier he had memorably proclaimed that the people of China had *stood up*—to the Nationalists, to imperialism, to the world. The War of Liberation was all but over, and now he addressed a crowd numbering in the hundreds of thousands to announce the establishment of the People's Republic of China.

China was emerging from a prolonged period of brutal foreign incursion, political infighting, and civil war—what Party propagandists later dubbed the "Century of National Humiliation." For the first time since the fall of the Qing dynasty in 1912, the nation was unified under a single revolutionary leader, who promised to restore its wounded pride. History has largely ignored the events that followed the speech and ensuing parade, but a second revolution quietly announced itself at that night's inaugural banquet. It involved what the freshly minted nation's leaders would drink, a decision that would predict and prescribe the future course of the Chinese alcohol industry.

Whisky, gin, brandy? Those were out, too foreign. Ditto for wine and beer. Huangjiu was Chinese, but it was also the drink of the effete Yangtze Delta and the ousted Nationalist Kuomintang government, which had made its capital there.

No. A proletarian revolution needed a proletarian drink. The people— ahem, the People—needed baijiu. Not just any baijiu, but a Beijing baijiu that reflected the grandeur of the newly restored capital. There was only one option: it had to be *erguotou.*

The Yuan Sheng Hao granary in Qianmen was a family operation. It lay in a narrow sliver of Beijing between the imperial and Chinese cities, a patchwork of dusty old Mongolian alleyways crowded with peddlers and mule carts. To the north and south, soaring forty feet in the sky, were the old Ming walls and sentry towers. Through their gates long caravans of camels passed daily.

Back in 1680, when a Manchu emperor sat on the Dragon Throne, the Zhao family's business fell on hard times. They had more grain than they knew what to do with and in desperation turned to distillation. That was when Zhao Cunli, the second of three brothers, hit on a great innovation.

At that time Chinese stills were roughshod, stacked-pot affairs. In essence, they had one big cauldron filled with fermented grains and topped with a pan of cold water. The alcoholic vapor would rise to meet the cool metal pan, thereby cooling into baijiu, which dripped into a funnel. As the pan of water grew hot, it was dumped out and refilled with more cool water. What Cunli discovered was that the best liquor flowed from the still during the second pot of water. This was the "head of the second pot," or erguotou.

Any distiller worth her salt will tell you that when the distilling temperature is too high or too low, the consistency of the liquid changes. What comes out the still first and last, what is respectively called the "head" and the "tail" in English, is where you find most impurities and toxins. What you want is the middle portion, the "heart," and that's essentially what Zhao Cunli discovered. It made the Zhao brothers' baijiu an instant success and inspired numerous competitors to follow suit. Before long the mild but potent sorghum spirit—frequently sold at an eye-watering 68 percent alcohol and known affectionately as the "burning dagger"—became the city's preferred tipple.

And this was a city that loved to drink. Most adult males in the capital consumed over four ounces of spirits daily, which they drank warm with meals. Though the laborers drank their fair share, the chief drinkers were the literati, who came to Beijing seeking government appointments, but often wound up waiting months or years for a vacancy. Largely out of boredom, they patronized the opera houses and brothels that sprouted like mushrooms around Qianmen. They drank at the local *jiuguan* (wine hall) or *jiulou* (wine building) or the more informal *jiubu* (wine spot). Those looking to drink on the cheap headed just beyond the city walls, where taverns called *jiudian* (wine shops) served duty-free beverages.

Within the walls, alcohol was taxed heavily but half-heartedly. A steady stream of smugglers traveled the roads between the city's liquor marts and local distilleries just east of the city. Dr. John Dudgeon, who lived in Peking in the late nineteenth century, described the racket thusly: "A Chinaman or woman, with their loose clothes and long gowns, can secrete 120 catties [about 132 lb.] in 5 or 6 catty pig's bladders around their waists. They carry a few of these bladders likewise quite exposed on their shoulders, and for these they perhaps pay a small duty to the petty officials. They make three or four runs daily."

Taxes were not the only corners unscrupulous baijiu merchants cut. They reportedly watered down or otherwise adulterated liquor. A Beijing shopkeeper once shortchanged the underlings of powerful Qing dynasty administrator Zhang Zhidong (1837–1909), and the shop erupted into fisticuffs. Zhang, ever the pragmatist, decreed that Beijing's spirits sellers begin using an officially approved pot of standard dimension to dispense alcohol.

By the twentieth century there existed in Beijing as large a spirits industry as anywhere in the country, and it hit all the right patriotic notes. When the Communists campaigned in the north against the Japanese and later the Nationalists, they used erguotou to fortify nerves and sterilize wounds. When the city bloodlessly surrendered to the People's Liberation Army in January 1949, many erguotou manufacturers also surrendered their distilleries. That's why Communist China's very first business license was issued to a hastily thrown together outfit called Hong Xing (Red Star) Erguotou.

Red Star was an amalgamation of twelve no-longer-private distilleries, including the erguotou originator, Yuan Sheng Hao. When the government tasked it with creating a baijiu to celebrate the coming Communist victory, workers drove more than a million pounds of grain to the capital in U.S. automobiles—China had yet to acquire any suitably proletarian vehicles from the Soviets. Red Star master blender Wang Qiufang watered down the erguotou from the standard 68 percent alcohol level to a more palatable 65. It was poured into brown beer bottles and the caps were emblazoned with a red star. In a pinch the cap could double as a shot glass, a trick that outlived the occasion. A Japanese Communist who fought against his compatriots in World War II designed the label, which also remains more or less unchanged.

When that first Communist cadre raised that first glass of Red Star Erguotou on October 1, China entered a new era. Liquor had for the first time become a fully industrialized state-run concern. The blueprint for the future was set.

Red Star was the first distillery formed in the People's Republic, but the national vision it realized was a century in the making. By the mid-nineteenth century China's imperial system had been pushed to the brink, as existential threats coalesced around it. British opium merchants forced their way into China at gunpoint on the pretense of free trade. As the London *Times*' Peking correspondent remarked in 1870, "The opening of the country is their cry, 'progress' is their motto, war is their object." Other European powers and the United States were quick to follow suit, followed by Russia and Japan. Little by little China's coastal and riverside ports became de facto foreign fiefdoms, self-governing and answerable to no one.

Meanwhile, the country's interior seethed with resentment. The people were angry at the foreign barbarians as well as their own Manchu overlords, whom they thought were little better. A series of rebellions broke out: White Lotus, Nian, Boxer. The deadliest of them all, the Taiping Rebellion, was led by a messianic lunatic who believed himself Jesus Christ's younger brother. It lasted more than a decade and claimed tens of millions of lives.

Everyone agreed, local and foreigner alike, that China had grown weak. Somewhere along the line the nation, which centuries earlier had impressed Marco Polo as impossibly advanced, had fallen behind the times. A group of reformist Qing bureaucrats embarked on an ambitious plan of "self-strengthening," in which they looked west for inspiration to modernize the nation's military, industry, and educational systems. It proved too little too late. In 1912 a popular rebellion swept the Manchus out of power and replaced the dynastic system with an equally doomed republic.

The dream of modernization lived on. Nationalists, inspired by China's revolutionary first provisional president, Sun Yat-Sen, sought to revitalize culture and commerce, to show the world that China could again be as great as any nation. For some this meant creating national brands that could compete with the foreign products that lined Shanghai storefronts. Others sought to create whole new industries employing the latest technological innovations.

Zhang Bishi, "The Rockefeller of the East," spent three million silver taels (more than $75 million in today's currency) to establish the nation's first modern wine producer: Changyu. In 1915 Zhang set sail for San Francisco as part of a Chinese business delegation to that year's World's Fair, the Panama-Pacific International Exposition.

Much was at stake for the fledgling Republic of China. To participate in a forum of great nations was to be seen as their peer, and China was desperate for any type of international recognition that might confer legitimacy on its government. It spent $1.5 million on its pavilion, in those days an outrageous sum that far exceeded any other country's expenditure. In the competitive portion of the exposition, Changyu's brandy, red wine, vermouth, and Riesling all garnered gold medals.

When Zhang passed away the next year, he left behind eight wives, fourteen acknowledged children, and a grateful nation.

There were other notable competitors at San Francisco that year. Baijiu distilleries from around the country presented their wares, collectively earning several silver and gold medals. Three even earned the coveted grand prize. One of the winners was a distillery from Xinghuacun in central China's Shanxi Province that made a drink called Fenjiu.

It was likely this victory that prompted a group of Chinese investors to establish the Jinyu Fenjiu Corporation in 1919. It was one of the nation's first modern distilleries, incorporating the latest industrial equipment and production techniques. Up to that point provincial styles of baijiu like Fenjiu had been closely guarded family secrets, passed down from one generation to the next. Now it was possible to produce baijiu on a massive scale. Even though Shanxi lacked the infrastructure to export, Jinyu produced about forty tons of baijiu a year by 1932, an amount roughly equivalent to eighty thousand bottles.

Baijiu's first efforts at industrialization could not have happened at a worse time. In 1916 then-president Yuan Shikai declared himself emperor, and the provinces splintered off one after another to form warring military dictatorships. The country would not be united again until 1928 under Generalissimo Chiang Kai-shek. Not long thereafter Japan invaded, and after the Japanese were defeated, the country erupted into civil war. All the while the grand modernization project stalled. Then the unthinkable happened: the Communists won.

In the first decade of Communist rule, the government built the baijiu industry from the top down. Across the county, wherever a county or village was famous for its alcohol, the government consolidated its various workshops into large state-run companies. This was not a choice but an order, and from this reckoning we got most of today's leading baijiu distilleries, like Red Star Erguotou and later, from Jinyu and others, the Xinghuacun Fenjiu distillery. At the first People's Consultative Conference in 1949, delegates toasted with Fenjiu.

What distillers lost in autonomy they gained in quality and precision.

Take the example of the Luzhou Laojiao distillery in southeastern Sichuan, makers of my first baijiu crush. It was founded in 1951 from the merger of dozens of distilleries, including the oldest operational workshops in China. Five years later the state sent researchers to Luzhou to study their techniques, publishing the results in the 1959 book *Luzhou Laojiao Big Qu Liquor.*

It was the first time in nearly five centuries of baijiu distillation that anyone had attempted to codify the elaborate Sichuanese techniques, which had all been passed down orally. Remarkably, not even a single sketch of a traditional Chinese pot still from the Ming or Qing dynasties survives today. Now distillers in other provinces could learn from and build on the Luzhou method. Across China a conversation began as to what baijiu was and how to make it better.

Baijiu had always been the everyman's drink, scorned by huangjiu-drinking elites but embraced by the laboring masses. Its rise had been slow and dependent on historical caprice. As Chinese spirits-making techniques became more refined, baijiu's commercial production capacity eclipsed that of huangjiu. Rice wine's popularity persisted in isolated pockets throughout China, but elsewhere it became all but extinct. Successful though it was, baijiu never shook its humble origins as a peasant's drink.

It took a peasant uprising, the Chinese Communist Revolution, to turn the tables. With the government ruling in the name of the people and controlling all stages of spirits production, the drink of the people began to achieve a level of prestige that matched its popularity. Powerful if not rich Party cadres made baijiu the preferred drink at official gatherings and state banquets, conferring elevated status to their favored brands.

Baijiu had, to borrow the expression, *stood up*. A nation would soon be falling down.

PART 3

The Journey of a
Thousand Drinks

A sober guest is a host's shame.

                        —Traditional saying

8 Party Favors

ELIXIR OF LIFE

PAUL MATHEW—*The Hide, London*

Stir over ice *two thirds of an ounce* each of **strong-aroma baijiu** and **sauce-aroma baijiu**; a *half ounce* each of **sweet vermouth infused with cacao nibs**, **Galliano**, and **Aperol**; and a *dash* of **walnut bitters**. Strain and garnish with an orange twist.

The year was 1972. For the first time in two decades of self-imposed isolation, the People's Republic of China was set to resume contact with the United States. Nixon was coming to dinner. Embedded within the reconnaissance party, U.S. deputy national security adviser Alexander Haig wired the following warning from Beijing: "Under No Repeat No Circumstances Should the President Actually Drink From His Glass in Response to Banquet Toasts."

Haig's concern was not etiquette. The White House understood the role of toasting in the Chinese dining ritual and that failure to return a toast would be seen as a gross affront to their hosts. The concern was that Nixon—a bellicose drunk with a low alcohol tolerance—would be undone by baijiu, the dreaded Chinese firewater.

The world would be watching. Eighty-seven U.S. print and television journalists would be following Air Force One to Beijing in two Boeing 707s: *Ni Hao One* and *Ni Hao Two*, *ni hao* being Mandarin for "hello." Competition was tight for the coveted assignment. Leading reporters jockeyed to be the first in their era to cross the Great Wall. Nixon despised the *New York Times* and repeatedly struck its reporters' names from the list of credentialed guests, only to have his staff add them back in each time. "It really was like going to moon," Barbara Walters later recalled in the documentary *Assignment: China; "The Week That Changed the World."*

The Chinese prepared a grand banquet to welcome the president at the Great Hall of the People, each table set with bottles of Moutai. Kweichow Moutai—Guizhou Maotai in today's romanization scheme—was the favorite drink of Premier Zhou Enlai, second-most powerful man in China next to Chairman Mao. Since the 1950s he had served it at every Chinese state dinner: Kim Il Sung had sipped Moutai, so too had Ho Chi Minh and Charlie Chaplin. With friends in such high places, it became the preferred baijiu of the Chinese Communist Party and assumed the mantel of Guojiu, "The National Liquor."

"Aided only in part by the *mao tai*," National Security Council adviser John Holdridge later recalled, "the atmosphere in the Great Hall was electric." He would know, having spent the evening engaged in raucous drinking games with the Chinese minister of electronics. Moutai may also have been partly to blame when Walter Cronkite mishandled his chopsticks and sent an olive flying across the Great Hall. Not everyone enjoyed the refreshment: Dan Rather compared the baijiu to "liquid razor blades."

At the appointed moment Premier Zhou Enlai took the stage and, speaking through an interpreter, said, "I propose a toast to the health of President Nixon and Mrs. Nixon, to the health of our other American guests, to the health of all our friends and comrades present, and to the friendship of the Chinese and American people." Stepping from the stage with a dignified expression, he walked to the Nixon's table, shot of Moutai in hand. The Chinese premier and the U.S. president, whose past ideological differences had seemed irreconcilable, looked into each other's eyes, smiled, and clinked glasses. Then they drank.

With one glass of Moutai, China made a grand entrance back onto the world stage. Whether or not Nixon dried his glass—close examination of the filmic evidence shows he sipped, not slurped—is immaterial, but ignoring Haig's warning was decisive.

Broadcast everywhere, this shot seen round the world changed everything. It was the most significant toast in modern history. As Henry Kissinger later remarked to then Communist Party chairman Deng Xiaoping, "I think if we drink enough Moutai we can solve anything."

Flash-forward forty years: a van shoots through the mist along a backwater mountain road. Guizhou is China's poorest province and has the infrastructure to prove it. Anything resembling a modern highway had ended an hour earlier back in Zunyi, "The Metropolis of the Future," according to an overly optimistic roadside billboard. Our driver had talked his way through a makeshift barricade that led to a shortcut that amounted to a muddy ramp to an unfinished mountain road, presumably the Superhighway of the Future. On we went along dirt roads, unpaved overpasses joined only by rebar, through unlit tunnels, past terraced rice paddies and tile-capped villages. All around us, rain and mist.

Not a year goes by without reports of a passenger bus careening down the side of a Guizhou cliff. I knew how our story would read: "There were no survivors." I tried not to think about it as we lunged over a rain-slick bridge suspended above chasms that disappeared into the fog.

The supposedly four-hour drive stretched into seven. The nearer we got to Maotai, ominous portents materialized around us: an overturned jug of wine, roughly twenty feet in diameter; an enormous titan's fist thrust out of a cliff's face, baijiu glass in hand; all manner of ancient wine vessels. All that was missing was "Abandon hope all ye who enter here," written in chicken blood.

Not including the driver there were nine of us: three French, two Thais, a couple of Chinese, an Austrian and me (the American). The French and Chinese were our hosts, representatives of Camus Cognac, Kweichow Moutai's international duty-free distribution partner. The Austrian was founder of the World Spirits Competition, at which Kweichow Moutai had just scored 95.7 points out of 100, its first international gold medal award since 1915. The two Thais were distributors. My reason for being there was less obvious.

A confession: I had bullshitted my way onto the trip. I got connected with Moutai through a friend attached to the *Wall Street Journal*, a fact I played up when reaching out to them. I had not exactly lied—I never said *I* worked for the newspaper—but I knew what I was doing. I was headed to Guizhou to drink, and to drink in style.

Kweichow Moutai is China's best-known baijiu. Bolstered by its reputation as the favorite drink of the rich and powerful, it had by the time of my visit become China's most valuable luxury brand. Its flagship Flying Fairy brand, which had cost only about a dollar a bottle in the 1980s, sold for more than three hundred at the time of my visit. Over roughly the same period, the growth of the company's stock price had outpaced Apple's.

Moutai has an enviable Communist Party pedigree. On Mao's Long March during the Chinese Civil War, the Red Army crossed the Chishui (Red Water) River four times to outwit their Kuomintang enemies. Troops sterilized their wounds with the town's baijiu and drank it to achieve martial fervor. In 1951 the state merged three famous Maotai distilleries into the Kweichow Moutai Company. (Two of the three original distilleries—Ronghe and Hengxing—have since reformed as private operations. Both have sued Kweichow Moutai for cashing in on their ancestors' reputations, but neither prevailed in court.) It achieved its exalted status through the patronage of Zhou Enlai, who publicly claimed that Moutai was in part responsible for the Long March's success.

The town is perched along a cliff face, nestled between mountains and the Chishui River. The place is entirely devoted to baijiu—its production, sale, and consumption. More than two hundred distilleries legally operate in Maotai, and more than a thousand others operate under the radar, according to a recent report in *Sixth Tone*. Everything is shrouded in mist and heavy with the sweet-and-sour funk of fermenting sorghum. Whether inside or out, the smell is suffocating.

Our van ground to a halt in front of a golden statue depicting two flying fairies with heaving chests, contorted into a ring, heels over head and joined at the hands by a chalice. This was the Mao Garden Hotel, the Kweichow Moutai Company's personal business hotel.

We reconvened at dinnertime. The lobby, empty when we arrived, was now filled to bursting with Moutai staff and local Party officials. Hostesses in red silk dresses showed us to our seats, directing the riffraff to a capacious banquet hall and the VIPs, our party among them, to a more sumptuous private room. At the head of our table sat Kweichow Moutai general manager Liu Zili, flanked by officials in order of descending importance. Stunning servers loaded the lazy Susan with a seemingly endless assortment of Guizhou delicacies and filled our glasses with a pungent liquid. The smell was dark and earthy, like a deep cavern in which someone has accidentally spilled a bottle of soy sauce.

Liu raised his glass and all stood. "Esteemed guests and foreign friends . . . welcome you to Guizhou . . . good fortune"—and a hearty chorus of "ganbei!"

Wow. The taste was bonkers: fermented beans, wild mushrooms, bitter herbs, roasted nuts—the flavors just kept coming. I had been sucker punched by the umami gremlin. I loved it.

Now the feast began in earnest. The day, which had started in the Agatha Christie oeuvre, now took a decidedly Hobbesian turn. None died but all competed for survival. One after the other, every Chinese diner snaked his way around the table, confronting each guest with a rapid-fire toast. I was quickly inundated at my own station of the cross. Manager Liu was not himself drinking—he said he had a cold, but I wasn't buying it—yet still he delivered a round of ganbeis. The company hacks and the Party cadres slammed me one after the other. I was ten to fifteen shots deep before the first hour passed.

"Each time someone toasts you, take note," said Pierre, one of the Camus Frenchmen. "You must return the toast before the meal ends." Fifteen shots became thirty.

A lull eventually set in and I surveyed the damage. Everyone was riotously drunk. Then a group of young women of a rough cut shuffled into the room. "What's happening?" I asked Pierre.

"We call them 'Demolition Girls,'" he whispered.

The job of a Demolition Girl, so far as I could tell, was to take whatever sobriety still clung to life and drown it in the bathtub. Before their arrival we had been toasting with thimble-sized shot glasses. Demolition Girls used rice bowls. As the least important member of the ensemble, I was spared the worst of the sirens' fury. But I could do nothing to help poor Wolfram—the rotund Austrian spirits aficionado—who received a series of bowls in quick succession and left the encounter red-faced and bursting with hilarity.

Who were these binge-drinking bruisers? What makes a harem (coven? gaggle?) of Demolition Girls? Were they the human avatars of Moutai's flying fairies? Were they KTV hostesses who had taken up the dark arts? I could not tell for certain. I had to know more.

After dinner I tracked them down in the lobby to ask them about their work. Most of them just giggled and pretended not to understand me, but a gruff, thirty-something with shoulder-length hair and a prison-stripe top stepped forward. "What do you want to know?" she said.

"How often do you have to drink this stuff?"

"Every day," she said, as if it were obvious.

"How much do you drink?"

"Half a liter."

"No," interrupted another Demo. "A whole liter!"

Impressive. I didn't know if I believed her, but I continued, "How did you find this job?"

"This is my hometown."

By now the riffraff was noisily filing out of the banquet hall with ties loosened. They hung off one another for support.

"But it's very unusual to drink alcohol for money," I tried, taking another tack.

"For money?"

She cocked her head, unsure if she had understood me. I asked her if this was her job. She repeated the words back to me. We were going in circles. I asked her how she found the job and told me she responded to a job posting after she left university. Then, after a slight pause, she repeated, "This is my hometown."

What I really wanted to know, I explained, was how they knew she could drink so much. Was there a placement test?

"I had to tell them my alcohol tolerance, but there wasn't any test. It all depended on how we spoke, how we looked, and our alcohol tolerance," she said. "I was hired. I like the job." Another pause. "We are ten girls."

"Ten girls?"

"Yeah, yeah, yeah," she confirmed in English.

Effusive good-byes and business-card exchanges were happening around us now. A bus had pulled around front to collect the drunks.

"How long does a career like this last. Ten years? Fifteen? How long have you been drinking every day?"

"Always!"

I laughed.

"All my life. Drinking alcohol makes people more beautiful, healthy, and open. It improves your demeanor." One of the other girls had begun pulling on her sleeve, and she would tell me no more. Some things are better left a mystery.

And then it was over. Team Moutai—Demolition Girls and all—receded into the mist, as if they had never been there.

Wherein lies a baijiu's greatness? What makes a bottle of Red Star Erguotou worth pocket change and a bottle of Moutai a small fortune? It seems a basic question, essential even, but whomever I asked gave me a different answer.

"It's simple," my Sichuanese friend Grace told me before I set out from Chengdu. "If you have a lot of money, you drink expensive baijiu— Moutai, Wuliangye, that sort of thing. If you don't have any money, you drink cheap baijiu." Chinese can at times be maddeningly literal. Of course she was right, but I was looking for something more qualitative.

Other friends, all seasoned baijiu drinkers, implied it was not so much about the immediate experience as what followed. You can purchase a number of very fine-tasting baijius on the cheap. You will probably even enjoy drinking them. The problem is you will feel like a fish slapped against the sidewalk the next morning.

This idea that the cheaper the baijiu the harder the fall never made much sense to me. I had always assumed that a hangover is less about the specific properties of a drink than it is the quantity one consumes: if you drink too much, you get dehydrated; if you fail to rehydrate before morning, you feel like death. And beyond a certain point of alcohol consumption there is no hope of redemption. It doesn't matter what brand you drink, so long as you are smart about it. Or something like that.

Kweichow Moutai, however, has for years claimed its liquor is hangover-proof. Moutai's factory director once told a radio host that, far from being harmful, his baijiu made one's liver function *better*. "Although alcohol is not good for your health," he said, "I dare to say that Maotai liquor is healthy."

Retired Moutai chair Ji Keliang—an adorable, elfish old man with whom I would years later clink glasses—went further, telling *Bloomberg* that in his forty-plus years of drinking Moutai, the total volume of which he conservatively estimated at two tons, he was fit as a fiddle. "One does not get headaches from drinking Moutai, or thirsty," Ji said. "It doesn't harm the head, and one can recover quite quickly from resting a little." The fact that he still holds his own at a banquet while pushing eighty is perhaps the most persuasive evidence.

I thought about their words when I got back to my room that night, after the banquet and the dozen or so beers that followed. There was no minifridge in the room, nor a single bottle of water. All I had was a miniature water dispenser, half full of a liquid that tasted of lead, and the tap water, which in China is about as sanitary as drinking from a Boston gutter the morning after Saint Patrick's Day. The point is I was barred access to the hydration I so desperately needed.

Then a crazy thing happened. I awoke feeling great: no headache, no nausea, not a hint of grogginess. To further drive home the point, the shower had no hot water. At breakfast the hotel provided us two choices of liquid, warm milk or warm soymilk. By then it felt like they were really rubbing it in.

Everyone else seemed chipper, too. Even Wolfram, who had taken the brunt of the damage, seemed in top form. Maybe there was something to this Kweichow Moutai stuff after all.

Before that morning I had never visited a Chinese state-run distillery, and seeing the scope of one up close was breathtaking. At European and U.S. breweries and distilleries, there are usually just a handful of employees who mind a few tidy rooms with vats and tubing and monitoring equipment, not so different from the dairy farms I visited on school fieldtrips as a kid in Kansas. Moutai was like a military camp gearing up for invasion.

The bottling plant was a squat gray building with a smokestack peeking out its rear. This was the central munitions plant, where hundreds of women in white lab coats and blue paper caps worked the line. It was a neat operation. A machine filled the bottles and conveyed them to inspectors, who searched for flaws. One group of women capped the bottles. Another tied red ribbons around them. Labels were affixed, boxes folded and filled, and a pair of distillery-branded shot glasses went in last—all the way down the line until the baijiu was loaded into shipping pallets.

From there we were ushered into the distillery: a long, dark hangar where legions of blue-uniformed men rushed about barefoot pushing wheelbarrows piled high with sorghum. Others stood ready with rakes and shovels. Shafts of light poured in through open windows, catching a curtain of steam wafting off mounds of fermenting grain. Through the haze I made out men raking cooling grain into long rectangles and industrial cranes dropping fermenting sorghum into deep, brick-lined pits.

Sauce-aroma style—the official classification for the umami type of baijiu that Moutai made famous—gets its flavor from a Byzantine, labor-intensive production cycle. The workers steam sorghum, mix it with the yeasty qu, and shovel the grain into waist-high piles to kick off fermentation. The fermented grains are buried in brick-lined pits and sealed with mud for about a month, before the workers unload and distill the grain mash a layer at a time. Fresh grains and qu are added to the mix, and the fermentation-distillation cycle begins anew. The mash is fermented and distilled eight times over the course of about a year, then aged several years more before a master blender mixes all the different distillates together, balancing its smoky, sweet, and savory flavors. A single blend can contain more than a hundred unique strains. In a glass it is exquisite, but in practice it is all sweat and commotion.

There were dozens more Kweichow Moutai workshops just like this one. In fact, every bit of usable land in town had been mobilized for the baijiu effort. The topography prevents locals from building anything up in the mountains, as the factories need access to the river, explained Cao Daming, a sixtyish production manager with jet black–dyed hair. "The Chishui is the only unpolluted river in China," he added, unblinking. I still wonder whether this statement was intended to reassure or alarm me.

To expand Kweichow Moutai's production, the town had recently relocated about a third of its inhabitants to nearby villages. Most of the resettled townspeople depended in one form or another on the distillery for their livelihood. "In France land ownership is private," said Cao, confusing me with one of the Frenchmen. "In China the land is public. The government owns everything and we move people around if we need to. But we compensated them for their trouble. Everyone is quite pleased about it."

Evicting townspeople for baijiu may seem extreme. Hell, it is extreme. But location is everything with baijiu. In 1975 the government tried to build a second Kweichow Moutai plant just a short distance upstream in Zunyi. Every detail of the original plant was meticulously copied, right down to the ceiling-beam dust motes, which were carefully transported to the new facility. Every aspect of the recipe and production process was re-created down to the minutest detail.

The trouble was that the baijiu just didn't taste the same. Because the qu cultures consist of microorganic life harvested from the air, which itself also plays a role in the fermentation process, the slightest change in climate can cause major changes in flavor. As with the French wine-making principle of *terroir*, the best Chinese alcohol is the product of its environment.

The last stop of the distillery tour was the aging cellar, a forest of evenly spaced, yard-high brown ceramic jugs. Moutai ages all of its spirits at least three years before bottling and sells the older baijiu to connois-seurs. Vintage Moutai has become a collector's item, sometimes selling at auction for hundreds of thousands of dollars. Perversely, the most coveted bottles date from 1958 to 1961, the period known as "The Great

Leap Forward," when disastrous central-planning policies resulted in mass starvation that killed tens of millions across China.

Maturation serves a different function in China than in the West, where wooden casks account for much of the flavor and color of brown spirits like whiskey and rum. In China distilleries use a more neutral substance like terracotta clay, which is more porous than wood and allows the spirit to freely interact with the surrounding environment. The oxygen helps break down harsh chemical compounds and mellows the spirit.

"You are all so lucky," Cao said, addressing our coterie, now seated around a long wooden table. His assistant poured us all glasses of a brackish yellow liquid from a laboratory beaker. "This is fifty-year-old Kweichow Moutai. This is something we normally serve only to visiting dignitaries and high-ranking officials."

We took a whiff, a sip, and a shot. This is the part of the story where I am supposed to wax poetic on the virtues of this rare and cherished vintage, to describe the transcendent experience that overcame my nose and palate. But that is not how baijiu works. One traditionally ages baijiu in porous ceramic vessels that allow it to interact with the air, which neutralizes the rough aldehyde edges and increases the concentration of esters. In laymen's terms it makes the baijiu smoother and more flavorful. Most of this happens in a matter of months or years, and it changes the overall character of the drink only slightly. The true secret to a great baijiu is proper blending, not overly long aging. So the spirit Cao served us was more odiferous than garden-variety Moutai, but it was also a bit more biting.

I told him as much later at lunch when he asked for my thoughts. "That's interesting," he said, exchanging glances with his coworkers. I recognized the look: it's the same one we reserve in Kansas City for someone who orders chicken at a steakhouse.

Moutai spirits again flowed freely at the ensuing feast, more than enough to wash down the home-style local delicacies like fish heads, chicken feet, and the dreaded spicy-sour dog pot.

Near the meal's close Moutai chair Yuan Renguo entered the room. A path was cleared and the executive currently occupying the seat of honor was brushed aside, causing a general reshuffling that literally cast the least important underling into the wilderness. Yuan had narrow eyes, a receding hairline, and the unsmiling countenance of a trained assassin. He was here to execute one duty, the generic toast: "Esteemed guests and foreign friends . . . welcome you to Guizhou . . . good fortune"—and a hearty chorus of "ganbei!"

Duties dispatched, he departed. The employee in exile slunk back to his seat, but Yuan's exit sucked all the oxygen out of the room. Team Moutai dutifully finished eating, then vacated the premises. Returning to the lobby, we could see the van waiting out front to take us back to civilization.

Half an hour outside of town, we stopped at the filling station. I went inside and bought an entire box of bottled water. It was the first real hydration anyone had had all day.

There were no headaches.

President Nixon's 1972 trip was a roaring success. Its signal achievement was the Shanghai Communiqué, in which China and the United States pledged to resolve their differences. This was the first step toward normalized diplomatic relations between the two powers. Nixon returned to Washington not just with mended Sino-American ties but with a pair of panda bears for the National Zoo and several bottles of Kweichow Moutai. It nearly cost him the White House.

When Zhou Enlai drank with Nixon in Beijing, he showed the president a party trick: if you held a match to bowl of Moutai, it would instantly ignite. Back in Washington the president tried to re-create the effect in a tea saucer for his daughter. The resulting flame was of such intensity that the saucer cracked and the fire consumed the table.

"So you nearly burned down the White House!" Henry Kissinger explained, recounting the story to Deng Xiaoping years later. A fast-thinking Secret Service agent thankfully snuffed out the flame before it caused any serious damage. It would not prove to be Nixon's last catastrophic miscalculation, but the free world was safe from the impending baijiu menace. At least it was safe for a time.

So why is Moutai called the National Liquor? Is it the rich history, the alleged health benefits, the deep coffers, the revolutionary bona fides, or the patronage of bloated bureaucrats? Or is it some combination of the above?

"The title of 'National Liquor' isn't just something one can wish into existence," Cao Daming said to me during our final encounter. "If the people didn't approve of us, we could not be called the 'National Liquor.' If everyone thinks we're a luxury brand, then we're a luxury brand. If everyone thinks that we're the national liquor, then we're the national liquor. Because we have the best baijiu, they have bestowed this honor on us."

He smiled broadly, adding, "Who are we to disagree?"

9 Song of the South

Northern Guangxi is at once seductive and uninviting. The Li River snakes across the land, creating a fertile basin. The people who have thrived here for thirty thousand years lived largely in cultural isolation, cut off by the province's harsh terrain. Limestone peaks, karst, mark the horizon, scars of a geologic battle fought tens of millions of years ago, when the Indian subcontinent slammed into Asia. The mossy green hills shoot from the ground like shark's teeth as far as the eye can see or the prevailing mists allow.

It is the dreamscape of Chinese watercolor made real: *shanshui*, the mountains and water that define the landscape form. As historian Meow Hui Goh writes in *Sight and Sound: Poetry and Courtier Culture in the Yongming Era*, "*Shanshui* is not nature as it is or by itself, but nature as beheld by humans." Deeply rooted in Daoist notions of natural balance, landscapes present an expressionistic rendering of the natural world— sheer cliff faces poking from cloud curtains, the gnarled branches of trees, valleys slashed by gentle rivulets. If humans are depicted at all, they appear in miniature, engulfed by their surroundings. A visit to Guangxi's countryside makes one realize this is not artistic license.

It is a rural rice-farming region dotted with small villages. The weather-stained homes are whitewashed with black tile roofs, and outside them sit stacks of round stone jars. The jars, approximately the size of beer kegs, store a sweet translucent wine, a kind of huangjiu called mijiu, or rice wine. Almost every family makes its own mijiu, emptied out a bowl at a time with meals until reaching the dregs. Then it is time to make the next jar.

Guangxi—officially the Zhong minority's "autonomous" region—is one of the more ethnically and culturally diverse parts of China, and its alcohol reflects this. Guilin, the region's historical capital, is known for a rice-based baijiu, while people in the modern capital, Nanning, prefer lighter fermented beverages. In the west people drink a clear mijiu, similar in taste and appearance to Japanese sake.

Todd and I set off from Yangshuo by bike to the intermittent clap of firecrackers. Smoke rose in small puffs from the karst hillside. It was Qingming Jie, the Tomb-Sweeping Festival, when families travel to the countryside to honor their ancestors by cleaning their plots, scaring off malign spirits with loud noises, and leaving gifts of fruit, paper money, and alcohol. In ages past, before China mandated cremation, families would disinter their dead every seven years to clean their bones and toast their spirits with a drink. Today the dead, incinerated and largely forgotten, drink only on holidays.

Todd pulled off the side of the road and stepped into a one-room shop, emerging minutes later with a large plastic bag full of explosives. It was a regrettable yet predictable development.

He had joined my quest for spiritual enlightenment in eastern Guizhou. We were old buddies from the Kansas City suburbs; our parents had been friends while we were still in the womb. The two of us connected in high school over a mutual affection for skipping classes and mood-altering substances. Together we developed a knack for brushing up against calamity—mortal, legal, and otherwise—without ever quite touching it.

An Eagle Scout with a mind for the sciences, Todd's chief virtue has always been his utility. On a camping trip I was good for unfolding the tent, cracking a beer, and, if pressed, finding kindling. He would do everything else, from scouting locations to starting the fire. Fire is also his chief weakness. I have a particularly vivid memory of a farmhouse party in the twilight of adolescence. I was listening to music in the back of someone's car, smoking cigarettes and watching the chaos unfold without. A towering pillar of flame danced on the prairie, growing bigger by the minute. A teenage Mephistopheles, Todd stood around the fire with his acolytes, stoking the pit and leaping around it with glee. Every so often a loud burst cracked like rifle shot as a dry-ice bomb exploded. It reminded me at the time of the Do Lung Bridge scene in *Apocalypse Now*. No one was in charge.

It was perhaps predictable that as a career choice he wound up as an engineer specializing in fire protection. At least now he can put out what he starts. I had asked him to join me on my travels because he is reliably good company and, whatever his pyromaniacal shortcomings, always handy in pinch.

We reached Xingping at midday. The village runs along a stretch of the Li so stunning the Chinese put it on the back of the twenty yuan banknote. It is a sleepy place with low-slung buildings with tile roofs, silent save the occasional holiday busload of Chinese tourists in safari gear.

I had been here years earlier, and upon my return the memories flooded back—narrow stone lanes, squat buildings, restaurants with large muskrat-like rodents caged out front. Then I saw something I had missed on my previous visit: a single large Chinese character *jiu* stenciled onto a shop front. We had not sought booze this day, but it found us all the same.

The Qingyang Hao Wine Shop was a single room filled with ceramic wine jugs and the thick perfume of rice alcohol. A perky young shop-keeper ladled us each a small glass of translucent yellow liquid. It was a sweet osmanthus-infused rice wine, smooth and light with a taste of flower tea. Next we tried the local *sanhua* "three-flower" baijiu, whose lightness belied its strength. Mellow, earthy, delicious.

"Our rice wine is some of the best known in the region," said the shopkeeper. The store had been in her husband's family for generations. His name was Chen Zhiming, and he was a tall, middle-aged man who that day sported a flattop and a teal windbreaker.

The Chen clan started as pastry cooks, he explained. In the late nineteenth century Chen Qingxiang went to Guilin for spices, becoming enamored of the local sanhua spirits. Soon after he began producing his own small-batch, pit-fermented liquor. A hundred years and four generations later, the family still runs the business. Chen lifted the lid of a sanhua jar. "Smells like Chivas—very smooth," he said. "It doesn't go straight to your head and it doesn't give you a hangover." Confession: all baijiu distillers make the no-hangover claim.

I told him how much the osmanthus wine appealed to me, and he said it is intended for women, to make them more beautiful. This was news. I had always been under the impression that others got more beautiful only when *I* drank. Todd asked if it could do anything for our looks, and Chen pretended not to understand him.

Chen led us down a narrow cobblestone alleyway to a sagging split-level wooden building that had been the original family shop. On the ground floor was another array of wine jugs, upstairs a cozy tasting room with wooden furniture. He motioned for us to sit while he ducked downstairs to prepare a tasting.

"You see that?" Todd whispered. I followed his gaze along the wall to what I will charitably call art—an assortment of photographs of the type normally found hanging in frat house bathrooms. Marilyn Monroe. Madonna in peak form. And the jewel of the collection, an intriguingly obese blonde nude reclining on a cushion, come-hither eyes staring into the lens.

An old woman wearing a vicious scowl startled us from our reverie. Presumably, this was Chen's mother, though she never introduced herself, and the local dialect was incoherent to us. She paced the room, tidying and making minor adjustments to the furniture. She offered a bowl of water chestnuts, which she demonstrated how to peel with a paring knife.

Chen returned with two plastic bottles filled with a white fluid that had the appearance and consistency of soy milk. "Freshly brewed osmanthus wine," he said, pouring. It was sweet and mouthwatering. The second glass was even better. It was a dark, rich brew: tangy and crisp like a good Argentine Torrontés.

Before we left we asked him for a bottle of his extraordinary osmanthus wine for the road. He walked us to the appropriate jug and pulled back the lid with a proud smile. "All sold out."

"Osmanthus wine?" said Li. "That's for bumpkins."

The next day we were at the headquarters of Guilin Sanhua, China's premier rice baijiu distillery. We sat in an unlit room on overstuffed leather couches opposite sales director Li Zhaolin. Guilin Sanhua is the modern analog to the folk wine-making tradition we had seen in Xingping. Founded from a number of smaller distilleries in 1952—part of Mao's great baijiu consolidation—it is the standard bearer of the local three-flower baijiu.

Tasting the floral notes in Guangxi baijiu, one is tempted to conclude that it is a baijiu infused with flowers, but the "flowers" actually refer to bubbles. In times past Guangxi distillers evaluated the quality of their liquor by surface tension, shaking the bottle and seeing how many bubbles formed. If three distinct bubble clusters appeared in the bottle, the baijiu was deemed first-rate.

Even in the diverse world of Chinese spirits, there is nothing quite like it. Guilin Sanhua uses qu made of rice flour and traditional Chinese herbs mixed with thrice-steamed rice. Earlier I mentioned that Chinese alcohols use qu to convert starches directly into ethanol, but this is the exception. Rice baijiu distillers use a more ancient process better suited to rice, performing these processes separately in stone jars. First they mix a little qu with water and rice to create a yeasty froth, then they mix in more rice and qu in a larger jar. And when I said all baijiu is distilled as a solid using traditional stills? I lied about that too. Guilin Sanhua triple distills a liquid mijiu—essentially clear rice huangjiu—in modern continuous stills similar to those used to make vodka. Sanhua spirit is made entirely from local rice and water from the Li River, then aged in karst caves. It is a synthesis of nature and technology, mountain and water.

Li's assistant entered the room with a tray of shot glasses, setting two in front of each of us. We were invited to try the first, the distillery's signature three-flower spirit. Smooth as silk. He invited us to guess how strong it was, before blurting "104 proof."

"Wow, that high?" said Todd, doubting my translation.

We moved on to the second glass. It was a drink called Lao Guilin made with sweet glutinous rice, like the local fermented rice wine. As we began to sip, an earsplitting bagpipe rendition of "Amazing Grace" erupted from Li's phone, which was appropriate, given the revelation that followed. Lao Guilin was viscous and syrupy, with wonderful honey-like sweetness. It tasted like a blended whiskey had a love child with sake. It is one of the finest Chinese drinks I have ever tasted, and any global spirits enthusiast would be happy to have a bottle of it on the shelf.

"You know sake? It's not so different from this rice baijiu," Li said, rejoining the conversation. "Our baijiu is similar in character to foreign wine and spirits. It has a light, elegant flavor. All alcohols have an optimal level of consumption, and Sanhua Jiu is no exception. If you drink it in the right quantity, it's as good for your health as deer antlers."

Deer antlers? Yes, you read that right. But antlers are a different story altogether.

It was a total horror show. Jars and vials, big and small. Glimpses of the bizarre and perverse floating in brackish yellow liquid. Each shelf revealed a fresh grotesquerie: partially identifiable bits of flora and fauna; herbs, spices, and their assorted detritus; whole animals—reptilian, mammalian, crustacean—milky white eyes frozen in a death stare. It was a scene plucked from the laboratory of Dr. Frankenstein, or of Dr. Moreau.

"I want to be sure that I'm getting this absolutely right," I said nervously. "Just what kind of dicks are we dealing with?"

"Deer dick, dog dick, and fur-seal dick," replied the stone-faced shopkeeper.

"I'm confused. What is it about three-penis wine that makes it preferable to a single-penis wine?"

"The seal penis and the dog penis serve different therapeutic functions," the man explained. "But neither of them is as potent as the deer's penis. That's the most important penis."

Clearly. "And what good is a deer's penis?"

"It's good for your kidneys; it strengthens your yang"—as in the yin and yang, the opposing Daoist forces, dark and light, feminine and the masculine. It puts more lead in the pencil. He slowly lifted a single finger skyward, in case I had missed his drift.

Todd was busy making a naturalist study of the various lab specimens and had settled on a bottle shaped like a weightlifter's torso. "That's a *very* good penis wine. Perhaps you would like some deer antlers?" the vendor suggested hopefully, holding up a vacuum-sealed package of something long and dark, sliced into rounds like salami.

This was Guangzhou, aka Canton, aka capital of Guangdong, China's easternmost southern province, where we would run out of real estate and veer north. We came looking for the region's infamous snake wine and thus far had succeeded only in finding trouser snake. But I'm getting ahead of myself.

A couple of days earlier in Guangxi, Todd and I returned from an outing to find Victor, our affable Aussie innkeeper, practicing martial arts on his front porch. His motions were slow and deliberate, punctuated by forceful kicks and thrusts. Seeing us, he let down his guard, grabbed a couple of beers from the cooler and asked what we had been up to. When he found out we were chasing Chinese alcohol, his face lit up and he retrieved a jug of dark-yellow liquid he kept stashed above his refrigerator. You could see from the coils within that it was snake wine. There appeared to be a lizard or two inside as well.

"Want some?" he said, pouring before we could object.

I gazed at the dark liquid. Reptilian sediment swirled around. Not promising. Todd furrowed his brow with uncertainty. We agreed to drink it shot for shot, drawing from the inexhaustible well of stupidity that has long guided our sex. Surprisingly not bad, I thought, picking a scale from my teeth. Gritty, obviously, but also herbaceous. All in all, it was an improvement on the cheap rice baijiu it had been before the snake.

It was a good thing too, because our next stop was Wuzhou, a blistering hot city in southeastern Guangxi, famous for serpentine delicacies and what I am told is the world's finest turtle jelly. I had received a hot tip from a friend who writes guidebooks that, for just a few dollars, you could spend a terrifying afternoon surrounded by thousands of poisonous vipers at the Wuzhou Snake Park. They even had a restaurant, where guests sip and slurp all the python, cobra, and krait they can stomach.

It seemed too good to be true, and so it was: the park had gone belly up. So we continued on to Guangzhou, where I hoped we would have more luck at the Chinese medicine market. It was crowded and full of pungent odors. There were stalls peddling all manner of herbs, mushrooms, and roots. There were starfish, sea horses, and turtles. One woman even had dried beetles spread across a blanket. But again the snakes eluded us.

This was not a pointless errand. Nor was it undertaken with the object of grossing out Todd or the reader, at least not entirely. We were there to learn more about the backbone of south China's wine-making tradition: medicinal alcohol.

It is easy to get lost in the weeds discussing traditional Chinese medicine, or TCM. In its purest form TCM is a school of preventive medicine based on thousands of years of collected folk wisdom. The mythical emperor Shennong supposedly taught the people agriculture and medicine. According to *Huainanzi*, the ancients lived off the land, eating wild plants, fruit, and raw seafood. Because their food often poisoned them, Shennong taught them how to sow the five grains: broomcorn millet, foxtail millet, rice, wheat, and hemp. "He tested the properties of the hundred plants, and the quality of the water, whether sweet or bitter; and thus he caused the people to know what to avoid." And thus Chinese medicine was born.

Its foundational text is *The Yellow Emperor's Inner Canon*, written roughly two thousand years ago, which sets forth a basic concept of wellness based around balance—between yin and yang, hot and cold, and the "five elements" (metal, wood, water, fire, and earth). According to Daoists, water is the only indestructible element, with the power to defeat both fire and earth. As wine scholar Peter Kupfer writes in "Amber Shine and Black Dragon Pearls," "one step further is *jiu* (alcohol), described as 'holy water' (*shensheng zhi shui*), applied to keep off evil spirits and influences, poison and illness."

Dr. Yu Jiazheng, a grandfatherly fourth-generation TCM practitioner, explained this to me back in Chengdu. "Western doctors look down on Chinese medicine, because Chinese medicine isn't rooted in hygiene and science," he said. "But contemporary TCM is continually developing and improving. Moreover, it's becoming more specialized, and it's learning from Western medicine."

It may sound like nonsense—some of it undoubtedly may be—but the underlying principle is sound: poor health results from an unbalanced body, and by maintaining a proper diet and healthy lifestyle you can avoid sickness. It is easier for the body to fight off an illness than to treat it after the fact. Or, as Dr. Yu told me, "You can't dig a well when you're thirsty."

Central to TCM, past and present, is alcohol. *The Yellow Emperor's Inner Canon* states that the ancient doctors prepared alcohol but hardly ever used it. But as time went by, the people lost their way and grew sickly. "By imbibing the wines and decoctions, they were able to stay healthy." It was believed that alcohol, more than just a treatment for illnesses, could ward off evil spirits that cause them.

In China tonics go by many names—*yaojiu* (medicinal alcohol), *yingyangjiu* and *zibujiu* (nutritional alcohol), *baojianjiu* (healthful alcohol)—but they amount to the same thing. Winemakers either incorporate Chinese medicine into qu, like Guilin Sanhua does, or they steep the ingredients in alcohol over days, weeks, or months. This latter method is also used to make nonmedicinal concoctions called *paojiu* (infused alcohols), popular with home brewers all over China, especially in the south.

Popular styles like chrysanthemum and *wujiapi* (Siberian ginseng) wine appeared around the sixth century, but the variety of medicinal wines has grown over time. There were about seven styles at the time of Chinese unification in 220 BCE and several dozen by the sixteenth century. Today there are around four hundred recorded recipes. The complexity has varied as well. Most wines rely on only one or two ingredients, but the Tang dynasty *danshen* wine used a record forty-five.

Medicinal alcohol is used to treat a wide range of ailments, such as joint pain, coughing, low circulation, and arterial blockage. Li Shizhen's definitive sixteenth century *Compendium of Medica Materia* explains,

> The wine of rice is the best suited as a medicine in disease, because it develops the efficacy of the medicine, causes circulation in the network of vessels, stirs the blood, and sets in motion the air, causing it to mount to the head, determines to the skin, and disperses to the extreme limits of the whole body. . . . A patient, laboring under the bite of a rabid dog, ought not to drink wine. . . . If bitten by a serpent, the wound is to be washed with cold wine. If a person has been subjected to a great dread, and death is feared, one or two cups of hot wine must be poured down his throat at once.

TCM has tonics to improve organ function, alleviate intestinal distress, boost a man's sperm count, prevent balding, extend longevity, soften wrinkle lines, and fight dementia. It can be applied as a topical ointment, an antiseptic, or an antidote to poison. In ancient China it was used to preserve royal corpses during funerary rites. Alcoholic tonics are even used to treat hangovers. "Of all the medicines," *The Book of Han* concludes, "alcohol is best."

The idea is that the medicinal ingredient possesses a curative property, which is transferred to the alcohol during the steeping process. There is also a simpler explanation: taste. Many of the common TCM ingredients are exceedingly bitter, so the alcohol functions as the proverbial spoonful of sugar. Meanwhile, the herbs round out some of a cheap alcohol's rougher edges. Both make the other more palatable, and that is no small feat. TCM ingredients run the gamut from inoffensive (flowers, bamboo leaves, ginseng) to disquieting (ants, bees, sea horses) and horrific (caterpillar fungus, quadruped fetus, human placenta)—which brings me back to snakes.

Snake wine is the most popular animal-based medicinal alcohol in China and greater Southeast Asia. A snake wine may be prepared in one of two equally shocking ways. To serve snake wine fresh, one cuts the gallbladder out of a live snake, squeezes the bile into a small glass, and adds a dash of alcohol. (This method was convincingly demonstrated by Leonardo DiCaprio in the opening scenes of *The Beach*.) The second, more popular, method is steeping, where one soaks gutted snakes in baijiu. Over time the transparent liquid absorbs the snake's slippery slurpiness and turns a deep ochre color.

Before crying foul, consider the story of TCM's introduction to the United States, when serpentine cure-alls became famous for all the wrong reasons. In the mid-nineteenth century Chinese flocked to the U.S. West Coast, first as miners in the California gold rush, then as laborers building the transcontinental railroad. The vast majority of them came from the snake-loving coastal provinces of southeastern China, particularly Guangdong, and they brought with them their cuisine and customs.

The ethnically European workers scoffed at the snake wines and tinctures the Chinese used to treat rheumatism. But when the white laborers tried them, they reluctantly admitted the snake's efficacy. U.S. hucksters saw a market opening and began making their own "snake oil," which of course had no effect. These salespeople were selling a potion made mostly from the U.S. rattlesnake or from no snake at all. When the U.S. government tested Stanley's Snake Oil in the early twentieth century, it found the recipe consisted mostly of mineral oil and pepper. Snake oil became synonymous with quackery.

Chinese medicine was not tarnished by the affair. TCM clinics proliferated and thrived in San Francisco during snake oil's rise, which is all the more remarkable, considering that it coincided with the high tide of anti-Chinese sentiment in the United States.

Later studies bore out the Chinese side of the snake-oil incident. Researchers have demonstrated that oil found in certain Chinese water snakes is rich in omega-3 fatty acids, which can supposedly decrease joint inflammation and boost cognitive ability while lowering blood pressure and cholesterol levels. Chinese snakes have even more omega-3 acids than salmon, whereas U.S. snakes have none at all. So perhaps the snake-oil salespeople weren't all quacks. They may just have been using the wrong snakes.

Todd and I strolled down the banyan-lined lanes of old Shameen Island, enjoying an early afternoon bottle of Filipino beer. Shameen is the old European quarter, poetically built atop a landfill. Next to the congested concrete bustle of Guangzhou, its relative tranquility and colonial villas are refreshing. Gone are the opium merchants of old, replaced by Chinese couples taking "Western-style" wedding photos in an exotic setting. The kapok trees were in bloom, and their red blossoms, the size of a small head of lettuce, had begun to drop from their branches. No sooner they made landfall than a passerby would rush to collect the coveted blooms for medicinal use.

The snake hunt was turning into a wash. I took a pull of San Miguel and looked back at the city across the canal. Then I saw it, not more than a block from where we stood. A large building on which was written "Chinese Medicine Shopping Center." The top two floors sold almost nothing but alcohol. This was the Chinatown backroom of popular imagination. Dusty jars of *disjecta* animal *membra* and anonymous roots lined the walls. Dried fish hung from the ceiling. A host of unidentifiable odors emanated from rows of satin-lined boxes containing dried deer penises. I half-expected to find a *mogwai*.

The shopkeeps showed us an assortment of wines, and, though I failed to bridge the Cantonese linguistic gap, they were able to convey holistic benefits by way of pantomime. One man pointed to one vat and made an exaggerated flexing motion. Pointing to another, he rubbed his stomach. And so on.

One imagines shops like these have changed little over the centuries, but what set the stores we saw apart from their ancient predecessors was their commercialization. Chinese medicine used to be an entirely localized craft industry. Patients bought medicine from what was available at their local druggist and mixed it with their own home-brewed alcohol. Today many medicinal alcohols are mass-produced by pharmaceutical companies, distilleries, and, yes, quacks. The popular energy drink Jing Jiu—kind of a Chinese Red Bull–Viagra hybrid—can be purchased by the flask at any bodega.

We retired to a nearby park with an embarrassment of potions. Spreading our bottles out on a bench, we set about our study. We had a bottle of snake-ginseng wine, some deer antler tonic, and a bag full of phallus phials, single-chamber and triple-barreled. To passersby we likely appeared a couple of foreign lowlifes on an epic bender. No matter.

First up, snake and ginseng. Much, *much* better than the first snake wine. Well worth the effort. Then we cracked a bottle of deer penis. It was delicious, and each bottle was better than the last, rich and full of syrupy cinnamon flavor. I cannot say if any of this made us any healthier. I do not know if I left the park stronger or more virile. But I liked it.

Say what you will, I had a delightful afternoon.

The sign read "Longyan," but every Chinese train station looks the same at four in the morning. Tile pathways, dingy and scuffed in the fluorescent light, lead passengers to a pack of scavengers waiting outside. We pushed past promises of warm beds and private cars, past motorcycles and bicycle rickshaws. Cabs are little better at this hour—you're getting fleeced any way you play it—but at least you can avoid sitting with your suitcase on your lap.

Our "four-star" hotel room smelled like half-smoked, full-tar cigarettes. An entire wall appeared as if it had weathered a tsunami, just barely: streaky wallpaper peeled away from the moldy black slab beneath. The carpet may once have had a pattern, but it was long since obscured by burn marks and murder stains. For the coup de grâce, the toilet refused to flush.

It felt like I had just closed my eyes when the phone rang. It was the welcoming committee from the Chengang Jiu Company. A shingle of light had already crept into the room, and, to my surprise, the direct sunlight did not cause the room to burst into flames or reduce it to a wailing heap. As I dressed, I wondered why the hotel service crew even bothered to make the beds.

"We were expecting two people," a man in sunglasses said when I met him outside. I told him Todd was feeling sick. It was a lie. The Judas had abandoned me for more sleep.

"Have you eaten?" he asked. I should have been ready for this, the most predictable opening gambit. It is a Chinese rhetorical device like "What's up?" asked any time, regardless of circumstance. You are not supposed to answer honestly, but my brain had not caught up with my body. I said no, and I walked right into the trap.

The Chinese built the Great Wall to keep outsiders out, so once you are in they make you pay for it. Chinese hospitality can best be described as ruthless altruism (if you have a Jewish grandmother, you already know what I mean by this). When a host makes an offer, it's happening. A refusal is a polite formality to be dispensed before inevitable acquiescence made with feigned reluctance. A "yes" also implies agreement. So short of a valid medical excuse, which may still be rejected, there is no way out. It is instructive to note that the Chinese language lacks a word that directly corresponds to the English "no."

So off we went to breakfast, where my hosts ordered and paid before I could object. While I worked my way through a heaping plate of rice noodles and tripe soup, we discussed the merits of snake wine, also popular here in Fujian Province. My failure to finish the meal, large enough for a family of six, visibly distressed them.

They assumed my lack of appetite had been a matter of suitability, so they frog-marched me to a Western-style bakery, hopeful that I would eat more. One by one, they picked up every item in the store, asking, "Will you eat this? How about this one?" By the third time I explained I would not require further nourishment—*seriously*—they relented.

We ventured beyond the city and backward in time, past paddy fields and sagging, centuries-old temples to Guanyin, Goddess of Mercy. At the top of a hill that overlooks a tiny village in the shadow of a rolling green hill was the Chengang factory. It was a boxy building, recently constructed, and upstairs in the corner office Party certificates and calligraphy scrolls adorned whitewashed walls. Company chair Wang Ruijin rose from his mahogany desk and invited me to join him for tea.

Wang wore a powder-blue polo. He had a wide face, side part, and a wisp of a mustache. He was not Fujianese but a Yangtze Delta man from Suzhou. He had come up in Guangzhou's textile industry and later worked a stint in Los Angeles. In 2007 a friend showed him the Chengang brewery, a two-hundred-year-old huangjiu outfit that had fallen on hard times. "I love huangjiu," he said. "So we decided to buy it."

The type of huangjiu they make in Fujian is a lustrous caramel color. It's based on a special kind of fermentation agent known as red qu, which was first produced by Song dynasty winemakers about a thousand years ago. It was one of the last major innovations in rice wine. Huangjiu made from red qu gets its color from monascus, a bright red and extremely stubborn mold. It can withstand higher levels of alcohol and acid than other common qu molds, so it crowds out competing microorganisms and ferments a very potent drink. In the old times they called it *hongjiu*, or red wine, but that name grew confusing with the rising popularity of grape red wine, so today it is considered to be a part of the huangjiu family.

Some of Chengang's wines are fortified with baijiu; others are brewed straight. The huangjiu's aroma is mild and its flavor complex, a delicate balance of sweet, fruity flavors that remind me of sherry. It is light on the palate and goes down easy. Given huangjiu's similarity to Western fortified wines, Wang wanted to know why foreigners in China, who have such strong opinions about baijiu, largely ignored it. I told him that most of us had never heard of it. And of those who had, most encountered it only as the cooking wine in Asian groceries.

He nodded thoughtfully. "Foreigners didn't even used to know where China was," he said. "They all thought Chinese people had pigtails and walked around in pajamas. It's not only that they didn't understand huangjiu. It's that they didn't understand China. Now there's better information out there, and foreigners are starting to get us." He held his teacup out in front of him, lost in thought. It had been like that for him in Los Angeles, he said. "Before I went to America I didn't understand the West, either. But eventually I started to get it."

A short, heavy-set man named Chen, the factory manager, led us outside, past piles of upended jars drying in the sun, and into the brewery. It was a modest, lightly staffed operation that annually produces about a thousand tons of huangjiu, roughly two million bottles' worth. We entered a dank, open room where hundreds of open stone jars crowded the floor.

Chen said the company was called Chengang Jiu, Sinking Jar Wine, because during fermentation carbon dioxide pushes the rice to the top of jar, and then it sinks. Three times this happens, with the best wine collecting at the bottom of the jar. Inside each of the jars was a crimson porridge of rice. Scattered throughout the dregs were black flecks of something that looked like sesame seeds. Medicine, Wang explained. The qu recipe was a jealously guarded secret, with more than thirty-two herbal ingredients.

Behind the factory was a wooden barn filled with sealed stone urns stacked two high. "My babies," Wang said. "There's not another wine like it in the world."

What makes the rice wine so special in Fujian is its connection to the Hakka community. Hakka means "guest family," though it indicates outsider more than visitor. The Hakka have their own dress, folklore, and cuisine. They speak their own language, which may be the purest surviving form of ancient Chinese. The Hakka are thought to have migrated from the Central Plain some two thousand years ago. Some believe it was the Hakka who first brought huangjiu to south China. Wherever the Hakka sought refuge, they were marginalized and denied access to the best farmland. An immigrant community in their own country, Hakkas formed tight-knit, insular clans to survive. In Hakka villages that bordered hostile local populations, they dug in.

In Fujian they built earthen houses, or *tulou*. The tulou are magnificent structures, part fortified compound, part communal dwelling capable of housing thousands. Typically three to five stories high, they are built square, round, or in interlocking semicircles. They are like castles—windowless lower floors, outer walls several feet thick, and a single stone-reinforced entrance. In the center are open courtyards lined with apartments. There's an oft-repeated story of dubious provenance that during the Cold War, U.S. spy satellites mistook the tulou—with their dense outer walls and cavernous centers—for missile silos.

Todd and I spent the afternoon hiking the tulou and surrounding hills in a Hakka village, drinking mouth-puckering rice wine from bamboo flasks. Between the sun and the wine, we fell fast asleep on the return ride. I awoke with a start to my phone's ringing.

"Derek, where are you?" Wang said through the receiver.

"On the road back to Longyan."

"Call me when you're done eating. We'll drink some tea, okay?"

I groaned inwardly, considering the implications. "Drinking tea" is as ambiguous a phrase as one encounters in China. It might be just an innocent cup of tea, but it can also imply debauched, liver-busting benders at third-rate brothels. It can even be sinister. When Chinese state security wants to intimidate subversives, they invite them for tea at the local police station.

In this particular instance I put my money on a KTV, as karaoke parlors are known. A further layer of ambiguity: I could not say whether this would entail singing karaoke with Wang or playing drinking games with KTV girls (hired companions: not exactly prostitutes but not exactly not prostitutes). I had once spent an entire awkward evening on a business trip forced by my superiors to shoot dice (not a euphemism) with a KTV girl named Miao Miao and found the experience uncomfortable in the extreme.

I put my hand over the receiver and told Todd to prepare for the worst.

"Give the phone to the driver," Wang said. "I'll tell him where to take you."

The cab took us to a Hakka restaurant, and, halfway through our meal, the phone went off again. "Are you at the restaurant?" Wang said. "Yes? I'm on my way!" Seconds later he burst through the door and barked his disapproval. "You haven't ordered enough food." We were stuffed full to bursting, but he brushed away our objections with a disgusted grunt, flagging down a server. "Three more Tsingtaos and a plate of spring rolls." Then, turning to me, "How'd you like the tulou?"

"Incredible. Good mijiu, too."

"How much did you drink?"

"Half liter each."

"That's nothing. I just drank two liters of huangjiu!"

A pitifully small plate of spring rolls landed on the table, shriveled oily husks. Inedible. "Let's get out of here," said Wang. He paid the server before we could reach our wallets. Face was at stake. Outside he flagged down a cab, and I sighed with relief.

"You think I'd drive in my state?" he said.

"Of course not," I lied.

As expected, the cab stopped in front of a neon mess of lights, unmistakably a KTV marquee. As we ascended a spiral staircase round a billion-watt chandelier, I told Todd to ready himself to leave at a moment's notice if things got hairy. In Chinese I told Wang we would not require any *xiaojie*, "little sisters." Escorts.

"Do I look like a *xiaojie* to you?" he laughed. And it was true—his moustache was a bit thicker than is customary. He led us to a small room with a wraparound couch and several middle-aged men, all there to see Wang's "American friends."

Karaoke is ubiquitous in China. In every city, town, and village with an electrical socket, you will find a KTV or eighty. Karaoke is not performed in a public space, as is the U.S. custom. It is an intimate affair, in which friends pile into dark, windowless rooms permeated with cigarette smoke. Sometimes there will be disco lights and lasers. There are always at least two microphones, and the reverb is set to eleven. If you are lucky, the room will have its own bathroom. If you are really lucky, you will not be sitting near it once the party gets going.

When Chinese and foreigners go KTVing together, it can get awkward. For many foreigners the only aspect of Chinese culture more off-putting than baijiu is the local pop music: long, rambling love ballads, dripping with schmaltz and tailor-made for late-night crooning. The foreigners, blissfully ignorant of the Chinese classics, sit bored to one side.

Conversely, Chinese eyes cloud over when foreigners sing the handful of available English tracks. Half the room always wishes it was somewhere else—a good recipe for drinking and little else. And at KTV one usually drinks lukewarm beer or a concoction of whiskey and green tea.

This night differed only slightly. As the guests of honor, Todd and I were allowed to choose the songs. Since our selections were all English, it also meant that we would be doing the singing. We started with "My Humps," and when that failed to excite our audience, we went more mainstream in the hope that someone might jump in and save us. When "Country Roads" got no play, we knew we were in trouble. By the time we hit "Hotel California," the lyrics morphed into grotesque self-parody: "You can check out any time you like, but you can never leave."

More of Wang's friends filed in to witness the spectacle. There was the KTV owner, a balding, chubby fellow who welcomed us to Fujian. There was the woman in the white dress with long black hair pulled back in a ponytail, too old to be a KTV girl.

"Pretty, isn't she?" he asked, instructing her to sit next to us so she could practice her English.

The ganbeis flew freely, and Wang grew more intimate. He put his arm around me and talked closer to my face than I would have preferred—some dudes get gropey when they drink. Neither Todd nor I have much talent at singing, and when the novelty wore thin, most of the onlookers left.

"Let's get out of here," Wang said.

"Where?" I asked nervously.

"Down the hall," he said. "That's where the women are." This was the turn I had feared. I told Todd we would soon be leaving.

"Let's see what happens first," Todd said.

Wang led us out into the bright hallway and stopped in front of a door. He pushed it open slowly, revealing approximately a dozen frumpily dressed women, median age fifty.

"Friends of mine from university," Wang explained.

Now well into his cups and still holding one of the microphones from the last room, Wang shouted, "Hey everyone, meet my American friends, Derek and Todd!" The woman who had been midsong was visibly annoyed. "Derek's here to learn about Chinese drinking culture." The woman resumed singing, and the others smiled at us politely.

When Todd and I were back on the mic, we unwisely selected the Beatles' "I Saw Her Standing There." The first verse went well enough. We had established that the girl in question was just seventeen, and that the others knew what that meant. From there it became increasingly apparent that we had forgotten the rest of the lyrics and with them a sense of rhythm. And that high note in the chorus? Missed it by a mile.

A peanut hit me in the face. I ducked the second one, but they kept coming. Wang still had half a bowl left. For Todd this was a teachable moment in the offensive ganbei. It was time to take Wang out of the game. When the song had drawn to a merciful end, I grabbed a handful of beers and led Todd over to Wang. I handed Wang a beer and cracked my own. "Ganbei," I said and downed the can in a long gulp. Any Kansan worth his salt can slam cheap beer, and Todd hit him with the next one. I passed out the remaining beers and proposed another ganbei. Wang was starting to look pale, so we left him to his nuts.

Now in the clear, Todd struck up a conversation with the woman in white. She asked us if we could give her an English name, and we settled on "Roxanne." Cue karaoke video. A woman with an eighties perm strides down an anonymous Eastern European city street looking for customers. MIDI keyboards swell in the background.

If the women thought we butchered the Beatles, we did them one better with the Police. But there was a glitch in the input system. As soon as "Roxanne" faded out, the video began anew. The lonesome Slavic streetwalker again took tentative steps down the street, and we redoubled the serenade of our newly christened friend. By the third time the song began playing, it was just me, Todd, and Roxanne—the one in the song. Everyone else had left.

On the cab back to the hotel, Wang slumped in the front seat almost to the floorboard. "I would hang out tomorrow, if I didn't have to go to Wuyisan," he said, slurring the words. "If you go to Suzhou or Shenzhen, give me a call. My friends will show you a good time."

"Thanks," I said. "You can call me the next time you go to Chengdu."

"I don't know," he said. "I've got a lot of friends in Chengdu."

The cab's taillights trailed off in the distance. We were finally free, after twenty hours of full-frontal hospitality. If this is what it means to be a guest in China, it is little wonder the Hakkas ran for the hills.

In the interest of full disclosure, Todd and I were wasted. We should have gone to bed. We should have rehydrated. This is what smarter people would have done. What *we* did was retrieve Chekov's bag of cheap Chinese fireworks, which Todd had carried in his luggage since Guangxi like an idiot.

We laid out our explosive stash on a bridge overlooking the Longchuan River, and Todd pulled the fuse out as far as it would go. Making sure no one else was near, Todd bent down with his lighter. The fuse hissed out quicker than you could say "kaboom!"

A great conflagration erupted behind us as we dove for safety. No one was hurt, Todd's lighter the sole casualty. And with this grand gesture we had conquered the south, checked mijiu country off the list, and presumably scared off any lingering evil spirits.

How wrong we were.

10 Yangtze Delta Blues

Yu the Great looks down on Shaoxing from his hilltop tomb on Kuaiji Mountain. He is remembered for many things. He tamed the floods of the Central Plain, founded the Xia dynasty, and tragically banished China's first winemaker, Yi Di, for her marvelous invention. If he knew what would become of Shaoxing, he would have had the good sense to die elsewhere.

Shaoxing is to rice wine what Bordeaux is to grape wine. Writing from Beijing in 1895, Scottish physician John Dudgeon remarked in *The Beverages of the Chinese,* "The [Shaoxing] wine is reckoned, at the present day, the best; its taste is acid and yet not acid, astringent and yet not astringent." It is a viscous amber nectar suited equally to drinking and cooking: many of the best Chinese recipes call for a dash of Shaoxing.

Todd and I rolled into the sleepy Zhejiang Province canal town on a rainy Friday night. The train ride had been brutal after the previous night's revel in Fujian. The trip spanned seven hours, and we spent almost all of it squatting in the smoky septic funk of the intracar bathroom passage. After that, the downpour was a welcome relief. It was late but not so late that we couldn't find a good bottle of huangjiu and a bowl of chilies and crawfish. The union of sweet and spicy was heavenly, and it conjured a dozen wonderful memories with it. It felt good to be back in the Jiangnan—South of the River.

In Chinese the Yangtze River is called Chang Jiang, the Long River. Flowing almost four thousand miles from the Tibetan Plateau to the East China Sea, it stretches farther than any other river in Asia. Symbolically, it is the Chinese Mason-Dixon, the historical dividing line between north and south, regions with different languages, traditions, and cuisines. Over the millennia China's political and cultural pendulum has swung back and forth between its poles, intermingling the disparate traditions and engendering a mostly healthy rivalry.

The Yangtze terminates in a fertile delta crosshatched with streams and canals, well suited to farming and fishing. It had access to China's interior as far west as Sichuan and China's north via the Grand Canal, so few regions were better situated for generating wealth than the Yangtze Delta. Elsewhere Chinese complain, always with a tinge of jealousy, that Jiangnan people are too materialistic. This was where I fell in love with the Middle Kingdom, and I have never known a better home.

Today the Yangtze Delta contains many of China's most vibrant and prosperous cities—Shanghai, Nanjing, Hangzhou, Suzhou—though in ancient times it was the seat of two warring kingdoms, the Wu and Yue.

Legend holds that their rivalry started when a Yue princess was forced to marry the king of Wu. Unhappy in her match, she fled her husband's palace on their wedding night. A bitter and bloody war ensued.

On the eve of the decisive battle the Yue generals presented their king with a gift of the finest wine. The king gathered his army, poured the wine into the river, and commanded his troops to drink of it. If he tasted glory, so too would they. The noble gesture was not lost on his soldiers, who delivered a crushing defeat to the Wu army. The kingdoms were thus united, and the culture of the Yangtze Delta region has since been dubbed Wu-Yue.

Then, as always, alcohol was the great leveler.

In China history and myth coexist in the present. After dinner we went for a stroll along a sleepy canal off the Toulao He, the River of Tossing Wine. This was where it happened, or at least where someone supposed that it did. Who can say two and a half millennia later? Our amble led us to an open courtyard, from which loud voices spilled onto the road. Peeking around the wall, we discovered a group of about eight twenty-something Chinese clustered around a stone table cluttered with Tsingtao bottles.

They were schoolmates, recently graduated from a well-known southeastern university. Most of them were teachers; the rest were working ill-defined entry-level office jobs in second-tier cities. They had come to Shaoxing for the weekend to blow off steam. They asked if we could help them with the remainder of their beer, and we gladly assented. It was easy to open up with them. They were outward looking, eloquent, and worldly, and through them we were able to restore some of the sanity that had eluded us in the blur of rice wine that had marked our time in south China. The conversation turned to the rapid pace of China's development in recent years, the good, the bad, and occasionally something that skirted the subversive.

I felt Yu the Great looking down on us from the hills. This was just the type of talk that he had feared alcohol might fuel. It is a risky business mixing authoritarianism with strong drink, yet perhaps the continuous cycles of prohibition and repeal reveal that the people will not tolerate one without the other.

But things in Shaoxing had indeed changed rapidly. Prior to "Liberation" people in Shaoxing brewed and sold huangjiu on every street. It was a family tradition, in which recipes and techniques passed from one generation to the next. In 1951 the Party merged most of the breweries into state-run companies like the Shaoxing Huangjiu Group, whose largest brand, Guyuelongshan, produces the majority of China's huangjiu, including the official huangjiu served at state dinners.

"Shaoxing is the true home of huangjiu. We've been making our own huangjiu here for the last 360 years," said Mr. Huang, a wine seller whose shop we happened on the next day. He was about sixty, wearing gold-rimmed glasses and a comb-over that had outgrown its last dye job.

When he learned we were American, his eyes lit up. He told us he loved our country and that his son was a student at the University of Virginia. "America is very good," he said in practiced English and gave us thumbs-up.

It was a narrow space, barely more than a counter in front of a row of clay jars. Huang walked over to one of them, lifted its cloth cover, and ladled two servings of its contents into flimsy plastic cups. "Try some of this. It's called *yuanhong*. This is the most traditional Shaoxing wine, and we make it ourselves with sticky rice."

We thanked him and sipped the bittersweet brew.

"If you want something sweeter and stronger, you just add more rice during fermentation," he continued. "It's called *jiafan*—add rice—wine." This is an ancient Chinese wine-making secret. You start fermenting rice in a jar with a wheat qu broth, which begins to liquefy into alcohol after a couple of days. Then you add another charge of rice, and then another, continually charging the alcohol until it kills the yeast and the last charge just adds sugar. This means that ancient Chinese fermented beverages could top thirty proof, whereas their Western counterparts maxed out at around ten.

Huang pointed to another bottle. "There's also this semisweet wine one called *shanniang*, which uses huangjiu instead of water in the brewing process. The sweetest and strongest type of Shaoxing wine is called *xiangxue*." I picked a small bottle labeled *nu'er hong* and asked him what it was.

"When a baby girl is born in Shaoxing, her family buries a jar of wine," he said. "After eighteen years, when the girl wants to get married, the *nu'er hong* is served to the guests at her wedding." *Nu'er hong* translates to "daughter red," red being the color of the traditional Chinese wedding gown and good fortune. "If you have a boy, you set aside a jar of *zhuangyuan hong* [valedictorian red]. You serve it at his wedding or when he sets off for university." He was a persuasive salesman. We left with seven bottles.

"Did anyone settle the tab?" I asked, zipping up. I had just made literal the age-old connection between southern Chinese rice wine and art, relieving myself in the canal that runs alongside the boyhood home of Lu Xun, arguably modern China's greatest writer. It was not my finest hour.

"I didn't give them anything," said James.

"They would have asked us for money if they wanted it," Todd suggested. This was a fair point, we agreed. In any case it didn't seem wise to go back.

What the hell had just happened? About nine hours earlier, an old colleague and comrade-in-drinks, James, made the trip from Shanghai for the Trial of the Seven Bottles. It took place at a restaurant called The Grandma's. One might reasonably infer from the name a rustic, homey setting—wicker chairs, flowery tablecloth, and the like—but this was a chrome palace, a kind of living monument to ostentation, so bright and reflective it practically necessitated sunglasses. Several servers made eye contact, but none proved brave enough to come to us. They would scan the room, see us looking back, and then dart into the restaurant's recesses. After ten minutes or so of this game, James got up and led a server to our table by the arm.

The three of us set about our task with deliberate precision, drinking a bottle at a time. It was unintentional, but it worked out exactly the opposite of how one wants a drinking session to transpire: dry to sweet, sweet to revolting, revolting to unpalatable. This is not to say that Shaoxing huangjiu is not good—it is in fact great, particularly the jiafan variety—but there is only so much saccharine alcohol a human can take in one sitting.

The pace of drinking slowed to a crawl. By the time we cracked the final bottle, most of the lights had dimmed and the night staff was mopping the floor. Desperate to put an end to the bottle, James flagged down the last two customers as they made their way to the door. "My friends," he said. "Come, drink with us."

One of the men ignored him and kept walking, but the other, a tall, heavy-set bruiser in a dark-blue suit came over and slid into the booth next to James.

"Here, friend, have some huangjiu," James said, passing him a full glass.

"I don't like huangjiu," said the man. "I drink baijiu."

"Just one glass?"

"All right." He raised his glass and looked around the table. "Ganbei!"

I set down my empty glass with a grimace. It was like chugging cough syrup at this point, but that was the end of our supply.

"Waiter!" shouted the stranger. "Two more bottles."

"No, you really don't need to do that," said James, imploring. "*Really*."

"I think the restaurant's closing," I added, noting the exasperated look on the manager's face. "We should get going."

"No, no, no," said the man, brushing aside our objections with his hand. "Don't worry about them. We're customers. They'll serve us." He barked instructions back at the server, acting like he owned the place. The manager was cowed. Two more bottles—another liter of sickly sweet huangjiu—arrived minutes later. The suit proposed another ganbei.

Our new friend was from Shanghai, but he spent a lot of time in these parts for work, he told us. We gave him our business cards, but he failed to reciprocate. "I left them in the car," he said vaguely. "I'll give it to you later." This was a red flag. Business cards are mandatory in China, and withholding one is a grave slight. Those rare professionals who fail to carry them usually have good reason: everyone already knows who they are; they are too powerful or important; they call the shots. They call *you*; you do not call *them*.

He demanded another ganbei. The man said he liked going to the Grandma's. A "classy joint" like this would be much more expensive in Shanghai, but in Shaoxing a man could live like a king. He told us we should look him up back in Shanghai. We would be there next week? Great, we could go out with his friends for hot pot.

Another ganbei. The man in the suit began to describe a woman he knew in Shaoxing whose proportions defied the laws of nature. We laughed nervously, and I started translating the conversation for Todd's benefit. Blue Suit cut me off: "Why aren't you two speaking in Chinese? I don't speak English." I explained Todd's linguistic limitations. Talking over me, he barreled ahead. "She's real, I tell you. Once we're done with these drinks here, we'll go to the KTV and I'll show you."

And another ganbei. One ganbei over the line, as it turned out. I ordered Todd to let me out of the booth and made a beeline for the men's room. I stared at the toilet. False alarm. I splashed some water on my face and walked back out. By the time I got back to the table, James was cornered. He had let slip that he worked for a financial news service, and Blue Suit started feeling him out for investment advice.

At the other end of the table, Todd and I began wondering aloud in English just whom we had invited to our table. Out-of-town guy with mysterious business dealings, ordering around the staff after hours, a personal "in" with the local brothel, money to invest offshore. It dawned on us that Grandma's had the look of a place that might appeal to a gangster. What had we gotten ourselves into?

James was doing his best to stay afloat, every so often turning toward Todd and me, mouthing, "Help!" or "Save me!" But we had to drink our way out of this one, and with a heroic push we finished the second bottle. After we politely declined several invitations to go to the KTV upstairs, Blue Suit walked with us outside, stopping us before we could hail a cab. Oh, god, what next?

He reached for something in his pocket. "I still need to give you my card." He produced a set of keys. With the press of a button, there was a loud whooshing sound, and a hydraulic door swung open next to us.

It was a tour bus. The man was a bus driver.

We laughed our way to the next bar. James belted a rousing rendition the Maoist anthem "The East Is Red" to the great amusement of our cabbie.

Yes, nine bottles deep and we still had the bad sense to continue. We found a surprisingly solid hole-in-the-wall with off-brand Germanic beer, run by a lively couple—both Jiangnan ladies in their thirties—and a cute server whom Todd and James both attempted to woo, albeit sloppily.

"You're not ugly, how could you think you're ugly?" James reassured her, slurring the words slightly as he spoke. By the time we left, the bottles were stacked so high it was becoming difficult to see across the table.

We left suddenly, shooed out onto the cobblestone streets by one of the owners. Somehow the bill did not enter into the equation. Perhaps one of them had offended our server, and we had been kicked out. Maybe the owners were being generous. Maybe we had paid after all. Inference was beyond any of our abilities at that point.

I awoke in a world of suffocating darkness and pain. The room was silent except for the whir of an air conditioner and the occasional miserable groan from one of the other cots. Shafts of light shot in from the corner of the curtain, revealing empty water bottles strewn about the floor, to no effect.

The king of Yue, who filled the river with wine, could not rouse our sorry lot to battle. Yu the Great, the legendary tamer of floods, could not have held back that morning's hangover.

Alcohol is the great leveler.

11 Dust Bowl Ballad

Little Yan cut the engine. The gravel crunched under my feet as I stepped from his Audi SUV. We had entered town along a quiet, dusty street. I was in Xinghuacun, Apricot Blossom Village, Middle of Nowhere, Shanxi Province. This was not a one-horse town; it was a town so small it has to share its horse with the next town over. A rooster crowed in the distance. The wind rustled. The absence of tumbleweed was palpable.

We stood before a showroom. A rainbow of bottles and Chinese floral vases lined the windows. There were several storefronts just like it on the block, though most were still shuttered at this early hour. The door opened and a modest welcoming party emerged, Yan the Elder at its lead.

"You're fatter than I remember," he said with infuriating candor. It was intended, I knew, as a compliment. He was remarking on my good fortune. Still, I wondered whether I should have worn a looser shirt.

"Good to see you, old friend," I said, part of me meaning it. I met Yan Fenguan a couple of months earlier in Chengdu at Tangjiuhui, the National Candy and Alcohol Fair. It is the biggest annual trade event for the Chinese alcohol industry, though this description belies its insanity.

For one thing, there is the official fair for the public, held at a convention center, and then there is the *real* fair, which happens behind closed doors before the other begins. All the wheeling and dealing takes place at Chengdu's major international hotels, where Chinese alcohol-industry personnel requisition every inch of usable space. The major distilleries rent floor space in the lobbies and meeting rooms, and some even hire female models or dancers wearing traditional silk costumes to lure potential clients. Others hire students to put on costumes in the shape of giant alcohol bottles. The smaller fish and hangers-on set up shop in the hotel rooms above, piling mattresses and box springs against the walls to clear a makeshift display space for shopping their wares.

Yan was at Tangjiuhui with a delegation of Xinghuacun distillers, all of them representing their hometown's world-famous spirit: Fenjiu. The name is a play on the region's historical name, Fenzhou, but if Mandarin is not your thing, just take my word for it. Yan was a short man, about sixty years old, with the sun-dried, sandblasted skin of a field hand. He had a slow manner of speaking, drawing out the end of his words until they trailed off in a high-pitched whine. In his mouth my Chinese name, De Li, became "Duh-liii*iii*," though ink doesn't do it justice.

Old Yan ran Gu Quan, one of about fifteen smallish local distilleries. A couple of decades after it opened, it had become a modest but successful operation, producing about five hundred tons of baijiu each year, most of it inexpensive low-end stuff. We exchanged cards in Chengdu, and he invited me to come visit if I ever passed through. I assume he figured I wouldn't bother.

I had arrived at the Taiyuan railway station early that morning. Even the nicest Chinese train stations are surrounded by lurkers and squatters, but Shanxi's provincial capital is far from the nicest. It had the usual dross lurking outside its terminal, but there was also an air of menace. A Chinese friend had told me before I boarded the train, "Taiyuan is a horrible place, awful people. Don't let your bags out of your sight for a minute." I took it for garden-variety regional rivalry. If you ask a Chinese person from anywhere, every neighboring province is filled with thieves and ruffians, much in the same way that the Portuguese call syphilis the "Spanish disease," and the Spanish and the Germans call it the "French disease," and so forth. But upon arriving in Taiyuan, I suspected my friend might have been on to something. I secured an easily defensible position with good visibility and waited for my ride.

Yan the Younger and his girlfriend picked me up in a black Audi SUV. They were wearing identical T-shirts, depicting the head of a cartoon monkey. Matching outfits are one of many public humiliations, like bag holding and period-costume glamor shots, to which young Chinese couples subject each other. They seemed curious, whispering in the front seat, but not enough to engage with me.

Out of my window was the real industrial north I had always read about but never encountered: a hilly, smog-choked hellscape slashed with smokestacks and church steeples. I smelled the pungent aroma of fermenting sorghum well before I could see the town.

The vast state-run Xinghuacun Fenjiu distillery was firing on all cylinders that morning. A row of grain silos at the town's edge bore Chinese characters writing out the name "Fenjiu Group." The facility was enormous, sprawling, and utterly incongruous with the surroundings, like an airport terminal in the middle of a pig farm. We pulled onto the main drag, really the only drag—Fenjiu Avenue—and soon reached the Yan family showroom.

Putting a paternal arm around my shoulder, Yan led me behind the showroom to the distillery, which comprised a few long, squat buildings that resembled an army barracks. In the bottling plant a group of five women sat hunched around a pile of empty plastic bottles with caps and fasteners spread before them. Using only a garden hose, petroleum tanks, and a funnel, they filled the bottles one at a time by hand. Accounting for differences of time and place, it is how I imagine U.S. Prohibition-era bootlegging operations must have appeared. Old Yan muttered a command at the woman manning the hose, who broke from her task and filled a glass. "Go ahead, try it," said Yan.

Pure hellfire. My esophagus convulsed as the rotgut tore its way down my system like broken glass. "How strong is this?" I gasped.

"It's 70 percent alcohol, give or take."

Dear god. I wiped the tears from my eyes with my sleeve. Leading me into another larger building, Yan pointed at a heap of grain raked into lines along the floor. "Sorghum." he said. "This is a unique feature of the baijiu process. It's mixed with water and left to sit all night. The next day it's steamed, spread out to cool, and mixed with qu." He picked up a brick of qu from a pile in one corner and handed it to me. It was a dense beige block about the same size as a large hardcover book. The fibrous exterior was patched with white wisps of mold. "Fenjiu qu," Yan explained. "We use only two ingredients: barley and peas, three-to-two ratio."

This simple gesture betrayed sincere respect and trust. Chinese brewers believe the secret to baijiu's complex flavors is qu—this is their secret sauce and the natural encapsulation of the local ecosystem. It is the one thing that makes every distillery different from its rivals. Recipes are fiercely guarded secrets, and samples are kept far from public scrutiny, lest someone steal some and replicate its germ colonies in a lab.

My friend Johan, who ran the baijiu company in Sichuan, once told me that he had worked with his Chinese partners for more than two years before they trusted him enough to let him inside their qu-production facility. When I had asked other distillers to see their qu, they either pretended not to hear me or responded as if I had asked them to drop their trousers.

In the fermentation room Yan pointed out several rows of holes dug into the ground, about two feet in diameter. All fenjiu is produced in stone jars, whose lips run level with these depressions to maintain an even temperature. During fermentation the holes are sealed with stone slabs, then covered with rice husks for insulation from the bitter North China cold. "Almost all light-aroma baijius are made in the same way," said Yan. "Shanxi is the birthplace of light-aroma baijiu. It's just like Luzhou [in Sichuan] is to strong-aroma baijiu."

As we walked back to the workshop, I asked Yan how he had decided to go into the business. "The baijiu business?" he said. "Originally, I worked in the village as a farmer." Old Yan started Gu Quan in 1989, getting in the industry at just the right time. The late eighties were a boom time for baijiu. Private enterprise had just been reintroduced in China after a three-decade hiatus, and everyone wanted a piece of the action. At the high-water mark there were as many as thirty-six thousand distilleries. State-owned distilleries suddenly found themselves forced to compete, and they responded by introducing a dizzying array of new products. But the rising baijiu tide came at a cost.

Ambition outpaced ability. Corners were cut. Counterfeit and unsafe spirits proliferated throughout the country. The government responded with tighter industry regulations, factory closures, and higher barriers to entry.

"Entering the industry now is an arduous task," Old Yan said. "You have to train for a while with a master. The particulars are difficult to explain." It would be much easier to show me. So we all piled back into the Audi, Old Yan, Little Yan, the girlfriend, a couple of miscellaneous employees, and a third-generation Yan, a devastatingly cute infant in a pink tutu. We headed down Fenjiu Avenue and hung a left onto Alcohol Capital Avenue, site of the Xinghuacun Fenjiu factory.

To one unfamiliar with Chinese central planning, the headquarters of a state-run baijiu outfit is difficult to comprehend, but Xinghuacun provides an illustrative example. In the compound's center are several acres of manicured green space surrounding a towering pagoda that celebrates the Eight Immortals of the Wine Cup. Ascending the pagoda, we passed statues depicting Li Bai and his ilk, and atop the vantage we could see production facilities—fermentation hangers, grain silos, smokestacks, and so on—stretching far into the distance in every direction. Immediately surrounding the park are offices and rows of identical Soviet-style dormitories, where all the factory workers live with their families. Each residential block has a small exercise facility and community bulletin board, which touts the latest company policy, safety advisory, or Party initiative. The distillery is a city unto itself, one far more substantial than the town for which it is named.

An electric tram collected us at the front gate and ambled to the museum at the other side of the compound. Just before we entered, there was a loud crunch behind us, the sound of the driver backing into another tram. He looked over both shoulders for witnesses and, seeing none, drove off without surveying the damage.

Despite being several hours from any major city, the museum attracted a steady stream of visitors, most of them less interested in the exhibits that day than its lone foreign patron. A man with childlike glee on his face walked over and said, "Hello." He squealed with delight when I returned the greeting in kind. "Do you speak Chinese?" he asked in Mandarin.

I told him I did.

"Which country are you from?"

"America."

Having dispensed with the formalities, he put his arm around me, lifted two fingers up in the air, and waited for his wife to snap a picture. With a click of the shutter the floodgates had opened. His wife, also in proximity of a short, pasty, and otherwise unremarkable American, naturally wanted her picture taken too. A woman from another tour group agreed the opportunity was too good to pass up. A line began to form. This is why China drove me to drink.

Near the end of the tour, we entered a room where a man in yellow period outfit ran a traditional wooden pot still. Old Yan escorted me past the velvet rope—visiting dignitary, special treatment—and ordered the man to bring us two shots of the piping hot liquid that trickled from the spout. Undiluted, it was another 140-plus proof jolt to the system. In the next room I was presented with more infused shots: rose essence (90 proof), Chinese cinnamon (90), medicinal wine (90), "Old White" (104), and more undiluted original spirit (130-plus).

For those of you keeping track at home, that brought the total to seven shots for the morning, most of them Herculean in strength. I was working on about three hours of train-pallet sleep and an empty stomach. I felt my fragile grasp on sanity begin to desert me. Everything was going pink elephants and tiger lilies. A dragon gently clawed at my liver.

But I rallied. I could do this, I thought; the worst was past. So it almost goes without saying that our next stop was a baijiu banquet.

With the promise of a free meal and my novel presence, the entourage swelled in number. A fifty-something woman in a knit purple shirt, hair dyed an unnatural shade of orange, initiated most of the drinking. (At least this is what I wrote in my notes. My memory gets a little fuzzy at this point.) Her husband, an affable giant in plaid, wanted to know *everything* about the United States, especially the intricacies of our visa process. He looked disappointed when I explained, as "trailing spouses" often must, that my wife's career did not endow me with any special immigration privileges. Instead I invited him to join me for a toast. His face lightened and, jangling his car keys, said, "Sorry, I'm driving."

"How about you?" I asked Yan Junior, raising my cup.

"No, thanks," he said. "I don't drink."

"You don't drink?" I asked in disbelief and turned to Old Yan. "And you *approve* of this?"

"He can drink when he wants to," he said. "It's no good for his health. He doesn't smoke either." Not that it would make any difference—the room was thick with the perfume of high-tar cigarettes smoked in succession, which, in fairness, was little worse than the air outside.

"It's so bad here that no one wears white," said one of the table elders, a qu craftsperson who had studied European wine making. "If you wear a white shirt to work, it'll be black by the time you get home."

The local cuisine was hearty fare: thick-cut vegetables and generous slabs of meat served with a dollop of viscous black vinegar. One dish tasted suspiciously like corned beef, setting my Semitic heart aflutter, but that might have just been the fog of war. We finished off with a gelatinous lavender mass served with a prickly pepper sauce and more vinegar. "Sorghum noodle," Yan explained. The crisp floral hum of fenjiu blended seamlessly with the tangy cuisine.

A far-gone stranger with his shirt partially untucked poked his head through the doorframe and staggered into our private room. Seeing me, he did an audible double take and stammered, "But you. You're a . . . you're a foreigner!"

"So it would appear."

"Welcome you to Shanxi," he said, toasting my health.

Another man, less drunk, but only marginally, followed him in and filled our glasses before toasting the table. He left the bottle on the table. I didn't need or want another drop, but etiquette demanded I continue.

When we returned from lunch, Yan's wife was sitting on a wooden chair, looking grimly out the storefront window. "So, what do you think of this place?" she asked. I told her Shanxi was a nice place.

"No," she replied. "Shanxi is not a nice place."

"Why do you say that?"

"The air. Just look at the cars." All of them were caked in dust. "It doesn't matter whether you wash them or not. They never stay clean for more than a few hours."

"Aside from the air, though, how is it?"

"Otherwise? It's all right," she said, her scowl still trained on the scene beyond the window.

Before I left, Old Yan led me into the building next door. Inside were paint buckets, exposed sockets, and the typical signs of new construction. It was two-story apartment he was building for the family. When it was finished, it would be spacious, well appointed and modern. Old Yan would live here with his wife and his son, he told me. Maybe one day soon the girlfriend would join them. It is traditional in China for parents to move in with the eldest son after he is married, and Yan the Younger's partner had been jockeying hard for the position all day, playing with the baby—Old Yan's daughter's—and otherwise ingratiating herself with the clan. In one room I noticed what appeared to be a secret passageway hidden behind a bookshelf. It fit in perfectly with the distillery's Prohibition-era mystique, but Old Yan denied that it was an escape hatch or panic room. I hope he was lying.

He spoke little that day, but there was a reason he showed me this. He wanted me to see what he had accomplished: the factory, the town, the new apartment, the Audi, and the mostly happy family. He had come far since his days as a field hand. He was too modest to put it in such blunt terms, but he was proud. Who could fault him for it?

"Business must be good," I said.

"There are lots of baijius out there nowadays," he nodded. "But we get by."

12 Yellow River Ramble

Zhengzhou came into focus as the plane descended. It was an uncharacteristically clear night, and the urban sprawl projected dull orange into the horizon. Staccato neon bursts swelled and disappeared below us. It was the first time I had seen fireworks from above. One of the minor springtime holidays was an excuse to set something on fire.

I boarded a bus to city center, taking a window seat in the last row—a schoolchild preference I never managed to shake—and fired up my laptop. The young man next to me leaned in and began reading the words over my shoulder. I tuned him out until he began slowly sounding out the words in tortured English. I shot him a look that would be difficult to misinterpret, but he returned it with a toothy grin.

"Hello," he said in English. The same old song and dance, drawing inexorably toward a carefully enunciated, "Welcome to China!" He turned to his girlfriend with a titter and began discussing me in great depth for the remainder of the ride, as if I were somewhere far away. It is not so much that I abhor casual conversation with strangers or that I am naive to the fact that an outsider elicits curiosity. What got to me was that

I had had the exact same conversation, word for word, a hundred times over the past several weeks. The only inflections were accent and setting.

Zhengzhou, capital of Henan Province, is one of dozens of anonymous Chinese megacities. Four million inhabitants, but god help the American asked to point it out on a map, let alone pronounce its name. Through the bus window it was indistinguishable from the other second-tier Chinese cities: shopping mall, KTV, garish nightclub, restaurant, hotel, brutalist Soviet plaza filled with waltzing septuagenarians, repeat over and over in a monotonous urban loop. Nothing suggested it had been the seat of a powerful ancient kingdom.

The once-mighty Yellow River lay to the north. Creator and destroyer, it used to flood so often, and with such lethality, that it is known as "China's Sorrow." Now it flows at a barely perceptible gurgle, invoking an altogether different kind of sadness. Perhaps its plight is a blessing in disguise. Over a third of its water is now so polluted it is unsafe for industrial use, let alone for supporting life. In 2006 a chemical spill caused the Yellow River to literally run red for a time.

North China's bleakness was wearing me thin. I had been away from home for a very long time, and the last stretch of my travels had been the loneliest. I had not spoken English since I parted company with Todd in Beijing a week earlier. I had been to Qingdao and Yantai and Harbin and a dozen points in between, fading in and out of good health. I missed Catherine, I missed my dog, and I missed my bed. I needed the kind of rest I could not find on the plank bunks of a ramshackle Chinese train. I needed to go home.

But Henan was a different sort of homecoming. This was where it had all started, where the Chinese had first learned the alcoholic arts. Without it there would be no Neolithic grog, without the grog there would be no huangjiu, and without the huangjiu there would be no baijiu. It was, in a sense, the force that had propelled me across China. And it had one last surprise for me.

From Zhengzhou I headed north across the Yellow River to Xinxiang. Three thousand years earlier it was there that the Zhou armies had rallied against the troops of Di Xin—China's Caligula, of wine-pool and meat-forest fame—and snuffed out the Shang dynasty.

A friend and former colleague of mine, Jessica, was born there, and she suggested I call on her aunt and uncle if I was passing through. I told her I would consider it. Her uncle, she said, was an enthusiastic baijiu drinker who had given her a first taste when she was only twelve years old. I asked for his number at once.

Uncle picked me up at the bus station. He was a tall, round-bellied man of about sixty, hair dyed jet black, who would have cut an imposing figure if not for the rhinestones on his sunglasses. He spoke freely and often with a clear northern accent that rose in pitch and tempo whenever he grew excited.

Auntie, seated in the back, was the spitting image of her niece. She was a sprightly woman with a broad face, a winning smile, and an accent almost beyond my comprehension. She handled the logistics, making sure everyone was well fed and hydrated, no mean feat considering what they had planned for me. She and Uncle argued in rapid-fire Mandarin as we drove, but the affection they shared for each other was unmistakable. Theirs were the practiced if halfhearted disagreements of the happily married.

My attention drifted in and out while they quibbled over directions, Ming history, food, and other pressing matters, only to be jolted back into reality by a pointed and unexpected comment from Auntie. "Could you repeat that one more time?" I asked her, a bead of sweat forming on my upper lip. If I concentrated and had a bit of luck, I could pick her meaning from the syllables.

My linguistic shortcomings had already made a hash of things. That morning I had accidentally committed myself to lunch with Jessica's entire extended family. While I had been unaware, blissfully contemplating Jiahu wine vessels at the Henan Provincial Museum, her grandparents were waiting for me impatiently at a restaurant an hour away. Thankfully, they decided not to wait. But Chinese hospitality is a juggernaut that cannot be stopped once set in motion.

"Do you like eating rice or noodles?" Uncle asked me as we pulled away from the bus station.

"I like them both," I said.

He asked again, as if I had not understood. "Well, which do you like: rice or noodles?" He was venturing into the realm of regional loyalty. Northerners eat noodles. Southerners eat rice. Pick a side, damn it.

"Rice," I said, tempting fate.

They drove me to an empty restaurant, and Auntie ordered enough food to feed a small elephant. For all three of us? No, she told me, she and Uncle had already eaten. Uncle set two bottles of his favorite baijiu on the table, Ruyang Du Kang, named for Du Kang, the legendary inventor of sorghum wine from nearby Ruyang. For all three of us? Again, no. They would not be drinking.

"I have to drive," said Uncle. "I'll have a glass or two, but that's it."

Gauntlet thrown, I began to make my way through a greasy bowl of pork belly, consuming several teacups of baijiu while they felt me out. Where was I from? Who was I? Why I was interested in baijiu? What was my *jiuliang*—alcohol tolerance? I gave what to my mind was an impressive gustatory performance, but Auntie was unimpressed. "Your *fanliang* (food tolerance) is awful," she said. It would not be the last time she made this observation.

Learning of my fondness for Chinese history, Uncle suggested we drive to the tomb of Bi Gan, King Di Xin's unfortunate adviser and uncle, whose compassion had left him literally heartless. Later dynasties rehabilitated Bi Gan's reputation, praising him as a model of self-sacrifice and civic virtue. They had even given Bi Gan and his descendants the posthumous honorific name Lin. It is said that all Chinese with this surname descend from Bi Gan, and each year Lins from around the world congregate at his tomb to pay homage.

As we entered the hallowed grounds, our guide pointed to the statue of Commissioner Lin Zexu, another statesman of the Lin clan who learned a hard truth about prohibitionist policy. In 1839 Commissioner Lin, charged by the emperor with cleaning up the opium trade, set fire to foreign drug caches in the Guangzhou harbor. The British responded with overwhelming naval force and crushed the Manchu armies in what became known as the First Opium War. The emperor exiled Lin to Xinjiang, in China's remote northwest. Later generations celebrated him as a selfless patriot who put country first.

"Do you know who he was?" asked Uncle.

"A great friend of the foreigner," I said. "We would have gotten along well."

It elicited a grin, though he withheld comment.

In the inner sanctum of Bi Gan's tomb, just before the tall ridge of the burial mound, stood a weathered stone slab. Four Chinese characters were etched into it, which translated roughly as "Here lies Bi Gan." The lines were rough-hewn, carved with a sword. Some of the detail had chipped off with age. At over 2,500 years old, it is among the oldest writing in China, and the only surviving text written by the hand of Confucius.

Just those four simple characters on the side of the rock remain, the only physical trace of the most influential thinker China ever produced. What hope do the rest of us have? But the Sage's legacy manifests in other ways, in attitudes and rituals, in the never-ending quest for self-betterment and social advancement.

"Let me ask you something," Uncle said later, back in the car. "In America, how do you determine status? Is it the price of your house? How much money you make? What kind of car you drive?"

What a question. I told him it depended, that everyone assigns value differently.

"No, no, no. I don't think you understand," he said. "Let me give you an example: you've got a boss and an employee, and they both buy cars. Clearly the boss *must* buy a more expensive car, right?"

"Not necessarily."

The sun was already setting, and Uncle removed the bejeweled spectacles. He looked at me with an expression that said, Come on, we're all reasonable adults here. Let's be straight with one another. "But how could a boss allow an employee to appear richer than he?"

"I don't know. Maybe he doesn't like flashy cars. Perhaps he has children and would rather save the money for their education or spend it on something else like travel."

Again he regarded me with suspicion. "But if you don't use money or possessions as the metric, how does anyone tell who the most important person is?"

I told him that some people in my country—maybe even most people— peg social status to wealth. Others value character or public service. Being a teacher or working for the common good are well respected, if not always well remunerated. Some people just don't care what others think about them.

"That's ridiculous," he said, shaking his head. "How does anyone in America know what to do with themselves?"

How indeed? If I knew the answer to that I might never have left.

We pulled onto a gravel road in a nearby village and got out in front of a single-story restaurant. In a private room in the back, my hosts' friends awaited us. Among them were a local Party official and her son. A handful of anonymous men, presumably drivers, sat at the far side of the table. Our guide from the tomb was there, along with his wife and teenage son, and they prodded him to practice his English with me. He told me he liked American rock music, especially Green Day and Guns n' Roses.

"I like them too," his mother said, blushing.

When asked, the boy told me he was too busy for girlfriends, and I assured him a man with his tastes would have more luck at university.

The table, like most found in private Chinese dining rooms, was round, with a lazy Susan at its center to facilitate family-style dining. One might suspect that this arrangement would engender an egalitarian seating arrangement, in which all positions are equal. This is not the case. Confucian values apply as much to food as to drink, requiring that all know their place in the social hierarchy. The seat farthest from the door—with the best line of sight to the comings and goings—is most coveted. The seats surrounding it are of decreasing value down the line, until those of limited significance, usually children or servants, sit with their backs to the door.

After making the necessary show of protest, I took the wholly undeserved seat of honor. To my left sat the Party official and to my right Uncle, himself a lower-ranking official. Precedence and order was thereby established. Across from me the guide's wife flipped through the menu. She asked me what I wanted to eat, and, as politeness dictated, I placed myself at her mercy.

"Can you eat spicy food?" she said.

"I can eat anything," I said. This was my first of several mistakes. A heaping pile of crispy caterpillars soon landed on the table. I know, I know, deep-fried food all tastes the same. But still. Caterpillars? With the arrival of food came baijiu. The cap was popped and the pouring began.

When serving baijiu, you start with the ranking member of the table as determined by age or status, ending with your own glass. With tea the glass must be filled halfway, but with alcohol you fill near to overflowing; to pour less would be a miserly affront to your guests. The drink recipient gives face to the pourer by tapping lightly on the table while the glass is filled.

This tradition supposedly dates back to the eighteenth century, during the reign of Emperor Qianlong, who liked to travel the country disguised as a commoner. While incognito he sometimes poured tea for a member of his entourage—a gross violation of rank—and the recipient, knowing his master's true identity, would tap his fingers against the table in thanks. The discreet gesture symbolized a kowtow, the act by which undeserving subjects prostrate and bang their head against the ground before the august presence. Today the finger taps are used to thank anyone filling your glass.

Uncle rose to make the requisite opening toast. Everyone stood with a raised glass, while Uncle thanked us for attending and heartily invited us to drink. After the group toast, individual toasting began. When clinking glasses, it is important to attempt to undercut the other drinker's glass, as the person whose glass is more elevated is accorded more face. This often results in an exaggerated gesture of humility that ends with both drinkers' glasses banging against the table. No matter how drunk one gets, hierarchy must be maintained.

Looking down at my cup, I grew concerned. In the south I was accustomed to having my baijiu poured into a diminutive glass, roughly a third the size of a standard shot glass. This thimble-sized glass is well suited to the down-the-hatch ganbei toasting, where sipping is frowned on. It gets sloppy fast, but at least it is reciprocal: if you make someone else drink, you also have to drink with them. They do things differently in the north, using teacups instead of shot glasses, and affecting a blasé attitude toward reciprocity.

The official to my left was a loud, imposing presence with a mop of curly black hair. She came with a tall son of gentle manner who drank only beer. He had clearly not inherited this gentleness from his mother, who delighted in steamrolling me.

She began by filling my teacup and inviting me to drink. She did not fill her own glass or make a motion toward her cup. Confused but not wishing to show disrespect, I met her gaze, thanked her, and downed the glass. "You don't need to drink the whole glass," Uncle chimed in one side, playing the part of better angel. "A sip will do."

"No, I don't mind," I said, not wishing to show weakness or offend her.

Curly proceeded to fill my glass back up to the brim and instructed me to drink. Again, no baijiu for her. Curious. I repeated the performance and downed the glass.

"You really don't need to drink the whole glass," Uncle said.

"No, no, it's fine. I like baijiu." I doubted the words, even as I was saying them. The ordeal was not yet over. Curly filled both our glasses and raised one, saying, "Ganbei!" What insanity was this?

Another teacup of baijiu might not have pushed me over the edge, but I hardly felt like risking the ignominious spectacle of pushing myself from my chair—farthest from the door, no less—and sprinting to the bathroom. "Thanks, I'm going to do a *slow* ganbei," I explained, taking a sip.

"Slow ganbei," Uncle repeated, chuckling.

Curly emptied hers in one go and slammed the glass on the table, maintaining eye contact throughout. She was judging me. I did not care.

"What the hell just happened there, Uncle?" I asked, turning to him.

"Normally when you clink glasses, everyone ganbeis. 'If feelings run deep, you drink deeply,'" he said, a common drinking refrain deployed to guilt friends into drinking more than they should. It sounds better in Mandarin. "Henan drinking culture is unique in that instead of downing glasses you 'present,' or *duan*, the glass to show respect. When people drink in China, they all clink glasses. You drink, I drink. In Henan if someone presents alcohol, he tells the other person to drink but doesn't himself drink."

"I find this lack of shared risk unsettling," I told him. "The host can just get her guest completely tanked and walk away scot free. It's not fair."

"No, it isn't very fair," Uncle said, amused. "But it is well intentioned. In the past we Henanese were poor folk, but we still wanted to be good hosts. When we received guests, we wanted them to drink first, even if there wasn't enough left over for us."

It was around this point that I learned another valuable lesson in keeping my mouth shut. The topic of conversation shifted to Chinese alcohol and, inevitably, my alcohol tolerance. "Just the other day I drank an entire bottle with an erguotou distiller in Beijing," I boasted. This was my second mistake. It is always wiser to swallow your pride and undersell your drinking prowess. To do otherwise is to invite grossly disproportionate retaliation, and I walked right into a minefield with a smile on my face.

A second bottle appeared on the table. "I don't know, do you think we really need a second bottle?" asked the guide, cracking the bottle and pouring before anyone could answer.

"The culture of the Central Chinese Plain is extremely layered, dating way back to the time of the ancient dynasties," he said while we drank. "After many years of war and bloodshed, from rise to fall, from fall to rise, it has accumulated substance. It's said that four words perfectly describe the people of the Central Chinese Plain: cultured, honest, kindhearted, and hospitable. That's what we are." Everyone agreed and we shared in a toast.

As we were leaving, Curly asked me, offhand, if I would like to see her dog. "Sure, why not? I love dogs." Another misstep, though a less obvious one. You see, it was not one dog she wanted me to see but many, and not the kind that jump on your lap and lick your face. Her house's two-story courtyard was lined with cages filled with bloodthirsty Tibetan mastiffs, barking holy hell at anything that moved. This was not how I had hoped to win my Darwin Award.

Curly led me upstairs to the cage of a couple of puppies, which were cuter if not less ferocious. Their mother paced in the adjacent cage, snarling angrily at us behind a dividing wall that stood at least five feet high. My jaw dropped and my legs went wobbly as I watched her easily leap into her pups' cage and lunge at us, fangs bared.

I jumped back and began plotting a survival strategy: Where's the nearest exit? Who looks the slowest? Which arm could I more easily do without?

Inside the house it was much what you would expect from someone who has devoted considerable energy to raising fluffy killing machines. Her husband, a bland-looking fellow of about sixty, was the local police chief. The walls were adorned with life-size, heroic man-of-the-people parade photographs with him at the center. They were the kind of adoring crowd scenes one normally associates with the Beatles at their highest ebb or with Chairman Mao. And here the man stood before me in his undershorts, robe wide open and an ashy cigarette dangling from his lips.

The reason for our continued presence had become obscure. Between the attack dogs and the fascistic imagery, it was all a bit much a couple of bottles deep.

I went with Uncle and Auntie back into the night. We swerved our way through weekend traffic, tearing past motorcycles and rickshaws on unlit country paths. The lines on the road danced and swirled, with only the stars to guide us home.

I had consumed every last drop of water in the hotel room by the time Auntie called, twenty minutes early, to say she was in the lobby. After I scraped my carcass from the bed, Auntie and Uncle ran me through a battery of local tourist attractions. Uncle offered more baijiu, though only as a halfhearted courtesy. Form dictated at least making the gesture, but he didn't insist when I declined.

We picked up Grandpa and Grandma. We ate, we took pictures, we went to another museum, we went to a tomb, and then we ate some more. Auntie continued to complain that my appetite would shame my family for several generations, offering me more nourishment at every turn. Grandpa, a slight man with a mat of white hair, added, "I'm an old man, but I can eat more than you can." We discussed what a model worker I thought their niece/grandchild was, and together we explored every permutation of the differences between our two countries. We played mahjong, and, though I can't prove it, I suspect they let me win.

Auntie and Uncle stayed with me until midnight, when my train was scheduled to depart. They even went so far as to walk me to the platform, gently reminding me to keep an eye on my luggage and mind my health. They were lovely, generous people, and it was one of those partially hungover days that felt like a fuzzy memory even as it unfolded. But there was a certain moment that sticks with me.

We were standing high atop a Ming dynasty burial mound, more of a hill really. To one side, faintly visible through the dense air, were nuclear cooling towers. To the other a solitary mountain peak, its visible face a sheer cliff with a patch of green on top.

"These mountains used to stretch for miles in both directions. They were much taller than they are today," said Uncle, a touch of sadness entering his voice. "This is all that's left. The rest has been turned into concrete." It was easy to see the rugged beauty the range must have imparted on the stark landscape. And what was it now? An apartment complex? A highway overpass? It was astonishing to contemplate a country that was literally moving mountains to feed its growth engines.

Bleak as the memory may seem in retrospect, a photograph snapped that afternoon tells a different story. There we are, the three of us standing atop the mound. I stand at the center, my arms wrapped around Auntie and Uncle, a genuine smile on all of our faces.

Before I boarded the train they asked me to call them the next time I was in Henan. I promised them that I would. Two strangers took me in, showed me their home, and gave me their wine. Just as has been done for thousands of years.

That was my lasting impression of the Central Plain, the place where it all started. Rivers run dry. Mountains turned to dust. But the people and the traditions endure.

PART 4

Warning Labels

When you drink with good friends, a thousand glasses are too few.
—*Common Chinese refrain*

13 Burning Questions

SHOT OF BAIJIU
Traditional Recipe

Fill your neighbors' glass to the brim with **baijiu** and allow them to return the favor. Serve neat at room temperature in a small cup, preferably alongside food. Consume in one swig following a well-considered toast. Repeat ad nauseam.

Nurse Jiang tightened the tourniquet and probed for a vein. "So, you're going to drink a lot of baijiu?" she said, finding a vein and sticking it with the needle.

"Baijiu, huangjiu, mijiu, a little bit of everything," I said. The blood crawled the length of the tube and into the first vial.

"Wow, you must know a lot about Chinese alcohol," she said. Less than she imagined. She capped one vial and replaced it with a fresh one.

At the outset I had decided to run tests. If in my foray into Chinese alcohol I were to turn myself into the proverbial canary in the coal mine, it seemed advisable to apply a modicum of scientific rigor. So I subjected myself to a battery of tests designed to measure liver functionality before I set off for Maotai. A second round would be conducted upon my return to Chengdu a couple of months later to assess the damage.

I did this less to silence skeptics than for my own piece of mind. A great many people regard baijiu—and Chinese food products generally—with suspicion. Some of their concerns are valid, others less so. When I told my friends and family I planned to make a study of baijiu, the first thing they said, after they stopped laughing and wiped the tears from their eyes, was some version of the phrase, "You're going kill yourself." They predicted liver failure and blindness. One person even suggested my wife take out a life-insurance policy in my name. I tried to push their taunts to the back of my mind, but it was impossible to entirely shut them out.

"Do you think drinking baijiu can kill a person?" I finally asked Nurse Jiang, who paused to consider my question.

"They say that drinking a little bit of alcohol each day is good for you," she replied, evading the question. She reached for another empty vial, and I began to wonder whether I would have any blood left at the end of this.

"How about a lot of alcohol every day?"

"That's probably not good for you."

"But I'll recover?"

"Probably," she said, mulling over her next words. "You might want to take it easy for a while once you return." She nodded with finality, emphasizing her point with the application of a cotton swab and a Snoopy bandage.

Not the bulletproof assurance I had sought. Yet if I ruined my liver, I would have the minor consolation of having done so in the name of science, or something near to it.

Up to this point in the story, I have presented an admittedly blushing account of China, its alcohol, and the many ways in which the two have shaped each other over the millennia. In doing so I have endeavored to focus on the positives, the aspects that made me fall in love with Chinese drink, absent consideration of the costs. In truth I have personal and professional incentives for keeping matters light and breezy. And though I sincerely believe Chinese alcohol deserves greater consideration from the outside world, I am not here to bullshit the reader.

As important as alcohol has been to Chinese society, it carries with it certain risks, and this narrative would be incomplete without addressing them. Over the next several chapters, I want to examine a couple of basic questions: is drinking baijiu inherently harmful to one's health, and what additional dangers stem from commercial malpractice and oppressive social custom? I also want to explore the enormous political pressure that baijiu exerts in contemporary China, how runaway economic growth, a taste for luxury liquor, and corruption combined to create one of modern China's greatest sociopolitical crises, and why its government has felt the need to respond to it with overwhelming force. In short, I want to consider the many ways in which baijiu reflects the aspirations and fears of China in the twenty-first century.

But let me begin with a basic question: will baijiu kill you?

The ancients praised the health benefits of libation. In combination with macerated herbs and spices, there was little alcohol could not treat, even hangovers. But classic Chinese doctors laid down their precepts and prescriptions in the age of huangjiu, and the character of baijiu, a distilled spirit, is much different.

Contemporary writing on the personal health implications of habitual baijiu consumption is virtually nonexistent, whereas the conclusions of earlier physicians are delightfully alarmist. My personal favorite is fourteenth-century imperial court physician Hu Sihui, who writes, "If you drink too much, the seven openings [eyes, ears, nose, and mouth] all run blood, and death ensues; and so also does blood flow from the anus and urethra, and death follows." Should you fail to die immediately, he continues, the pain will be worse than anything a seasoned torturer could dream up, a condition known as "flowing fire."

Dr. Hu believed that though a boozer's plight is "all one's own doing," the drinker poses an even greater threat to society. Baijiu production requires a considerable expenditure of grain, leaving ordinary people to wallow in hunger. Drinking in this context is an act bordering on treason: "Hence no pity can be extended to such."

Hu reluctantly concedes that liquor has some medicinal benefit, though "its evils are unspeakably great," adding, "People with blood diseases, if they do not give up spirits, medicine has no effect upon them; and, if the bones be fractured and the flesh contused, and the man drink spirits, he is lost. If pregnant women drink spirits, their progeny break out with small-pox, and the children are few. If a man has sons and grandsons and still drinks, his posterity will rapidly disappear. If three generations drink, posterity becomes defunct."

His warning culminates with the story of Zhou Wei, magistrate of Suzhou and a drunk of the most lamentable sort who neglected his official duties and drank himself to death. When mourners came to offer libation to his corpse, as is customary at Chinese wakes, Zhou's coffin burst into flames, leaving behind not a trace of the bumbling magistrate. "Was this not a reproof from heaven for his drinking?" asks Hu. "And was this not a necessary punishment?"

Hu was typical of Confucian killjoys, molding the story to fit his ethic. The same cannot be said of the normally reliable Lazarist missionary Évariste Huc, who said that baijiu was "absolutely like liquid fire." And he meant this literally.

During Abbé Huc's nineteenth-century journey through the cities and villages of China, he collected tales of Chinese tipplers who died fiery deaths due to their love of baijiu. These men "absorbed such a quantity of alcohol as to have become fairly saturated with it, and to have, in a manner, exhaled it at every pore." At the tiniest accidental spark, something as innocent as lighting one's pipe, the "wretched creatures" burst into a fiery inferno. Though Huc never personally witnessed this macabre spectacle, he writes in *The Chinese Empire*, "many persons, on whom we can place the most perfect reliance," said it was "far from uncommon."

Such tales of alcohol-related spontaneous human combustion were a uniquely nineteenth-century phenomenon. You need look no further than Charles Dickens's *Bleak House*, in which the perpetually besotted Mr. Krook dies a death "inborn, inbred, engendered in the corrupted humours of the vicious body itself, and that only—Spontaneous Combustion." Both Nikolai Gogol and Jules Verne crafted characters whose desultory ways sublimated in fire, and one of Herman Melville's came awfully close to meeting the same fate. It was a pressing concern of the era and thus one that Huc may have been predisposed to accept.

The popular theory at the time was that a drunkard's body could become so suffused with alcohol that it became an accelerant. A slight frisson at the cellular level and—poof!—no more Mr. Krook. To one who has experienced the residual effects of a good baijiu sousing, there is much to recommend the theory. In the hours following baijiu intoxication, its taste lingers on the palate and resurfaces in full force in every subsequent belch. When you wake the following morning, hungover or not, you can smell baijiu's funk in the sweat leaking from your pores. Of more unseemly morning rituals, the less said the better.

And why is this? For the answer we turn to the keen scientific mind of Dr. John Dudgeon, early twentieth-century instructor at Peking's Imperial College. In *The Beverages of the Chinese,* Dudgeon identified fusel oil—a natural byproduct of the fermentation process—as the principal cause of baijiu's mischief, saying, "It exhales a powerful and peculiarly suffocating odour, and leaves a burning taste." Fusel oil, he continues, can cause "flushing of the face, mounting into [drinkers'] heads, burning sensation in the stomach which it disorders, causing vertigo and next day a feeling like one threatened with immediate illness . . . although they are not really drunk." Fusel oil muddles the nervous system, intoxicating tipplers before the ethanol (the *good* alcohol) has had a chance to get them properly drunk, and lingers long in the system thereafter.

Fusel, a term derived from the German word for "hooch," is not actually oil at all but a combination of deleterious substances. Amyl alcohol, the chief offender, is used in the manufacture of varnish, rubber, petroleum, and even explosives, which helps explain some of baijiu's uniquely industrial bouquet. Direct exposure to amyl alcohol can produce effects ranging from mild skin irritation to nausea, headaches, and vomiting. Since the human body takes longer to expel fusels from the system than ethanol, it was long believed that fusel oil prolonged hangovers and increased their severity.

In a remarkable 2006 experiment, a group of Japanese scientists set out to test the effects of fusel oils by feeding them to mice alongside whiskey. Contrary to prevailing wisdom, results suggested that fusel oils actually *reduced* the severity of hangovers. More surprising still, they suggested that mice drink whiskey.

Fusel oils may have strong odors and contain trace amounts of unsavory compounds, but they should not cause the drinker any lasting discomfort.

Still, there is a simpler reason not to avoid baijiu on account of these substances: their presence is not unique to baijiu. Fusels are found in low concentrations in many popular drinks, such as beer, cider, and whiskey. In small amounts fusel oils and related chemical compounds are harmless and even desirable in beverages as flavoring agents.

In Dudgeon's time, baijiu may indeed have been more toxic than it is today. Recall that contemporaneous Beijing distillers were, after all, adding arsenic and pigeon dung to their erguotou. Accounting for the vast improvements in modern production techniques, I have concluded that baijiu is as safe to drink as any other spirituous beverage one might imbibe.

At a minimum there is no evidence suggesting it can make you suddenly burst into flames. This is no guarantee that you might not accidentally light yourself on fire while blind drunk, what most historians agree is the likeliest cause of the Victorian combustion epidemic. But who could blame baijiu for that? Not I.

I returned from my boozy jaunt around China exhausted, mind and body. Most of the first few days back in Chengdu, I spent shaking off the dust and catching up on sleep. But by the end of the week, I was seated once more on the health clinic's plush table, needle in arm.

"So you drank a lot of Chinese alcohol?" asked Nurse Jiang.

"A lot," I agreed.

"And you enjoy it?" she said, eyebrow cocked.

Several more vials of blood and half a week later, I got a call from the chief U.S. nurse. "I have your lab results," she said. "But before getting into them, could I ask just how much baijiu you consumed since your last visit?"

My accounting had been inexact, but my tally put the number at about 160 shots over a couple of months. I had consumed just as much, if not more, huangjiu and mijiu. I heard a barely audible gasp on the other line. "One hundred and sixty shots?" she repeated. "Of baijiu?"

"Give or take."

"I see," she said, regaining her clinical composure. "We tested your levels of protein, uric acid, potassium, and globulin, all of which are at healthier levels than when we tested you the first time."

"Come again?"

"The tests we ran suggest that by every metric your liver is functioning as well or better than before you left."

"You mean the drinking actually improved my health?"

The nurse paused a moment before answering, "There's no *statistically significant* change in your lab results. But, yes, your results were either the same or better than the first time we checked your blood."

I know, I know: "what doesn't kill you" and all that. But still, this was a shock.

"All the same," she concluded, "I would advise you to reduce your current rate of consumption." Sound medical advice.

I add here as a parenthetical afterword the story of the only time alcohol made me violently ill in the course of my research. It was the day of the 2012 summer solstice. Johan, the aforementioned Swedish baijiu impresario, invited me to attend the Scandinavian community's annual Midsommer festivities at a small Swedish café, where much of the earliest draft of this book was written. (The existence of both a sizable Swedish community and a Swedish café in Chengdu is no doubt as much a surprise to the reader as it was to the author.)

Catherine is a quarter Swedish on her mother's side, which lends us certain privileges in Scandinavian company. Having met her Swedish family and befriended a number of Swedes, I will say this: one could not hope to know a friendlier, more considerate group of people, and in their presence I have never felt more Jewish. To enter their company is to become the furriest, schlubbiest animal in the elven forest. At least both our peoples understand the value of smoked fish.

The point is that Dani and Soojin—the café's owners and fellow travelers on the baijiu road—had prepared a herring-laden feast where the schnapps flowed freely. Swedish schnapps are traditional grain alcohols, generally vodkas, flavored with various herbs, fruits, and spices. They are to be consumed before, after, and during meals, and with the kind of abandon one might expect of the descendants of Vikings. Dani had made two kinds of schnapps, one infused with honey and dill, the other a more potent blend of cardamom, anise, and other things that generally tasted of Christmas.

By the time Johan arrived with his wife, Johanna—that is really her name—I was already deep in my cups. All the same I volunteered to drink his shots when a drinking game broke out nearby. By the time the meal had finished, I was having a merry time learning Swedish drinking songs and feeling a full foot taller than at the meal's start.

The rest of the story I must relate secondhand because, quite frankly, I do not remember it. It seems at some point my speech became incomprehensible, and I was shoved into a taxi by my wife. Once home I grew violently ill and nonresponsive. At some point I became covered in a dark red rash from head to toe, though mostly in the extremities: hands, feet, face, and areas best not discussed in polite company. Needless to say, this is not how I normally react to drink.

In a panic Catherine called U.S. Poison Control. "Help! My husband is having a horrible reaction to Swedish schnapps," she said, tears streaming down her face. (This is how I prefer to imagine the scene.)

"Ma'am, your husband is drunk," they told her.

"No, I've seen him drunk. He's nonresponsive and turning red," she pleaded.

"He's drunk," said they.

It turns out she had been in the right, but we would only learn that a couple of days later when the rash had still not subsided. A doctor diagnosed it as an allergic reaction to something in the schnapps.

I learned later that I had not caught the worst of that night's dubious tonic. Schnapps-induced tragedy had claimed two other victims, both executives of the local branch of a well-known Swedish company, which for the sake of professionalism (and libel laws) I shall not name. The top boss had gotten fired for getting frisky with one of his subordinates after leaving the café. His deputy had gone face-first down a flight of stairs and had to be rushed back to Sweden for emergency dentistry. Considering their fates, I am inclined to think I got off lightly.

As previously mentioned I was raised in the Jewish tradition, and our holidays start and end at sunset. In this spirit it was important that my suffering carried over into the next day. By some unholy coincidence I had arranged a meeting with the leadership of a major Chengdu distillery, Shui Jing Fang, at nine o'clock the following morning. Never mind that I had a hangover that could derail a freight train. I did not know in which country, let alone which hemisphere, I had awoken.

Catherine, saint that she is, saw to it that I was properly dressed and presentable, going so far as to cover my facial rash with a healthy swath of foundation. She explained the previous night's excitement, Poison Control, journey to the Ivory Kingdom, and all. I had barely begun my apologies when she pushed me out the door and onto the road to the distillery, just three blocks from my apartment. But her efforts could go only so far in masking my condition.

"Had a rough one with the boys last night, did you?" asked Kenneth Macpherson, the then general manager of Shui Jing Fang, upon my arrival. I tried to explain, but he did not believe me. Nor should he have, if I may be brutally honest about spirits writers. Then it was off to a tour of the distillery, followed by an elaborate baijiu banquet. It was the only time, theretofore or since, that I have ever declined even a single swig of baijiu with a producer. I just couldn't do it, not even for the sake of politeness.

There is a moral to this meander. Before we may accuse the Chinese of poisoning themselves, we must first look in the mirror. Whether its Swedish schnapps or Appalachian moonshine, grappa, or slivovitz, the Western canon is hardly blameless. Dodgy alcohol is dodgy alcohol. A poorly made spirit is as debilitating in France as it is in Fuzhou.

But in discussing baijiu there is a borderline-pathological compulsion in some circles to doubt Chinese distillers, to suggest that they are somehow less skilled, or at least less careful, than their Western counterparts. When drinking baijiu, they say, you take your life into your own hands. Thus I come to skeptics bearing a grim message: believe these lies at your own peril. The danger is indeed real, but you approach the problem from the wrong angle.

The problem with Chinese alcohol is simple, and it all boils down to quality and quantity.

14 Quality Control

Drinking baijiu is safe. More precisely, it is no less safe than drinking any other variety of liquor. I wish that the discussion ended there. I wish I could leave readers with an unqualified recommendation to go out and drink China dry. But China is a large country with continually shifting terrain, and things are rarely as simple as they initially seem.

The problem is that while drinking baijiu may be safe, one cannot safely say that what she is drinking *is* baijiu. This may sound cynical, and of course it is. Living long enough in China will make a cynic out of anyone.

In some parts of the world one worries about war and famine, in others crime and disease. In China one worries about the basic stuff of living: the food you eat, the water you drink, and the air you breathe. Pollution is so rampant and food safety scandals happen with such alarming regularity that neither merits serious debate. I state this as fact, like the sky being blue in most countries not named China.

As a matter of growing domestic and international concern, the Chinese government treats this situation like the existential threat that it is. It invests heavily in renewable energy—hydroelectric, wind, and solar—and in 2014 passed sweeping environmental-protection reforms. When industry watchdogs find toxins in foodstuff, as was the case when melamine-laced milk poisoned hundreds of thousands in 2008, heads roll. Usually only a token offender is disciplined as an example to other miscreants, but as an American I still find it refreshing to see white-collar crimes punished.

The state is also quick to remind its critics that it is a country in transition. Much as Europe and the United States had Industrial Revolutions—coal-darkened skies, dirty rivers, and the rest—China is simply following suit. Hiccups are to be expected. While this notion contains a kernel of truth, and more than a little obfuscation, historical context is small comfort for those living through the transition. When people's health, or the health of their families, is at risk abstract notions of progress and modernity are scant consolation.

If there is one area in which the Chinese people have repeatedly demonstrated a willingness to mobilize against entrenched interests, it is public health. People want their government to respond to threats quickly and decisively and have pounced on perceived breaches of public trust. None are immune from their collective wrath, and 2012 demonstrated that one of the country's seemingly invincible industries could be brought to its knees. For the first time in its brief existence, the baijiu industry showed vulnerability.

Business had never been better. The level of commercial alcohol production grew six times from 1952 until 1978 and another nine times by 1997. By 2007 the baijiu industry was estimated to be valued at twenty billion dollars and growing. Over the next five years baijiu experienced an annual average expansion of around 30 percent, according to China's National Bureau of Statistics, and sales reached about sixty billion dollars in 2011. Over that same half decade annual profits grew 50 percent per year.

More than just successful, baijiu had become monolithic. In every Chinese city Chinese distilleries plastered advertisements on billboards and the sides of buses and buildings. Ads for Shui Jing Fang appeared alongside those for Rolex and Hermès. One could not turn on the TV or scan the radio without being pitched Luzhou Laojiao's flagship 1573—*yi wu qi san*—in sultry baritone. In 2012 bottles of top-shelf baijiu regularly sold for hundreds, if not thousands, of dollars. According to the China-based research firm Hurun, Kweichow Moutai and Wuliangye were then among the world's ten most valuable brands, with a combined brand value estimated at $19 billion.

It had all happened in the blink of an eye. Until the eighties the baijiu industry operated more like a public utility than a business. Under Mao all the distilleries were state-owned and usually served a specific province or municipality. Each made a single beverage or two that was rationed off to the local citizenry, but it rarely operated outside of its own territory. The distilleries produced drinks of higher quality than their preindustrial ancestors, but their managers lacked imagination. There was no concern for product differentiation, even less for consumer preference.

All that changed with the rise of Chairman Deng Xiaoping in 1978 and the reintroduction of market economics soon thereafter. During the eighties and nineties China invested heavily in agriculture and the food-service industry, and many of the first private businesses were restaurants. In a country where it is commonly said, "It isn't a feast without alcohol," baijiu's concurrent rise was inevitable. Entrepreneurs were quick to enter the alcohol industry, and by the early nineties China is believed to have had an astonishing thirty-six thousand distilleries.

Almost overnight China had a diverse and competitive national spirits industry. What had previously been exclusively regional products could now be sold anywhere in the country. The geographic and cultural boundaries that for centuries separated different styles of baijiu began to blur. Entirely new categories of Chinese spirits began to appear, as did premium baijius aimed at the emerging luxury market. The older state distilleries had a significant advantage in terms of resources and pedigree and jockeyed for market position with advertising and diversified product lines. Upstart private distilleries rushed to capitalize on the low- and mid-range sectors.

For consumers the rapid transformation was a blessing and a curse. On the one hand they could, for the first time, enjoy the full diversity of Chinese spirits. The increased competition forced established brands to improve their products' flavor and quality. However, as was true of the country's larger economic transformation, market growth outpaced the government's ability to regulate the industry. Many opportunistic new producers lacked the skill or inclination to distill their baijiu properly.

Substandard distillation can be lethal. If a distiller does not know what he is doing, he can produce spirits with high concentrations of dangerous substances like methanol, a chemical that strongly resembles ethanol—the alcohol we drink—in smell, taste, and appearance. This is fearsome not only because methanol is highly toxic but because its effects are slow to appear. Just a little over a sixth of an ounce of a 40 percent methanol product can cause alcohol poisoning, about a third of an ounce can cause blindness, and an ounce can kill. It is because of rampant methanol poisoning during the United States' ill-fated Prohibition that moonshine is associated with blindness.

In 1987 thirty-three people in Guangxi Province died and dozens more suffered illness when two unscrupulous entrepreneurs mixed methanol and water and sold it as baijiu. The local authorities captured and convicted the men responsible, but the problem was more widespread. "This fake baijiu killed many people," Zhang Zhengjun, deputy director of the Beijing Yongfeng Erguotou distillery told me, shortly before asking me to share an entire bottle with him over lunch. "So the government moved in and began strictly controlling baijiu production. If a distillery is unqualified to produce baijiu today, the government will not issue them a license."

Methanol poisoning happens with less frequency today, but reports of fake baijiu sending unsuspecting drinkers to the hospital still appear from time to time. I have met a few victims of fake baijiu, all of whom thankfully survived without lasting injury. But drinking dodgy alcohol in China is still risky. In 2009 at least four villagers in Hubei Province died from drinking unbottled bulk alcohol containing high levels of methanol.

The risk of drinking is limited not just to liquor. In 2005 there was minor outrage when the *Global Times* published a report by Du Lujun, beer secretary of the China Alcoholic Drinks Association (CADA), claiming that 95 percent of the nation's beer was made using formaldehyde. Toxic in high concentrations, formaldehyde can be an effective aid in mashing grains, a practice once common in the West. Only a negligible amount of formaldehyde survives in the finished product, so it sounds scarier than it actually is. Unfortunately, the government muddied the waters by issuing contradictory responses, one claiming that major Chinese beer producers did not use the additive, and the other that formaldehyde levels of Chinese beer were well below domestic and international standards.

The alleged story of Laoshan spring water, once used in the brewing of all Tsingtao beer, may be added here as an aside. The factory producing Laoshan entered negotiations to export its water to the United States in the early eighties. According to a source with knowledge of the deal, the plan went awry when investigators discovered that the water contained an unhealthy level of fecal matter, providing a grim if poetic comment on China's reliably shitty mass-market beer.

CADA again found itself at the center of a public relations fiasco during baijiu's single biggest product safety scandal. In late November 2012 Li Er, in the Chinese daily *21st Century Business Herald*, reported that a Hunan Province industry watchdog had found high levels of phthalates—industrial chemicals known as plasticizers, used to soften plastic for molding—in the products of Jiugui Liquor. While harmless in small doses, high exposure to plasticizers has been linked to liver damage and problems of the digestive and reproductive systems. Jiugui, at the time a respected industry leader, responded by issuing a statement that the report was inconsistent with internal tests.

Doing little to reassure consumers, CADA said that the distillery could not have violated national standards, as no alcohol-industry standard existed regarding the use of plasticizers in drinks. Worse still, the association suggested that most mainland distilleries' products contained levels of the offending chemical well above the corresponding standard then on the books for food products. The source of the contamination, CADA said, was unsuitable plastic used in the lining of bottle caps and in the tubing from the production process. Rumors also tied the use of certain flavoring compounds, which most distilleries denied using, to plasticizers.

Another possible source of contamination was the plastic containers used to transport baijiu cross-country between distilleries. Demand for baijiu was at the time so great that many of the most popular distilleries lacked the ability to produce baijiu fast enough to meet it. Some distilleries raised their prices, while others settled on the ethically dubious solution of buying baijiu in bulk from other producers and then selling the blend under their own names until they could expand their production facilities.

These were the growing pains of an industry experiencing an unprecedented spurt. And in adolescence, things get awkward. Someone leaked unsubstantiated but apparently authentic internal CADA documents showing that the organization had known about the plasticizer-contamination problem at least seventeen months before the scandal broke. Even while a contemporaneous plasticizer scandal surrounding a Taiwanese sports drink erupted across the strait, the government dragged its heels in implementing an industry-wide solution.

Now both the producers and the government regulators drew heavy public fire. Within days of the revelation, the stock prices of many of the most successful baijiu producers had dropped by as much as 9 percent. By the end of the week baijiu industry stocks had lost more than $5 billion, then about 5 percent of their total value.

The next week an anonymous blogger alleged that industry leader Kweichow Moutai's products also contained excessive levels of plasticizer, which sent that company's stock into a tailspin. Moutai denounced the rumors as the dirty trick of a competitor and published exonerating results from three independent laboratories. But the damage was already done: so great was the public anger that the value of Moutai's stock had already dropped by more than $3 billion. When subsequent tests bore out the initial claim against Jiugui Liquor, the company identified the culprit—a specific tube temporarily used on its production line—and issued a recall for all of its products. Its stock lost 42 percent of its value in less than two weeks and has failed to reclaim its prescandal position in the years since.

The situation had grown so dire that the government was forced to step in, not to punish the offending parties but to silence critics. On December 18 the Central Propaganda Department issued a directive, "with regards to negative news on the baijiu industry," media was "to discontinue production of all reports and commentary," with the sole exception of copy prepared by state mouthpiece *Xinhua*.

In early 2013 China implemented strict limits on plasticizer levels in alcoholic beverages, leading to the unexpected blockage of several shipments of French cognac by Chinese customs officials at Shenzhen port. According to local media reports, all three of the cognacs seized— Rémy Martin, Camus, and Frapin—contained plasticizer levels above the new legal limit.

The incident suggested that the problem might have been more widespread than originally suspected. A more conspiratorial reading might conclude that the seizure was a smokescreen intended to deflect attention away from problems affecting state-owned interests. In any case the improved standards marked an important victory for consumers and a step in the right direction for an industry in dire need of more rigorous regulation. Though the plasticizer scandal eventually blew over when the industry corrected the problem, it revealed an unsettling weakness in the previously unstoppable baijiu juggernaut: consumer confidence.

China has continued to raise its baijiu standards since the scandal, but still there are snags. In August 2015 reports emerged of two small distilleries in Guangxi Province lacing their baijiu with sildenafil, a chemical better known by its commercial name Viagra. Police seized over five thousand bottles of the baijiu, which had been marketed as a health tonic. The incident appears to have been contained to a single province and a handful of Western headline editors vying to find the most puerile use of "stiff drink."

Best practices can help consumers only up to a point. Industry regulators can monitor only producers who operate within a legal framework, and there is a large subset of the Chinese alcohol world that exists beyond the law.

It is a truism in contemporary China that anything worth doing is worth counterfeiting. And in baijiu pirates have found an attractive target. Respect for intellectual property, or lack thereof, is one of the great hazards facing China-based businesses and consumers. Success is punished by imitators and knockoffs—the more successful the brand the more acute the problem.

Moutai provides a telling example. By the early 2010s a bottle of its flagship Flying Fairy brand sold in excess of $250. In 2011 authorities seized almost a 160,000 bottles of fake Kweichow Moutai in a single province. How many more evaded detection? Contemporaneous commentators estimated as much as 90 percent of all Moutai sold in China at that time was counterfeit. Moutai management protested that the figure was a gross exaggeration, but how does one reliably measure the size of a black market?

During a 2012 police raid in Hunan Province, an alleged counterfeiter told police that all of his liquor came from a professional private distillery in the town of Maotai. "He boasted that the quality of their fake liquor products were [sic] almost as good as the real thing," reported *Want China Times*. Indeed, most counterfeit baijiu sold in China is perfectly safe off-brand liquor masquerading as the good stuff. But every so often counterfeiters, hardly the most scrupulous sort in the best of times, will bottle something toxic—methanol, formaldehyde, or god knows what else—and it's off to the hospital for the unfortunate drinker.

Sadly for consumers, the piracy is not limited to baijiu. International Western spirits brands have been plagued by fakery for decades, and the wine industry has been particularly hard hit. Chinese authorities shut down and recalled the products of almost thirty wineries in Hebei Province for selling fake wine in 2010. The largest of these producers, Jiahua, was then selling an estimated 2.4 million bottles of wine per year to a customer base that included Walmart. It used toxic coloring agents that caused headaches and heart arrhythmia. There have also been multiple reports of wines cut with methanol, especially troubling in that Chinese consumers are attracted by wine's purported health benefits.

Piracy can also injure reputations. Château Lafite Rothschild is a high-prestige French vineyard long favored by connoisseurs. A bottle of their wine once sold for as much as $8,000 at Chinese hotels and restaurants, which marked them as an obvious target. According to a 2011 report in *Shanghai Daily*, a counterfeit Lafite operation working out of a "secret wine factory on a cargo ship" was blending low-end French wines and unloading them in bottles identical to the Lafite originals. To give a sense of the scope, the report added that, while it was estimated that China imports only 50,000 bottles of Lafite annually, a single hotel in Guangdong Province reported annual sales of 40,000 bottles. Zhejiang Province alone supposedly consumed 300,000 bottles of "Lafite" in 2011. Consumers grew wary, and Lafite's retail price dropped 20 percent the following year.

While attending an alcohol industry event in Chengdu, I once encountered a wine seller who had laid out racks of their products for prospective customers. On one row I noticed several bottles of the high-end Australian wine Penfolds Bin 707. Next to those sat several near-indistinguishable bottles whose label used the same font and color scheme: Panfaids Bin 28. It almost goes without saying that both wines were likely fakes.

In response to this crisis of confidence producers and industry associations have introduced a number of antipiracy measures. Distilleries have turned to increasingly elaborate packaging and unrefillable bottles and bottle caps that cannot be resealed. Many distilleries use designs that require the drinker to physically damage the bottle to open it. Still, the incentives remain, and counterfeiters have proved remarkably adept at keeping pace with antipiracy measures. Copycats have even gone so far as to make vendors accomplices by offering substantial kickbacks for used bottles.

One of the most promising consumer innovations in recent years has been the increasing popularity of online alcohol retailers. Though the internet marketplaces may not be entirely immune to the piracy that has tainted their brick-and-mortar counterparts, several websites have attracted a steady business by acting as trusted intermediaries between consumers and distilleries.

Internet sales of alcohol in China grew more than 230 percent from

2010 to 2015, by which time they accounted for about 5 percent of the total market. Specialty websites like T-Mall and Jiuxian have sold tens of thousands of bottles online, most of them baijiu. In the period from 2015 to 2017 the website Jingdong Mall—the current leader in online alcohol sales—claims its baijiu sales doubled each year. At the time of this writing Jingdong has more than a thousand online retailers accounting for about 64 percent of all online alcohol sales.

These new digital platforms are still susceptible to human weakness. In May 2018 a user of Jingdong complained that he received counterfeit Kweichow Moutai Flying Fairy. The website acknowledged the problem, saying that an unscrupulous person in the supply chain had switched genuine products with fakes prior to delivery. Moutai's chair initially expressed confidence in Jingdong's founder Liu Qiangdong, but as the public outcry grew the producer announced it would temporarily halt all sales on the website.

Ironically, baijiu enthusiasts may be safest when purchasing Chinese alcohol outside of China. Many of the leading baijiu distilleries sell their premium products in airport duty-free shops around the world, and a small but increasing number have begun exporting drinks for retail in the United States, Europe, and elsewhere. Since these products ship directly from the source, the risk of forgery is almost nonexistent. Moreover, each bottle is subject to the safety regulations of the country in which they it is sold. So foreign drinkers, who currently consume little baijiu, have access to a far more reliable supply than the Chinese who drink it to great excess.

Yet the most significant health risk posed to Chinese drinkers is not found in any drink, or in any dubious knockoff thereof. The greatest threat lies in the social pressure that informs the consumption of baijiu. It is a uniquely Chinese public health crisis thousands of years in the making. It is the enabling and self-destructive phenomenon known as "ganbei culture."

15 The Cost of Doing Business

"God, grant me the serenity to accept the things I cannot change, the courage to change the things I can, and the wisdom to know the difference." Teacher Gang read the prayer aloud in Mandarin, pausing after each line for the others to repeat.

It was Thursday night, when the local branch of Alcoholics Anonymous holds its weekly meeting in a cramped white room in Chengdu's Huaxi Hospital. On one wall was a whiteboard gone gray from overuse, a smattering of barely visible words staining its surface: physical dependency, psychological addiction, and so forth. There were six attendees: two of them in recovery and four family members of people with alcohol problems. We sat in a circle, some of us on stiff metal chairs, others on ancient olive hospital beds folded into chairs. Foam burst from the ripped upholstery.

At the prayer's conclusion the meeting ended, and the group began filing out. "I want to show you something," Teacher Gang said, taking me paternally by the arm. He led me down a hall. In the first room was a line of beds with patients, some of them hooked up to intravenous drips. Nurses and visitors sat to one side. This is the hospital's substance-abuse ward, Gang explained. In one room a man in a suit sat in a crouch and joked with a man in the bed next to him. In the next room a nurse helped a teenager with vacant eyes as he staggered toward the door. I was feet away but he seemed not to see me.

"What kind of substances?" I said.

"Alcohol, drugs, the internet. Any kind of addiction," he said. "This the biggest unit of its kind in Sichuan."

"It's full of patients. So many of them."

"That's right," he said. "Five years ago I was one of them."

In February 2008 Guo Shizhong, family-planning commissioner in a small Henan town called Xinyang, collapsed from a fatal brain hemorrhage. The local government rushed to posthumously name Guo an "outstanding communist," citing his long overtime hours. Others should learn from his selfless example, they said. Guo received the "level three order of merit," a commendation bestowed on the rare patriot who dies at his post in the service of the People's Republic.

Guo was no ordinary martyr. He had not died in defense of a grand ideal, nor had he succumbed to the normal stresses of bureaucratic life, inundated by mounds of paperwork. No, Guo's was a peculiar end: he had drunk himself to death at a karaoke parlor.

When the truth was revealed the public responded with furor. Xinyang was then in the midst of a public campaign prohibiting officials from drinking during the workday. At the time of Guo's death, the municipal government boasted it had already reprimanded more than four hundred cadres and was saving an average of about a million dollars a month in liquor expenditures. It was to be a model of civic virtue for the rest of country. The town's reputation was dashed overnight, and, facing intense outside pressure, it withdrew the award.

Such incidents were then the norm. A year after Guo met his end, an unnamed Guangdong official fell into a coma from excessive drink. A week later public servant Jin Guoqing of Wuhan, Hubei Province, lost consciousness while drinking baijiu at a banquet. He died before he reached the hospital. A few months after that Chen Lusheng, a Shenzhen police officer known for his Herculean alcoholic prowess, choked to death on his own vomit while drinking off-duty. He received a martyr's burial, and his family got almost double the standard death benefit. Less than a month later Shen Hao, Party secretary of Xiagang Village, Anhui Province, failed to rise from his bed the day after he had feted three separate groups of investors. And those are just the stories that made the news.

Drink killed these people, but none had been poisoned in the understood sense. In none of the reports is a single mention of toxic additives or counterfeit products—nor would one expect there to be. In those halcyon days of official extravagance, only the finest would do for China's cadres. They died not because of *what* they drank, but because of *how* they drank. Binge drinking killed them. Ganbei culture killed them.

China has long recognized the connection between economic success and alcoholic excess. Since the days of Di Xin's wine pool and meat forest—since Wu of Zhou's first alcohol prohibition and the dozens that followed it—conspicuous consumption has been a hallmark of power and wealth. It is unsurprising then, that in a period where the country rapidly acquired both, indulgence would follow and in many cases swerve out of control. It was simply the cost of doing business. Moreover, when its victims were elevated to the status of martyrs, binging became a sacred service to the state.

Necessity is at the heart of this societal transformation. In her aptly named book *Occupational Hazards*, Elanah Uretsky argues that *yingchou*— "involuntary toasting" and the dining, smoking, and paid sex work that surrounds it—is "essential for establishing and maintaining the personalistic relations, known as *guanxi*, that are necessary for political and economic success in post-Mao China."

This kind of informal wheeling and dealing is legally prohibited but tacitly expected of officials in the service of their duties. Those who don't partake in the ritual are considered untrustworthy, she explains; "refusing the offer of a cigarette or invitation to drink is considered insulting, disrespectful, and a sign of someone who is not willing to engage in mutual exchange." Whereas in other East Asian countries like Japan much of the same after-hours entertainment is expected of white-collar workers, only in China is a worker's performance in the extracurricular arena, "the relationships he builds over food, drink, and entertainment," deemed of equal or greater importance than his daytime professional abilities.

Given the sensitivities surrounding state employees, the extent of the resulting public health crisis can be difficult to gauge. But what we do know is alarming. When Chairman Deng Xiaoping's "Reform and Opening Up" began to transform the economy in the 1980s, the number of people suffering from health complications related to drinking, dining, and smoking spiked.

Stroke is the predominant cause of death for men in China today. In a study conducted between 1991 and 2000, a team led by Lydia Bazzano of Tulane University surveyed more than sixty-four thousand Chinese men over the age of forty, all of whom were initially free from stroke. "Alcohol consumption was significantly related to increased stroke incidence and mortality," the authors concluded. "At the top level of alcohol consumption (at least 35 drinks per week), risk of stroke incidence was 22 percent higher and risk of mortality was 30 percent higher than among nondrinkers."

A 2011 report by Wuhan University's Zhongnan Hospital's Physical Examination Center, directed by Zou Shiqing, concluded that among the government officials in Hubei Province as many as 90 percent suffer from poor health. Working with data from officials' hospital visits, the researchers further indicated that up to 34 percent of officials suffer from liver damage. The second most common set of ailments, predictably, were those affecting kidney function.

In 2017 medical company iKang surveyed three hundred thousand civil servants and found the majority of them were overweight or obese. More than half of the men in the study (and over 30 percent of the women) suffered from fatty liver disease, compared to a rate of about 20 percent of men throughout broader China. The condition is typically associated with poor diet and alcohol abuse.

Few high-level decisions in China are made without the aid of a strong drink. So closely is professional advancement tied to one's drinking ability that the more successful one becomes, the more they must drink. China is thus the world's only nation where an adult's likelihood to binge increases with age.

This was the startling conclusion of a report published by Beijing's National Center for Chronic and Non-communicable Disease Control and Prevention in 2011. The study looked at the drinking patters of almost fifty thousand Chinese adults and concluded binge drinking in Chinese society had reached epidemic proportions. The study defined a binge as consuming about 1.75 ounces of alcohol—roughly five beers' worth—over the course of a day, slightly less for women. Just 55 percent of men and 15 percent of women in China said they had consumed at least one drink in the past year, but of them a majority of the men and more than a quarter of the women binged. Among both sexes the overall frequency of drinking corresponded with the tendency to binge. "Analytical results showed that excessive drinking, frequent drinking and binge drinking were most common among drinkers of middle-age or above," Dr. Alex Li Yichong, who led the study, told me. "This was markedly different from findings in Western countries [where] alcohol consumption peaks in the early twenties or late teens."

In this environment, known collectively as "ganbei culture," alcohol tolerance is a professional skill and alcohol poisoning an occupational hazard. Recruiters often list drinking ability among desired qualities in a job listing. Some even go so far as to indicate that applicants must be able to drink as much as an entire bottle of baijiu—about half a pint of pure alcohol—in a single sitting.

Professional advancement is so closely related to one's drinking ability that many companies keep on staff a "public relations" specialist whose primary responsibility is to bear the brunt of the drinking when hosting important visitors. "Of course, you can choose not to drink. But it will be difficult when dealing with other officials. Drinking at the dinner table is an unspoken rule for doing business," an anonymous Tianjin official told *China Daily*, commenting on the string of binge-drinking deaths. "We just have no choice." This sense of helplessness, of being in thrall to a system that devastates bodies and families, was a theme repeatedly expressed by Chinese officials at the time.

When I spoke with Uretsky, she explained that the men suffering from what she calls *yingchou bing* (involuntary toasting sickness) believed their condition was culturally derived. "Their perception was really that their disease comes from what they had to do," she said. "They had no choice in the matter." In this context it becomes clear why these men were viewed by their colleagues as martyrs. People were participating in a system that was involuntary, lethal, and in many minds necessary. How did it come to this?

Drinking was not always a deadly business in the Middle Kingdom. Chinese have happily sipped alcoholic beverages since prehistoric times without many major incidents. And the marriage of business and alcohol has always been a part of Chinese society. Libations have long been essential to forging and maintaining relationships with allies and rivals. Between colleagues and kin the ceremonial toast strengthened bonds of camaraderie and demonstrated respect to superiors. In delicate negotiations a stiff drink can weaken an opponent's defenses and resolve, or reveal a hidden agenda.

Since the Confucian *Book of Rites*, a rigid set of prescriptions guides every aspect of a drinking session. Knowledge of these guidelines helped establish a man's erudition and social status. The current form of social drinking and dining as a means of socialization and trust building among bureaucratic elites began as a minor ritual about a thousand years ago. The Song poet Lu You (1125–1210), for example, complained he had grown too lazy in his old age to participate in the toasting ritual. But although the tradition of professional drinking is ancient, drinking to dangerous excess is a uniquely modern phenomenon.

Until recent decades the means to overindulge in alcohol was limited to a small elite. Alcohol was an expensive habit that only the aristocratic scholar-official class could afford. Merchants and artists also occasionally drank heavily, but their limited social status limited their influence.

The agrarian peasantry, who constituted the country's overwhelming majority, drank little. For most Chinese drunkenness was an aspirational state achieved only once or twice a year, if ever. The cost of a few jugs of alcohol could be justified only to ring in the New Year or celebrate a betrothal. Many farmers brewed a small supply of rice wine at home, but it was simply too expensive, and the grain too precious, to become habit forming.

Several factors limited wealthy Chinese's consumption, foremost the alcohol itself. Spirits arrived relatively late in Chinese history, and early baijius were of such atrocious quality that the aristocracy preferred drinking mostly huangjiu until the mid-twentieth century. Chinese drawn to drink could either imbibe a beverage too weak to get them drunk quickly or a very potent beverage so foul it would be difficult to countenance in large quantities, what Qing-era physician John Dudgeon called in *The Beverages of the Chinese* "a most happy self-moderating, self-regulating quality."

There were also genetic considerations. Remember that a significant portion of the population of China—more than one in ten—suffer from the debilitating "Asian flush," which turns drinkers beet red and makes even moderate consumption highly unpleasant. It has always provided a strong incentive against widespread alcohol abuse.

Moderation was also imposed from without, as the heavy hand of Confucianism kept the bottle at a safe distance. Although it was the duty of the host to provide his guests with alcohol while banqueting, his discretion determined when and how much would be consumed. A host was generally liberal with pours, but the goal was to make his friends and associates comfortable, not to force drink on them. Guests were expected to down the first glass in entirety as a show of respect, but beyond that point they were free to drink as much or as little as they pleased at their own pace.

In *Social Life of the Chinese*, U.S. missionary Rev. Justus Doolittle describes the laxity of premodern Chinese drinking in 1865: "Many drink only a part of the contents of their cups at a round. Sometimes, and even frequently in the case of the wealthy, and of those who are fond of the cup, from twenty to thirty, or even forty rounds are drank. Those who can not drink wine so freely without becoming drunk, let their cups stand filled in front of them on the table, excusing themselves from drinking, offering some apology to the company; or they take their cups and raise them to their lips, with or without tasting, as they please, while the others drink."

On the other side of the Pacific, at roughly the same time, Mark Twain made a similar observation of the Chinese immigrants in Virginia City, Nevada. "They are quiet, peaceable, tractable, free from drunkenness, and they are as industrious as the day is long," he writes in *Roughing It.* "A disorderly Chinaman is rare, and a lazy one does not exist." Since alcohol was consumed almost exclusively with meals and in small quantities, public drunkenness resulted only in the rarest circumstances. This is not to suggest that binging never occurred. Then as now, drinking games could get out of hand. According to Canton-born Englishman James Dyer Ball in *Things Chinese*, in 1903 these games were so "exasperating to any Europeans who may unfortunately have their residences near to those of the Chinese" that Hong Kong enacted a prohibition against them.

Daoism provided the ideological counterweight to Confucian restraint, especially in artistic circles. The Seven Sages of the Bamboo Grove, the Eight Immortals of the Wine Glass, and the artists who followed their example praised the transcendent powers of drink. Every town in China had a drunk or several, a situation aggravated by the fact that early baijiu distillers ("pushers" might be a more apt term) extended drinkers credit for periods up to a year.

In *The Chinese Empire* Abbé Huc describes the pitiful circumstances of drinkers who "ruin themselves" on baijiu, who "pass whole days and nights in drinking successive little cups of it, until their intoxication makes them incapable of carrying the cup to their lips." When this insatiable thirst waylays the family patriarch, "poverty, with all its lugubrious train, very soon makes its entrance into the house."

But the intemperate were outliers in a land that drank well but not often or too deeply. Problem drinkers like Di Xin and Li Bai were the exception, not the rule. To become a *jiugui*, a "wine ghost" or drunkard, was to fail in one's most basic societal obligation and become an object of universal contempt: the antithesis of today's "successful" professional tippler.

In the time since, China has transformed from a principally poor, agrarian society into a rapidly urbanizing global economic leader. In the three decades preceding the 2010s the Chinese GDP grew by almost 2,000 percent. In 1990 China was the world's tenth-largest economy, but in 2010 China displaced Japan to become the world's second largest behind the United States. During the same period the disposable income of urban families jumped by a factor of ten. China's alcohol industry expanded rapidly but struggled to keep pace with demand.

China's craving for drink may therefore be a perverse form of wish fulfillment. For thousands of years drinking to excess was an exclusively elite pursuit. The less fortunate masses were consigned to drink what they could when they could. All at once alcohol became accessible to everyone in great quantities and priced to any budget. Anybody with a fistful of yuan could drink themselves into oblivion, and many have tried: according to the World Health Organization, alcohol consumption in China jumped more than 300 percent from 1978 to 2000.

It is much the same with nourishment. In a country that only decades ago struggled to feed itself, as much as a quarter of the adult population is overweight today. Type 2 diabetes rates tripled in the decade ending in 2012, according to the International Diabetes Foundation. As of 2016, the *Global Times* reports, China became home to the world's largest obese population. Under Mao the primary challenge in terms of nutrition had been survival. Possessed of newfound wealth, many Chinese are struggling to learn restraint.

"An increasing percentage of the population can afford to consume alcohol, and do so more regularly," Dr. Li told me. "But as Chinese culture has evolved and become influenced by other cultures, traditional Confucian norms have lost their impact with regard to imposing restrictions on drinking behavior."

With a surfeit of drink and no tempering influence, the so-called ganbei culture developed—a drinking problem scaled to China's boundless ambition.

It boils down to trust. An enormous amount of the Chinese government's resources is controlled by a class of officials whose success or failure depends on self-reported statistics, the reliability of which is virtually impossible to independently corroborate. "*Yingchou* is employed as an informal mechanism for demonstrating the trust, respect, and loyalty necessary for governing distribution of China's state-controlled resources," Elanah Uretsky writes. As a result, "governance is often conducted outside the official halls of government and instead is influenced by activities that take place in top-tier restaurants, karaoke clubs, massage parlors, and saunas."

For proof one need look no further than recent high-level diplomatic negotiations in China. Richard Nixon traded toasts with Zhou Enlai, Bill Clinton with Jiang Zemin, and Barack Obama with Xi Jinping. When the results of these meetings were reported in the Chinese media, it was not alongside a picture of a handshake, as is customary in the West, but with a picture of raised glasses.

But this behavior extends far beyond the professional realm. One sees it on full display at every festive occasion, at wedding receptions and family gatherings. As is the case in the West, China's heaviest drinking happens during the holiday season. What sets China apart is the strength of its alcohol and the compulsion to drink more than is necessary or desirable.

This is not a recipe for holiday cheer. Over the ten-day period that encompassed the National Day and Mid-Autumn Festival holidays in 2012, Chinese media reported that more than a hundred people were hospitalized for alcohol poisoning in a single city.

From a public health perspective the consequences have been dramatic. Sustained heavy drinking causes a wide range of maladies, chief among them heart and liver disease. The aforementioned Asian flush also elevates one's risk of life-threatening illness. The fact that China's heaviest drinkers tend to be older than their global peers further exacerbates the risk. One must also account for increased rates of domestic violence, accidental injury, and vehicular homicide.

The Chinese government has attempted to curb drunk driving at the national and local levels, instituting harsher penalties and implementing random roadside tests for blood alcohol levels. The absence of reliable accident data and consistent enforcement make the impact of such policies difficult to gauge, but these measures have accomplished something more significant than statistics could indicate.

By raising public awareness of the threat posed by drinking and driving the state has provided a plausible excuse to avoid binging. An automobile provides a desperately needed out for reluctant bingers. In the course of my travels around China, I lost count of how many times someone responded to one of my toasts with an apologetic jingle of a key ring. But this is an insufficient solution, available only to those who can afford it.

Sober Chinese have struggled to escape from the requisite ganbei sessions. Potential victims proffer excuses—spouses, work, and health foremost—but success is contingent on the acceptance of other drinkers, an outcome far from guaranteed. Passing out or even vomiting may buy drinkers a moment's respite, but they may soon be drafted back into service. So long as they agreed to the first toast, they tacitly agree to all that follow.

For men in particular there is more than professional courtesy at stake. From Bamboo Sage Liu Lin to the tiger-bludgeoning Wu Song, Chinese have celebrated the heroic manliness of drinking. To drink is to be *one of the guys* and to refuse is to call one's manhood into question and risk exclusion from the tribe.

"Alcohol, food, and sex are fun. But in China, the culture of banquet and brothel has become largely joyless, a business tool chiefly directed at transactional relationships with other men," James Palmer explains, writing in *ChinaFile*. "It comes with a sniggering puerility, even though the majority of the men involved are well into middle-age. Drinking games, groping, crude jokes, and the bullying hunt for weakness, whether over drink or women, are the norm." A part of the game is sharing a dirty secret, Palmer explains. "Like schoolboys' playing hooky, being bad together moves a relationship along fast. As one saying that went rapidly around the Chinese Internet in 2011 put it, 'It's better to do one bad thing with your boss than a hundred good things for your boss.'"

So great is the pressure to ganbei that former U.S. ambassador to China John Huntsman, a teetotaling Mormon, drank baijiu to avoid offending his hosts. Supposedly, he would drink the first toast with baijiu and switch to water thereafter, but nonetheless local social pressure outweighed religious proscription.

Alcoholic subterfuge may seem ridiculous to outsiders—on some level it undoubtedly is—but it is commonplace in modern China. Many drinkers hold the liquid in their mouths after the toast, then spit it out while pretending sip tea. My friend Duan Li told me that when her grandmother was a government official, she was considered a formidable drinker by her peers. Her secret was the handkerchief she always carried in her pocket, into which she would spit out shots while pretending to cough or pat her lips.

There is also the mercenary solution: hiring professional drinkers. When an employer hits his baijiu ceiling, stunt drinkers can step in and start taking shots for him. A friend in Chengdu's sober boss used him in this capacity. It is notable that the important thing, where maintaining face is concerned, is only that the toast is received, not where it lands. In certain business circles, however, this method may send the wrong signal or invite ridicule.

Uretsky related the story of an acquaintance of hers, a gastric surgeon in Changchun, who felt binging was a professional necessity. "As doctors we need to do this," he told her. "As doctors we compete for patients. . . . They go to who they trust, and we need to build up trust with them, and this is the way we build up trust with them." No one is safe from the pressure to drink. Even alcohol epidemiologists like Dr. Li, who understand the cost better than most, must binge to facilitate cooperation between the national and regional branches of China's Centers for Disease Control. "In some circumstances," he said, "drinking is mandatory."

All these stratagems and equivocations indicate most Chinese are still unwilling to consider abstinence an acceptable social practice. The belief that drinking is a social obligation—the guiding principle of ganbei culture—leaves little room in society for those who cannot drink. There's a traditional Chinese expression, "Alcohol does not intoxicate man, but man intoxicates himself." It reveals an attitude similar to the old NRA chestnut, "Guns don't kill people; people kill people," and both are equally unhelpful to a society hoping to address a crisis.

I met Teacher Gang outside the hospital's main gate. He was the representative of Chengdu's Chinese Alcoholics Anonymous chapter—foreign and Chinese AA members meet separately. He was slight, aged beyond his years, with a flat face and protruding eyes, one of them lazy. He wore plimsoll shoes, a sweater with a sailboat on it, and a painter's cap with a metal decal that said "Sports." His wife, Liu, a woman with a kind face and wavy hair dyed brown, accompanied him. My friend Duan Li came along with me to help decode the impenetrable Sichuanese dialect.

"You're the American?" he asked as he approached us. I told him that I was. He gestured for us to follow him inside. The Mental Health Division of Huaxi Hospital had the same tired, worn-down look peculiar to hospitals in the developing world; it was something between a stuffy bureaucratic workspace and prison. Rows of metal seats were bolted to the ground in front of reception windows. Some waiting rooms had many seats and few patients; elsewhere there were many patients and no seats. Everywhere was the perfume of high-tar cigarettes.

While Gang sought out an empty room, Liu explained that a woman with an alcohol-abusing father had founded the local AA chapter. He died a couple of years ago, and now Gang lead the meetings. "He's been sober longer than anyone else in the branch," she said. "Almost *five* years." A buzzer sounded and the door to the ward clicked open. Gang led us past a nurses' station and into an empty doctor's office. It was where his journey to recovery had begun.

Gang was just shy of sixty when I met him. In his youth China was still ruled by Mao, and alcohol was a strictly regulated commodity. Most people drank baijiu, but government rationing determined the amount they could purchase. Grain was too scarce to distill much of it, so drinking sessions rarely got out of hand.

When Gang reached middle age, China was a different country. The rising economy transformed scarcity to surplus. Gang gained a reputation as his office's drinking specialist. His superiors regularly sent him out to wine and dine clients. When not drinking with clients, he was drinking with friends.

"People used to try and get me to drink with them all the time," he said. "When I went out to eat, everyone wanted to sit next to me." He nodded toward his wife, who wore a pained expression. "She doesn't drink, but when I drink I totally lose control. It hurt our marriage. And then there was also our daughter, always wondering why Mom and Dad were fighting."

"We didn't know what we were supposed to do," Liu said. "We thought we could help him ourselves but we couldn't. We thought that by yelling at him we could make him stop. It just made him angrier, and then he just drank more. It was a nasty cycle."

"The people close to you try to persuade you to drink less. It goes in one ear and out the other," said Gang. "When you're an alcoholic you've already lost the ability to control yourself around alcohol." Gang drank himself unconscious some nights, and finally Liu had had enough. She literally dragged him to the hospital.

When the doctor examined him, he said Gang was critically ill, in mortal danger. "It terrified me," he said. He made up his mind that night to get sober, checking himself into the clinic just down the hall from where we sat.

"The first day back from the hospital I sat down for dinner and reached for the wine glass without thinking about it. When I realized I was doing it, I picked up the glass and threw it to the ground." Gang stood from his chair, throwing down the imaginary glass. "I walked to the back of the kitchen and picked up the baijiu." He grasped for the invisible bottles and shattered them against the linoleum.

He said his closest friends and family have been supportive, but coworkers and casual acquaintances are confused by his decision. Mental health and addiction carry social stigma in China, and few people understand that chemical dependency can be fatal.

"When I came back from the hospital to my home and my job, they asked me, 'Gang, where were you?'"

"I said, 'I was quitting alcohol.'"

"Then they asked, 'Where did you quit alcohol?'"

"I replied, 'Huaxi Hospital.'"

"They were really surprised. 'You need to go to a hospital to stop drinking?'"

"I said, 'That's right. With a scientific approach they help you get it under control. Using a combination of injections, medicines, and psychiatry, they helped me quit.'"

He has attended the AA meetings every week since, but he knows he is the exception to the rule. It is just too easy to slip back into old habits. Everyone tries to convince you to have another drink, and in many professions the pressure is just too great. "It's really difficult not to drink in China, especially if you work in certain jobs," he said. "We have one guy in the hospital who's been in and out of treatment eight times. One time they had to strap him to the bed to keep him from leaving.

"Just yesterday, I was walking down the street on my way to this week's meeting, and I bumped into some friends. They tried to make me go drinking with them." He declined, as he has declined many such invitations in the past five years. When others drink baijiu, he drinks tea. They don't get it. In China the colloquial expression for a fair-weather fiend is *jiurou pengyou*, an "alcohol and meat friend." Absent a banquet, the friendships vanish.

By some estimates more than forty million Chinese suffer from alcohol-use disorder, and the number has increased significantly since the 1980s. Multiple studies conducted in recent decades conclude that overall rates of alcohol dependence in China are comparable to those found in the United States and Australia. Yet in those countries drinking problems are more evenly distributed between the sexes and age groups, and, according to a 2015 study led by Cheng Hui of the Shanghai Mental Health Center, the rates of alcohol abuse in China are close to zero among teenagers, and women are thirty times less likely to abuse alcohol than men.

Gang has made a mission out of helping problem drinkers and their families by bringing them into AA's support network. Liu accompanies him to the meetings most weeks. He is lucky to have her and to live in one of the handful of Chinese cities with treatment options. AA has only a dozen or so chapters in China. "It's not like it is in America," Gang said, "where there are many organizations doing this kind of work, and everything is already well developed on a grand scale."

In the United States Alcoholics Anonymous has dominated treatment for alcohol abuse since its establishment in 1935. It was the first organization to treat dependence as a disease rather than a moral failing, though some argue it has failed to keep pace with our understanding of substance abuse and addiction. Critics accuse AA of lacking scientific rigor and relying more heavily on faith than science—five of the Twelve Steps make explicit reference to God or a higher power. AA has no standardized certification for counselors, and in many cases they are not trained medical professionals. The program's efficacy has never been persuasively demonstrated in a peer-reviewed study, and studies suggest AA's focus on absolute abstention from alcohol may be counterproductive for some drinkers.

Many newer approaches to treatment focus on fostering healthier drinking habits rather than eliminating alcohol altogether. Prescription drugs like naltrexone and naloxone inhibit the soothing sensations alcohol produces in the brain and have proved highly effective in reducing cravings for drink. In combination with behavioral therapy, medication-based approaches are often more effective for addicts. Some problems are so severe that moderate drinking may not be possible, but that's the point AA's detractors make: treatment should be tailored to the patient, not the other way around.

In China options are extremely limited. Most of the medications commonly used to treat alcohol dependency in the West are currently unavailable, and none have been officially approved to treat alcohol-use disorder. There were essentially zero treatment facilities in the country before 1990, and today few exist outside of major cities. This means Chinese seeking treatment often rely on a combination of emergency room visits, antidepressants, and traditional Chinese medicine.

Unsurprisingly, the Chinese public remains skeptical in its attitudes toward the disease model of alcohol abuse. In a public survey published in the *Chinese Mental Health Journal* in 2009, about 70 percent of respondents said it was pointless to treat those with drinking problems. Another study published that year in *Alcoholism Clinical and Experimental Research* indicated that as few as 2.4 percent of dependent drinkers in Beijing sought any kind of treatment.

"I trust that in the future Chinese society can develop a culture of alcohol abstinence," Gang said. "If you can have a drinking culture, then you can also have a culture of sobriety."

He stood, took off his hat, and gave me a deep bow. He took my hand in his and thanked me for listening to his story. We left the room and started walking to the elevator. When I reached for the door to let myself out, it wouldn't budge. "You can't let yourself out of a mental hospital," Gang explained.

Outside the elevator, a group of patients stood waiting. A Tibetan man stood among them with an intravenous tube sticking out of his arm. Partially visible under his bandage was a Buddhist swastika tattoo. Where I come from a tattoo like that would make him virtually unemployable, but in China sobriety is a much bigger threat to one's prospects.

The situation is stark. Tens of millions of Chinese are drinking themselves to death. And the act of seeking help makes them outcasts, relegated to meetings in an unused room in a mental hospital—the only place where people understand them.

"Will you come to our meeting next week?" Gang asked.

I told him I would.

He took me by the elbow as we stepped outside. "So when you finish writing about alcohol, then what?" he asked me.

"I'm not really sure."

"You should write a book about Chinese food," he said. "There are lots of different types. Many people would be interested in that."

I told him I would consider it and thanked him.

"Derek," Duan said in a hushed tone and pulled me aside. "I don't think you understood. When Teacher Gang came to meet us, he thought you were an addict. He met with you today because he thought you needed help."

I joined his meeting next Thursday in the small room on the top floor of the hospital. A sixty-two-year-old recovering alcohol abuser named Peng read aloud the "Alcoholics Anonymous Preamble" in Mandarin with a strong Sichuanese accent. When he finished a middle-aged woman named Shu, whose son suffered from a drinking problem, read aloud the organization's famous Twelve Steps.

When she finished, Teacher Gang turned to address the group. "This American would like to learn more about our culture and what it's like to give up drinking," he said. "Don't be shy, he won't use your real names. Tell the world your story."

16 Red Tape

On July 28, 2012, protesters hit the streets of Qidong, a sleepy Jiangsu fishing town some fifty miles north of Shanghai. At issue was the construction of a pipeline from a Japanese-owned paper mill that would spew 150,000 tons of sewage daily into the port. According to Reuters reporter John Ruwitch, a thousand Qidong residents marched through town chanting slogans—Chinese bloggers inflated the number to between fifty and a hundred times that—before storming local government offices, overturning cars, and bloodily clashing with police.

The protesters carried the day. Local officials quickly announced that the paper mill would be permanently closed. The crowd dispersed, and the incident was quietly swept under the rug.

Protests of this type were common in those years. According to the Chinese Academy of Governance, so-called mass incidents had been steadily increasing each year, reaching 180,000 in 2010. The same year as the Qidong incident, protests in Shifang and Dalian similarly led to halted construction of potentially polluting plants.

Anti-Japanese sentiment was a factor in Qidong, but a more notable

feature distinguished the revolt. When protesters ransacked government offices, they went in search of expensive cigarettes and booze,
the outward trappings of bribery and corruption. In one photograph
taken at the scene—later posted on the popular microblogging site Sina
Weibo—protesters lined up several bottles of luxury baijiu in an office
window for the crowd to see. "There are people everywhere, on walls,
cars, rooftops, in streets," wrote blogger Jiaojiaotaotailang. "The air is
filled with the smell of alcohol, and there are sounds of breaking glass."

A seismic shift was at hand. Baijiu had long been the beneficiary of
government patronage, but now it had become a political lightening
rod. At a moment when its fortunes never looked brighter, when prices
and profits were soaring, when a national culture of binge drinking
made it indispensable, the baijiu industry suddenly found itself in a
precarious position.

The government faced a stark choice: change course or risk further
provoking the mob. The impact of any response, or the lack thereof,
would reverberate throughout the alcohol industry.

Just days before I first visited the Kweichow Moutai distillery in 2012,
Beijing dealt the company a serious blow. Premier Wen Jiabao, then the
country's second-most powerful official, pledged to prohibit the use of
public funds on high-end alcohol, cigarettes, and luxury goods, saying,
"Corruption is the biggest danger facing the ruling party. If not dealt
with properly, the problem may change the nature of, or terminate, the
political regime." In the wake of this announcement, Moutai's stock fell
almost 6.5 percent in a single day.

Momentum behind Wen's bombshell had been building for years.
Despite a closed, entirely state-run media and a restrictive internet
censorship regime, the Chinese public was becoming increasingly vocal
against what it saw as official abuse of state funds. The so-called three
publics—use of public funds to finance officials' international vacations,
purchase of automobiles for private use, and wining and dining—had
created a confidence gap between the government and the governed.

The excesses were well documented. In 1997 Wu Zhaoren, deputy director of Anhui Province's Agricultural Committee told *Reference News*, "Mao Zedong said, 'The Revolution is not a dinner party.' Now this has been transformed into 'The revolution *is* a dinner party.' Even the often-quoted lines from one of Mao's poems—'The Red Army fears not the long march, mountains and rivers they will take in stride . . .'—has been changed to a popular saying: 'The official fears not a drinking match, ten thousand cups he will down with pride.'"

"Officials eating at public expense have tired of the usual delicacies of chicken, duck, fish and pork; they are familiar with turtles and have tasted wildlife in all forms," write Chen Guidi and Wu Chuntao in the now-banned *Will the Boat Sink the Water?* "They have passed the 'test of alcohol' as their predecessors passed through and survived the 'crucible of revolution.'" Writing in 2004, Chen and Wu used figures from the National Statistics Bureau to show that official dining expenditures had approached one billion yuan (then about $125 million). By their informal estimates, this was "enough to host four Olympic Games, to build two dams like the Three Gorges, or wipe out the disgrace of the widespread phenomenon of children being kept out of school because there are insufficient funds."

Five years later, in a 2009 conversation with *China Daily*, a professor at Peking University's school of government, Li Chengyan, estimated that the government spent about 500 billion yuan ($79 billion) in public funds on official banquets, approximately a third of the nation's annual dining bill. Another estimate reported in *Global Times* in 2011 said that the Chinese government's annual liquor tab was at 600 billion yuan ($94.5 billion), an amount roughly three times that year's stated national defense budget.

The issue came to a head in April 2011, when employees of the state-run energy giant Sinopec leaked their office's alcohol invoices online. The total bill—which included 696 bottles of red wine and 480 bottles of premium Moutai—was $243,604. A single bottle of Château Lafite Rothschild had cost taxpayers $1,813. Sinopec pinned the purchase on a single man, Guangdong branch general manager Lu Guangyu, vowing that he would be punished for his transgressions.

In the face of such damning evidence, and Sinopec's plainly absurd explanation, even the reliably pro-government *Global Times* joined in the criticism. Noting the "mass public skepticism" regarding Sinopec's claim that one person could consume a quarter-million dollars' worth of alcohol in one pay period, journalists Li Xiang and Zhang Han quoted four anonymous Sinopec sources, saying, "huge spending on alcohol is omnipresent." The liquor, explained one of them, is used to "bribe local authorities," to give the company preferential treatment, and to overlook legal transgressions. "Clearly, Lu is just a scapegoat," said another.

The paper further suggested that the price of Kweichow Moutai is a barometer for official corruption. And if there is a link between the cost of Moutai and malfeasance, then the picture was indeed grim. Moutai's flagship Flying Fairy brand retailed for about 11 yuan in 1982, but sold for 140 yuan a decade later. In early 2012 the same bottle sold for around 2,500 yuan, or just shy of $400.

Two high-ranking Party officials echoed the paper's sentiment in speaking against corruption in January of that year. Wang Rong, mayor of the major southern metropolis Shenzhen, said, "If it wasn't being purchased with public funds, Moutai wouldn't have reached such an expensive price." Going a step further, deputy to the Shanghai Municipal People's Congress Shen Haixiong said, "The price of Moutai keeps soaring and drinking the liquor is considered a luxury. To consume the liquor is actually an abuse of public funds."

Amid the growing tension Moutai general manager Liu Zili—the man who presided over the trial of the Demolition Girls—did his best Marie Antoinette impression, publicly responding, "If Moutai was banned, I would be confused what drink could be served at government receptions. Should it be Château Lafite instead?" Indeed, let them drink Lafite.

Regrettable though the statement may have been, his point was sound. Targeting high-end alcohol attacks a symptom of corruption rather than its cause. If someone is abusing the public trust, is his taste in alcohol the pressing issue? This nuance was apparently lost on Beijing. Kweichow Moutai was not alone in benefiting from the prevailing trends, but as the most famous national brand it was the most exposed. Or, as the Chinese idiom says, "The bird that sticks out its head gets shot."

It was the Party's old nemesis capitalism, specifically the law of supply and demand, that created the poor optics. For years government officials and military brass had relied on a steady stream of baijiu to lubricate business dealings. Practically, this meant various government offices and agencies purchased a large stock of baijiu distilleries' output outright each year. Since the government's outlay would primarily enrich state-run distilleries, this had an added benefit of supporting local governments and economies across the county.

According to *Caixin* reporter He Chunmei, "Cases of the best [Moutai] liquor are set aside, for example, for the Great Hall of the People in Beijing, members of the Chinese People's Political Consultative Conference (CPPCC), the military's Central Guard Bureau, the navy's North Sea Fleet, the Chengdu Military Command, telecom giant China Mobile and the utility China Southern Power Grid."

Meanwhile, China's private sector had also grown wealthier, and thirstier. The increased demand provided distillers a strong incentive to expand production, particularly for more expensive products: in the decade ending in 2011, baijiu production more than doubled, while ultrapremium baijiu (over $200 per bottle) grew by a factor of almost fifteen. Unfortunately, the most coveted types of baijiu take years to produce, so it was almost impossible for distilleries to meet unforeseen spikes in demand. Thus, an increasingly large population of wealthy Chinese began fighting for the diminishing amount of baijiu that had not been earmarked for government use. Supply dwindled and prices skyrocketed.

The consequent political risk was twofold. As prices of baijiu soared, the government's annual liquor expenditure likewise rose to a level that became increasingly difficult to defend. And as individual bottle prices grew to hundreds or thousands of dollars, their potential to be used as bribes also dramatically increased.

Gift giving is a practice with deep roots in China. The idea is to demonstrate respect and loyalty to one's superiors or potential allies. Selection of a gift is undertaken with care, as certain objects hold symbolic meaning and an inappropriate offering invites offense. When an ancient duke once offered his king a wine that befit a lower station, war was the inevitable result.

Elanah Uretsky related the story of accompanying a group of Senate staffers to Shenyang around 2014. At an official banquet, she told one of her hosts, "It's so embarrassing that you come to the United States, and we can't do this for you. You host us—and it's so nice the way you host us—and when you come to the United States, we can't reciprocate, both because we just can't, and it's not a part of our culture."

"We get it," the official replied. "You don't have the budget to do that."

Always gifts come with an expectation of reciprocity, whether it be expanded opportunities, preferential treatment, or protection from rivals and regulators. Mayfair Yang says in *Gifts, Favors, and Banquets*, "There is a common saying that male officials, when requested to help out in a certain affair over which they have jurisdiction, are always given to declaring that the matter needs more 'study' (*yanjiu yanjiu*) on their part." In Mandarin *yanjiu* is a homonym of "cigarettes and booze," Yang explains. "The suggestion is that officials are essentially asking for an inducement to render service." If there is a practical difference between gift giving and bribery, I have yet to determine it. That said, the practice is long-standing, widespread, and culturally acceptable in China, at least up to a point.

As China's fortunes rose, so too did the appetite for extravagant gifts. Luxury goods—Rolex, Hermès, Apple, Louis Vuitton, and so on—proliferated, growing 30 percent in 2011. Baijiu, which connotes camaraderie and leisure, was always a popular gift. And with the market for premium baijiu trending ever upward, baijiu could double as an off-the-books and rapidly valuating currency. It became a symbol of decadence and abuse of station.

In a discussion with a leading baijiu CEO in 2012, I asked him to justify the $1,250 retail price of one of his products. Surely, I said, there could be little qualitative difference between this blend and a slightly less premium expression he sold for about $200. "You don't understand, Derek," he said. "I can't make this stuff fast enough. Every day I get calls from customers, asking, 'Why only 8,000 yuan? Can't you make something more expensive?' Whatever we charge, it's never enough."

Lavish banquets and gift giving fueled the growth and expansion of the premium baijiu sector. One Chinese research firm, according to Oliver Duggan in the *Telegraph*, estimated that by 2012 as much as 70 percent of industry profits came from these two sources. In early 2013 an executive interviewed by *Caixin* reporters Qu Yunxu and Wang Chen claimed that between 30 and 50 percent of all high-end baijiu production went directly to the government and military. In another unusually candid moment, a major Chinese alcohol producer confirmed to me that the government bought half of his annual stock.

All these government sales of course came at a substantial discount, further pushing up retail prices. So even as government officials were coming under increased public scrutiny for drinking expensive baijiu, distilleries had strong incentive to make more—and more expensive— products. The major state-operated, publicly listed distilleries found themselves in the uncomfortable position of rewarding shareholders at the cost of embarrassing their Party bosses. It was a political time bomb.

Within just months of Wen's announced crackdown, it became clear that the government was only paying lip service to reining in booze budgets. Moutai announced that it would raise its prices by about 20 to 30 percent. Its stock again moved almost 6.5 percent, this time in the right direction. The celebration proved premature. In November 2012 the Eighteenth Party Congress convened in Beijing to select a new national leader, tapping Vice President Xi Jinping for the job. In what was effectively his acceptance speech, Xi said that of the many problems facing the Party, corruption was foremost. Throwback propaganda posters appeared around the country announcing Xi's vision for the future, what he called the "Chinese Dream." Then down came the hammer.

"How long do you think it's going to last? Are they actually serious this time?"

"From what I hear, through this Chinese New Year and the next. Maybe longer."

It was the last conversation I had with Kenneth Macpherson, shortly before he stepped down as general manager of Shui Jing Fang in early 2013. The British businessman had overseen international spirits conglomerate Diageo's acquisition of the distillery, a deal that had taken about a decade to complete and had cost Diageo more than a half billion dollars. Under his guidance Shui Jing Fang had transitioned from a young and relatively low-profile brand into one of the most popular luxury spirits in the country, largely through clever and aggressive marketing campaigns. By mid-2012 Shui Jing Fang's shares were valued 50 percent higher than they had been in 2007, when Diageo first bought in.

What Kenneth and I had been discussing was newly anointed President Xi's antigraft campaign. In the first weeks of Xi's term, the Party announced a blanket ban on extravagant spending by government agencies.

Gone were the days of red-carpet receptions, of officials greeted by smiling hordes of children and elaborate floral wreaths. Motorcades were out, as were cushy overseas "business" trips. Officials dining together would be limited to "four dishes and a soup." Luxury purchases were off-limits, and industry sources said that the three top baijiu brands—Luzhou Laojiao, Wuliangye, and Kweichow Moutai—were expressly forbidden. Any of the outward trappings of corruption had to vanish from the public eye.

Not long after the military followed suit. Its Central Commission issued a directive banning many of the same practices with a notable addition: all banqueting and luxury goods were forbidden. Within days the stock prices of many leading baijiu brands—still nursing their wounds from the previous month's plasticizer scandal—began to tumble, and the value of Kweichow Moutai's stock dropped two billion dollars.

The anticorruption campaign extended beyond baijiu, snaring a handful of officials in the early days. I had witnessed countless disciplinary crackdowns in my time in China, most of which withered before the ink had dried on the *People's Daily* announcement of their arrival. In the five years preceding Xi's ascension, the government reprimanded 668,000 officials for corruption, but the conditions facilitating corruption remained largely unaddressed. Most reporters and academics agreed there was little reason to think this campaign would be any different—just the new boss coming in and making examples of flagrant offenders and eliminating a few rivals in the process. It would all be over in a few months.

They were wrong. We were all wrong.

At first the anticorruption campaign had a comic aspect. Stories circulated of pampered military officers forced to share hotel rooms at the National People's Congress and, worse still, bring their own toiletries. Modest buffets replaced gluttonous banquets. *People's Daily* reported some officials now smuggled baijiu to dinner in water bottles to avoid detection. The public roundly applauded, and many professionals, no longer forced to endure nightly ganbei sessions, expressed relief.

"Officials were actually happy about the reduction," *Foreign Policy's* James Palmer told me. "Now, they weren't happy about the crackdown on corruption, the losing out on money and having to try to live on something, if not quite their official salaries, much closer to their actual salaries as before. But so many people found the culture really uncomfortable and unpleasant and still had to participate in it. . . . It was work, and work that most people involved in did not enjoy."

Not everyone welcomed the change. Upscale restaurants and banquet halls were hit hard by the new policy, as were florists and tobacconists. By early 2013 retailers of luxury goods reported a 20 to 30 percent drop in sales. But their losses were nothing compared to what happened to the baijiu industry.

Deprived of their best customers, distilleries were adrift. It was not simply a question of losing half of their annual profits—to which the government orders often amounted—it was about sunk costs. Many distilleries had invested heavily in expanding their production capacity, undertaking massive construction projects that would take years to complete. The majority of these efforts had focused on increasing yields of the best, and costliest, baijius in the belief that ever-increasing retail prices would more than justify the outlay. They were left in the lurch: a glut of high-end baijiu, half-completed factories, and a broken market.

The double-digit annual growth that propelled baijiu through the century's first decade crashed. In the first half of 2013, Wuliangye's sales were down more than a quarter. The sales of other significant players like

Tuopai Shede dropped by as much as 80 percent. Kweichow Moutai's Flying Fairy, the alleged "corruption barometer," saw its sales price drop to just over a hundred dollars, less than a third of what it had been. And as Moutai's price dropped, other premium baijiu brands had no choice but to lower their prices as well.

Though he could not have known the dimensions of the impending catastrophe, Kenneth Macpherson got out at the right time. Months after his 2013 departure, international spirits conglomerate Diageo finalized a £233 million payment to obtain full control of Shui Jing Fang. At the time Diageo had tendered its bid a year earlier, the company projected 10 percent growth year on year through 2015. Instead, sales fell 79 percent in 2014. A massive new facility Diageo was building in Qionglai, a baijiu-production hub just outside of Chengdu, quietly halted construction. The project's estimated costs had been £237 million. The next year the company announced it had no plans to resume construction later. And by the end of that year Jim Rice, Macpherson's replacement, had also stepped down.

Chinese New Year 2013, the Year of the Snake, came and went. The antigraft measures remained in place. So too did they outlast the Year of the Horse and the Year of the Sheep. Industry experts began revising their estimates. Things would be back to normal in three to five years, they said, still hesitant to admit the obvious.

The longer the sting wore on the more it resembled a purge. The government had caught thousands of officials in its dragnet, some of them very high ranking. Longtime Jiannanchun chair Qiao Tianming, who had once traded shots with Bill Clinton, vanished without explanation in May 2015. Qiao briefly resurfaced at company headquarters in December of that year to sign a few documents, including his resignation. He was released on bail in early 2017 while awaiting charges for corruption and bribery.

Kweichow Moutai's deputy general manager, Tan Dinghua, left his post in early 2015. A year later the Central Commission of Discipline Inspection announced that it was investigating him. Even the *21st Century Business Herald*, which broke the plasticizer scandal in 2012, was forced to shutter its doors under allegations of extortion. By 2018 the transformation was complete. On March 11 the People's Congress abruptly announced that it had amended the constitution to remove presidential term limits. Xi Jinping's presidency was now, if he wished it, a lifetime appointment.

On the evening of April 29, 2015, a group of fourteen officials sat down for dinner in Yongzhou. At the end of the meal the total bill came to 7,707 yuan ($1,241), a staggering sum in those parts. It was never reported what happened in the interval, but one may reasonably assume that a great deal of food and drink was consumed. The only people who really knew were the thirteen survivors and an unnamed woman who died of alcohol poisoning.

It was a familiar story. Anyone who had witnessed the string of official binging deaths just a few years earlier, or the endemic baijiu sousing that caused it—which is to say, anyone in China with a pair of eyes and at least half a brain—could have predicted ganbei culture would strike again.

What set this incident apart from its predecessors was the severity of the government's response.

The provincial government fired Yongzhou's mayor and deputy Party chief for allowing it to happen under their watch. This was no small matter. Readers will be forgiven for not having heard of Yongzhou, a city in Hunan Province with more than five million inhabitants, but its mayoralty is a position of influence and responsibility. Other municipal officials lost their jobs or received official reprimands. This in a country where, not long before, alcohol poisoning was celebrated as martyrdom, where there was a line for alcohol tolerance on job applications, where investors speculated on premium baijiu that was so coveted it was impossible to separate the real from the fake. But that China had evaporated like spilled liquor from last night's banquet.

There are occasional indications that China's elites still test the boundaries. There are rumors that some wealthy businesspeople have opened underground restaurants with private chefs in their homes. Others allege that the uber-rich have moved their orgies to luxury cruise ships and far-off destinations like the Maldives—"out of the watchful eye of Mordor," as James Palmer put it.

To the extent that any of this actually happens, the outward trappings of ganbei culture are no longer visible. For many who partook in it, this has robbed the behavior of much its allure. After all, what's the point of conspicuous consumption if it is no longer conspicuous? "Developmental corruption still seems to be pretty heavily reduced," said Palmer. "It's still very hard to get shit done in business because you can no longer bribe people directly, but that has been replaced by legalized ways of doing things."

Ironically, the efforts to restore public trust in the government may have eliminated the primary mechanism by which intragovernmental players established trust among themselves. "One unintended consequence of this campaign has been bureaucratic paralysis," John Osburg, author of *Anxious Wealth: Money and Morality among China's New Rich*, told Ian Johnson in the *New York Times*. Another consequence, he notes, is that avenues that once offered social advancement have disappeared. "It used to be that ordinary people could in a sense work their way up through bribes and cultivating connections."

So did the crackdown at least achieve its initial aim of restoring public trust? It is impossible to say. The news detailing corrupt dining practices had all but vanished, but a good deal else had vanished with it.

Elanah Uretsky had planned to follow up *Occupational Hazards*, which primarily focused on HIV rates in official circles, by examining the public health dimension of official banqueting, but told me she was forced to abandon the project. "People won't talk to me about drinking anymore," she said. "It's too sensitive." If they told her anything, they would just say that the situation was much better. "They were just scared."

Palmer echoed the sentiment. "I don't think most people have taken onboard just how bad it's been. It is a complete destruction of any form of watchdog culture, civil culture. I mean just totally complete," he said. "With so many things we're in best guess territory."

The baijiu industry had grown too large too quickly, and a reckoning was inevitable. That the government used such a heavy hand suggests that its assessment of the crisis was starker than the experts had predicted.

But a moment of pause, a chance to slow down and forge a more sustainable path forward, was long overdue; the market was in dire need of a corrective.

It was not the end of baijiu's story. The nonofficial class still gathered around the table for business and holiday celebrations, and more often than not they still toasted with baijiu. It may have been off-limits for the Party of the people, but the people still partied.

By 2015 the baijiu market had stabilized, and in 2017 the industry was posting profit growth of 25 percent, compared to a mainland average of 14 percent for other industries. In April of that year, Kweichow Moutai's market capitalization had climbed to $71.5 billion on the Shanghai Stock Exchange, displacing Diageo as the single-most valuable liquor company in the world.

A few months later at the Nineteenth Party Congress, Xi Jinping met with a Guizhou Province delegation that included a baijiu manufacturer. President Xi inquired as to the distillery's retail price and was told ninety-nine yuan. "Ninety-nine yuan isn't cheap," Xi told her, indicating that price does not necessarily reflect quality.

The woman vowed to immediately lower the price.

"No, no no—that's a market question," he said, laughing. "I was just giving you my personal opinion. Follow the markets."

But producers were free to follow the market only so far. By early 2018 the retail price of Kweichow Moutai's Feitian brand—the erstwhile "corruption barometer"—reached a five-year high of around $300 a bottle. The National Development and Reform Commission summoned Moutai representatives to Beijing for a "warning meeting," and shortly thereafter the company told its retailers to cap their prices at around $220—well below the market rate.

In recent years the baijiu industry has undergone the painful transition to becoming a more traditional, unsubsidized industry. A more competitive market has emerged, one in which distilleries fight for existing customers and seek out new customers in unlikely places.

Baijiu has entered a new era. And once the hangover passes, Chinese alcohol will face its greatest challenge: the world.

PART 5

Matters of Taste

The average American, when he first approaches the Chinese table, does so in fear and trembling. Vague presentiments of ragouts or rats, mayonnaises of mice, and similar luxuries float through his mind. Nine times out of ten he leaves the table with the conviction that he has learned something, and that the almond-eyed sons of the queue are the best cooks in the world.

—*Wong Chin Foo, "Chinese Cooking" (1885)*

17 Reinventing the Flavor Wheel

On June 26, 2013, in Shanghai, I was in the Yuan Lounge, a chic bar, crimson with vaulted ceilings, wooden Qing furniture, and assorted chinoiserie. Yuan first attracted my attention for its drinks menu, which featured baijiu and huangjiu cocktails. Back then these were novelties, even in China. This was to be the staging ground for the Great Baijiu Blitz—one day, ten tasters, eighty-odd baijius.

It is impossible to grasp the breadth of the Chinese spirits category until it is laid out before you: sauce-aroma style, light-aroma style, rice-aroma style, medicine, fat and phoenix styles. Each table was a little forest of bottles—short and bulbous, tall and sleek, square, and round; glass, plastic, porcelain, and terracotta; red, gold, green, and blue, but mostly red; sorghum, rice, wheat, corn, and millet; 40 proof, 80 proof, 130 proof. The variety was endless. Once the caps had all been twisted, cracked, and otherwise prized open, the smell was strong enough to singe the hairs in nostrils ten blocks out.

Our mission was simple: sample as much as we could before our taste buds melted. I had divided the bottles into six sections, loosely organized by flavor and production method. Another table was set aside for huangjiu and mijiu. There were buckets for spitting, bread and water for palate cleansing, tasting forms and pens for scribbling notes. Yet despite the appearance of order, all was chaos.

As is often the case for my best worst ideas, a book was to blame. Somewhere along the way I had been entrusted with the task of penning the English-language's first comprehensive guide to Chinese spirits. It fell to me as much by default as merit, and I was only marginally qualified to do it. My publisher showed me a couple of guides to whiskey and asked me if I thought I could put together something similar for baijiu.

Of course, I said, because that is what I say when wholly out of my depth. Get ink on paper. Sort the details later.

My friend Grace—a no-nonsense Sichuanese woman from Ya'an—acted as my assistant, and between us we cold-called several hundred distilleries, begging for samples. Some obliged, some asked who the hell I was and why the hell they should help me, and others just hung up before I had finished introducing myself. I took what I could get and cobbled together the rest from my local supermarket and online vendors. All of it was mailed to my editor Mike in Shanghai. When I arrived at his office, he was barricaded behind a wall of baijiu.

From an invite list of about three dozen alcohol writers and bartenders in greater China, less than half RSVPed. When the doors opened at ten in the morning, only two of them showed, both wine writers and neither from Shanghai. (I later learned Hendrick's Gin was hosting a concurrent Shanghai event, thereby poaching all the local bartenders.) More filtered in as the day progressed, and occasional passersby would approach to observe, drawn no doubt by the pungent odor wafting from the bar's open French doors.

What we lacked in taster quantity, we compensated for in quality. Our evaluators represented at least five nationalities and diverse alcoholic pedigrees. Among the attendees were master of wine and sake aficionado Jeannie Cho Lee, prolific Beijing drinks writer Jim Boyce, and the editorial team of the bilingual magazine *DRiNK*, which included a mysterious character introduced as "Madame Moutai." Any way you sliced it, there were few of us and a great many bottles to get through.

The tasting was slow and methodical. I explained the stylistic differences between the various categories and set tasters free to roam the room, sipping as they liked. The liquor was spit after each sip to protect our fragile sobriety. The evaluators had clear preferences for certain brands and styles, but they were mostly just curious and excited about the spirits category with its infinite complexity. In the final tally we managed multiple sets of tasting notes for each bottle—guerrilla spirits research at its finest. And if I could turn our findings into something practical, we would have the increasingly rare satisfaction of breaking fresh ground. We would be inventing a new language.

Nothing like this had ever been attempted. I do not mean that no one had ever assembled a range of baijius to assess their relative merits—the Chinese government has done this regularly since the 1950s—but this was taking their work a step further.

The challenge was fundamentally linguistic. It was translating baijiu across cultural boundaries. I was not attempting to assign ratings or classifications but to create an original lexicon for Chinese spirits. This was inventing the wheel.

I knew then how baijiu was made and from where it came, but I lacked a proper vocabulary to describe its flavor. Having passed from baijiu skeptic to proselyte and finally to evangelist, I wanted to share what little I knew with the world and bring more converts into the fold. But this would involve addressing a primarily English-speaking audience, most of whom had never tasted a single baijiu. And baijiu is, of course, many different things.

Baijiu is a range of at least a dozen distinct types of liquor, each with a particular taste and odor. Casual Chinese drinkers recognize baijiu instantly, if not the subcategory or distillery from whence it came. If they dislike it, they might say it is too harsh or too bitter. A positive reaction most often elicits, *hen xiang*! (how fragrant!). Even industry insiders rarely get more specific than *chunhou* (rich and smooth) or *shuang* (crisp and refreshing), occasionally rhapsodizing on the mouthfeel and length of an aftertaste. More often than not it is just "how fragrant," a remarkably imprecise descriptor.

For most of baijiu's long history, this has sufficed. In premodern China the baijiu one drank was whatever the local distillers produced. A simple comment on quality, potency, and pungency was as much detail as a drinker required. In the more crowded and diverse contemporary market, consumers demand more.

Food scholar Sierra Clark told me that a similar divide has emerged between producers and consumers of bourbon whiskey in the United States. Among Kentucky distillers most talk centers around whether a whiskey is good or bad, strong or weak, and perhaps whether they detect fusel oils or other chemical compounds. But bourbon's increasingly urban national and international customer base expects more descriptive tasting notes. "Now [distillers] have to learn the flowery language of the wine folks to be able to describe their whiskies," Clark said.

In the case of baijiu, describing a brand merely as odiferous is further complicated by the fact that baijiu is categorized in the Chinese language by aroma. The government's first attempt at aroma classification came in 1952, when it named categories after four major state-run distilleries: *Lu* aroma (for **Lu**zhou Laojiao), *Mao* aroma (Kweichow **Mou**tai), *Fen* aroma (Xinghuacun **Fen**jiu), and *Feng* aroma (**Xifeng**jiu). The limitations of this system, and its favoritism, were obvious. The government replaced it in 1979, creating four primary styles of baijiu—strong aroma, light aroma, sauce aroma, and rice aroma—and a handful of minor categories, some so specific as to refer to the products of a single distillery. The names are awkward in translation and lack unity of purpose. Strong and light aroma derive meaning from relative intensity, but (soy) sauce from flavor and rice aroma from ingredients. Then there are nonsensical classifiers like *feng*, a holdover from the first system meaning "phoenix." It is difficult to fathom a mythological bird's odor.

Tasting notes and flavor profiles—the substance of Western wine and spirits appreciation—are little used or understood in China. Never will a baijiu connoisseur speak of a drink's grassiness or floral notes, nor of detecting hints of cardamom and gooseberry. It is not simply that this rubric is rarely applied, but that it is an ill-fitting garment.

The Chinese culinary tradition from which baijiu originates favors bold and pungent flavors. The Guizhou cuisine is intensely spicy and sour, served with a dazzling array of pickled vegetables. Its sauce-aroma baijiu is fermented in stone pits and distilled seven times to produce a smoky, bitter, and earthy umami mélange that perfectly accentuates the local dishes. Bordering Guizhou is Sichuan, deservedly famous for its numbing spice and bold flavors. There one tempers the heat with a sweet and fruity strong-aroma baijiu, fermented in mud pits and aged to perfection. When one consumes a spicy-sour fish hot pot with a bottle of Moutai, or boiled beef in a sizzling sea of chili oil with a carafe of Wuliangye, she gets the full flavor complement. Without baijiu the meal is like listening to your favorite album with the bass muted—a good thing rendered strange by omission.

Context cuts deep. If a drinker cannot recognize the flavors a distiller champions, success can be mistaken for failure. An exquisite strong aroma like Jiannanchun, with notes of tropical fruit, white pepper, and anise, might draw an unfavorable comparison to paint thinner to the untrained nose. A subtle northern light aroma, like Xinghuacun Fenjiu, which smells of roasted herbs, chrysanthemum, and pine, might become rocket fuel to one unaccustomed to eating sorghum noodles with black vinegar. One must train his tongue to detect the culinary similarities.

A translational disconnect is not simply a matter of conflicting aesthetic preferences but also of cultural expectations. Within the Chinese culinary context, the food preparer is expected to achieve balance, not just between drinks and dishes on the table but within the individual drinks and dishes themselves.

Every baijiu is blended, sometimes from more than a hundred unique spirits. A distillery's most prized employee is thus the master blender, who ideally achieves complexity and depth of flavor in each blend. A strong-aroma baijiu that contains distinct notes of pineapple, apple peel, licorice, and grass is the result of an elegant combination. But to the untrained Western drinker, the mixture of flavors becomes a cacophony or "like six kinds of flavors at the same time," to quote my uncle Larry.

This suggests not only that our respective cultures disagree on how to describe a flavor, but that we disagree about what makes a drink worth drinking. This disconnect is so fundamental it casts doubt on any attempt at mutual intelligibility. Yet with wine this has been done, and done well.

Since the start of its civilization China has experimented with grape wine but rarely developed a lasting fondness for it. It was not until the arrival of Western colonialists over the past three centuries that European-style wine gained a foothold in China, and only the past three decades that it became widely popular. From 1999 to 2008 the domestic wine market grew an average of 20 percent each year. In 2014 China became the single-biggest global market for red wine. When the Communist Party assumed power in 1949, China had only seven modern wineries. Now as much as 80 percent of wine sales in China come from domestic production.

This did not happen by accident. Much of the credit for the wholesale adoption of a foreign beverage can be attributed to the early attempts of wine producers and educators to adapt to Chinese consumers. Wine educators have learned over the years to adapt their tasting notes to the local audience. Instead of black currants, meadow grass, and sea salt—common wine descriptors in the West—they substitute dried plums, Chinese medicine, and bone broth. They go with what works in a Chinese context rather than try to force impractical and impracticable language from a distant culture. "Where the object of inquiry is not itself a textual product like literature, but an ephemeral one or one destroyed in the process of engagement, such as gastronomy," Sierra Clark writes in *A Liquid Spirit*, "actors must communicate their fleeting sensations through a common vocabulary and a stable discourse of value."

What I was hoping to create with my team in Shanghai was this stable discourse. Rather than compare the salty umami swell of Kweichow Moutai to vinegar-glazed cabbage, I could use dark soy sauce instead. Kiwi and pineapple have greater resonance with an English-speaking audience than dragon fruit and lychee. Worcester could serve as an approximation *doujiang*, the inimitable condiment made of fermented black soy and peppers. And rice? Well, that could remain rice. No need to overthink it.

It was an imperfect solution. Adopting Anglo-centric language to describe Chinese liquor still leaves Western connoisseurs unable to participate in meaningful discussions with their Chinese peers. Absent a universal language, we might drink the same drink but speak at cross-purposes. "A stable lexicon provides a foundation for a taste community, demarcating both belonging and standing within it," says Clark. "Those with a sensorium conditioned to the norms of the field and those able to apply the accepted vocabulary to their taste experiences are marked as qualified insiders."

But this was messy stuff. I did not need the Rosetta Stone, just a trailhead. I just wanted to get something going. Others would build on and improve what we started. And the more curious drinkers out there would in time begin incorporating the Chinese terminology—aromas and all—into their education. "Taste is a collaborative endeavor," Clark told me. "We experience something in our tongue, but how we communicate it shapes the experience of it."

So long as baijiu had a workable language, so long as it got people thinking about how the rest of the world drinks, that was enough. The details could be sorted later.

In retrospect, I cannot help but wonder whether the Shanghai endeavor rested on a false foundation. Is it really possible for a shared language to reveal objective truth about a tasting process that is necessarily intimate and subjective? A collective understanding of taste requires two things. First, there must be an intrinsic physical characteristic of the drink that can be identified by the taster. Second, one has to be able to trust that the individual tasters can be trusted to independently identify the drink's characteristics.

A baijiu's smell and taste are matters of scientific certainty. Researchers have lately identified hundreds of chemical compounds within baijiu, using a technique called gas chromatography. A team from Shanghai

Jiao Tong University and the National Engineering Research Center of Solid-State Brewing led by Yao Feng analyzed eighteen varieties of strong-aroma baijiu from the Luzhou Laojiao distillery and found that they shared more than three hundred aromatic compounds. The most prevalent chemicals the scientists identified were ethyl hexanoate and ethyl acetate, which also happen to be the leading aromatic compounds in a pineapple. Thus, we have an empirical basis for the subjective experience of pineapple candy that foreign strong-aroma baijiu drinkers often describe.

Any style of baijiu can be described by its molecular components. Ethyl acetate, which tastes of pear drops and can be found in nail polish remover, is especially abundant in the light-aroma of north China. Dank and earthy sauce-aroma style is chief among baijius in concentration of furfural, a savory chemical that resembles bran or bitter, slightly skunky beer.

Variations in the chemical makeup of a baijiu can be attributed to many things—production methods, ingredients, and, most of all, the local microclimate. In 2018 a study by scientists at China Agricultural University in Beijing noted that one of the chief bacteria responsible for light-aroma baijiu's fruitiness, lactobacillus, is not present in any of the baijiu's ingredients but in the air itself. Moreover, the amount of bacteria present in the air fluctuates depending on the season. So the taste and smell of a baijiu depends not just on how and where it is made but *when* it is made.

Yet knowing how the molecules fit together excites chemists more than palates, and it is impossible to separate the drinking experience from the drinker. Flavors are never experienced in isolation but in complex combinations.

Luckily, we possess a far more precise and reliable barometer than can be found in a modern laboratory. "The tongue is in fact a much more tuned machine than any scientific lab machine in terms of identifying the chemical compounds," says Sierra Clark, noting that many of the larger bourbon producers employ teams of highly experienced human tasters. The human tongue is not a back-up instrument; it is the best tool we have. A gas chromatograph can isolate chemical compounds, "but that is only so precise, and there are certain tastes that we can identify in our tongue that come down to only a couple of molecules."

A controlled tasting can still feel artificial insofar as it fails to reflect the actual drinking experience. We don't spit in the wild, nor do we always cleanse palates between drinks. We sip, savor, and enjoy, and, critically, we experience the effects of the alcohol. "The reactions of the chemicals suspended in the liquid spirit with the body are inseparable from the value attached to the experience," Clark writes. "While critics disregard the influence of ingestion, proclaiming the effects of alcohol to be consistent and thus irrelevant to judgment, in daily practice the experience of inebriation and the perception of value are inextricably intertwined."

Comments on the "minerality" or "subtle vegetable notes" say nothing of the joy many find in a glass of baijiu. Intoxication with baijui is a different kind of intoxication. It is exhilarating and wild. It is the all-encompassing buoyancy one finds only sweating alongside friends over a spicy hot pot. "I don't drink baijiu for its taste or smell," a Chinese friend in Chengdu once said. "I drink baijiu to see the face of god." His words are an eerie yet reassuring echo of alcohol's ancient origins in the Stone Age séance.

The subjective experience of drinking, like the production process, is also highly dependent on place. For better or worse there is no real social stigma attached to insobriety in China. Absent shame or fear of social censure, drunkenness is a different feeling. Yet to study a drink by getting drunk is itself a doomed endeavor. On both a physical and mental level—which modern science makes increasingly clear amount to the same thing—drinking baijiu taxes you. It fatigues the tongue and dulls the senses. The closer you get to knowing the thing, the further you are from being able to perceive and reflect on it.

Baijiu's truth is revealed only at a distance and can never be appreciated in an undiluted form. And that is another kind of truth. It is the Daoist truth of the Seven Sages and the Eight Immortals. It is a thing that can be known only by drinking. "The things I feel when wine possesses my soul," says Li Bai, "I will never tell to those who are not drunk."

A year after the Shanghai Baijiu Blitz, I was speaking about Chinese alcohol with a small audience in Beijing's Sanlitun neighborhood. My English-language guide to baijiu had just been published, and I was there promoting it at a friend's bookstore. When I introduce people to the intricacies of baijiu, I like to bring tasting samples. I try to have four styles of baijiu on hand: light aroma, strong aroma, sauce aroma, and rice aroma, one of each of the four primary categories established in 1979. Inevitably, the tasters will dislike at least one of them (usually the light or sauce) and enjoy at least one of the others (usually strong or rice).

To me it is irrelevant whether the baijiu wins over the room. My goal is to plant a single idea in the tasters' heads: not all baijiu is created equal. It might not seem like much, but it is the first step toward demystifying baijiu. This is especially important in a place like China, where there are so many expats with a negative impression of the drink. If they can learn to see baijiu as just another type of liquor, not some impenetrable Chinese monolith, I consider it a small victory. It is the end of a diatribe and the beginning of a conversation.

As I finished signing books in the back corner, a thirty-something American approached me. He was compact and intense, with receding hair cropped close. His name was Bill, and he was in the business of inseminating cows in Inner Mongolian and Hebei (not personally). A few years back he had run a modestly successful bar not far from where we were speaking. He told me he had enjoyed the talk, loved the tasting, and had gotten a notion in his head to open up a baijiu bar in Beijing. Not sure how seriously to take this earnest bovine impregnator, I told him I thought that he should. I would drink there. We shook hands, exchanged cards, and I thought little more of him until much later.

What interested me more at the time was what was transpiring in the room's opposite corner. After the tasting I had left the unfinished baijiu bottles sitting on a couple of high-topped tables. A crowd, mostly young and foreign, had formed around them. They held paper cups in their hands. They were drinking and toasting, laughing and smiling. I was smiling too.

A few days later I was back in Arlington, Virginia. Catherine and I had left Chengdu in late 2013, this time without definite plans to return to China. After so many years gathering friends and memories, it was more difficult leaving the second time. It felt more permanent. But what I saw in Beijing gave me heart.

Maybe the China to which I one day returned would be a place where foreigners drank baijiu unironically, and the segregated liquor store had gone the way of the Peking mule cart. And maybe, just maybe, I could one day taste my favorite Chinese liquor without having to fly halfway round the world.

That would be something.

18 Exclusion

In 1878 Paris hosted the Exposition Universelle—the World's Fair—where the great colonial powers gathered to take stock of their holdings, and the middling players jostled for room at the table. It was the Exposition Universelle where the world first saw the Statue of Liberty's face. It was where Victor Hugo argued for an international copyright law to protect writers, and where the world adopted Louis Braille's system so that the blind might read the writers' work. In Paris Alexander Graham Bell unveiled the telephone, megaphone, phonograph, and arc lamp, precursor to the filament light bulb. Other proceedings were less enlightened, such as the "negro village," a human zoo filled with four hundred inhabitants.

This was the high-water mark of colonialism, when sneering white supremacy darkened everything it touched. Not even so benign a diversion as liquor tasting was spared its condescension. This was baijiu's first documented landfall on European shores, and the response was as cordial as one might expect.

George Augustus Sala, whose irreverence made him one of Victorian England's most popular writers, related the scene in *Paris Herself Again in 1878–9*, saying, "the flavour of the Celestial 'schnick' was found by the experts to be so atrocious that, after making various wry faces and undergoing fearful qualms, they were about to pass Chinese spirits by altogether." Then one of the judges was struck by a "happy thought." If Europeans' tastes were incompatible with baijiu, then why not find someone with compatible tastes and judge by proxy. What they needed was a Chinese person, and any Chinese would do. Settling on a random passerby with whom they communicated by "pantomimic gestures," they awarded medals as follows:

> When a sample of spirits was submitted to a Celestial, and he made, while imbibing it, a hideous grimace, the sample was classed as "zero." If, on the other hand, the Chinaman's countenance assumed a dubious expression, the spirit was allowed the benefit of the doubt, and was voted worthy of "Honourable Mention," which, I may parenthetically remark, a disappointed French exhibitor lately defined to me as a distinction just a little worse than having your ears boxed, and just a little better than being kicked downstairs. When, however, the eyes of the heathen Chinee [*sic*] glistened, and he licked his lips, the [baijiu] was at once set down for a Bronze Medal; and finally, if he broke out in exclamations of delight, and passed his hand approvingly over the region of the stomach, a Silver Medal was accorded to the fortunate liqueur.

A gold medal, it seems, was unattainable within the Parisian rubric. Sala's English readers shared a knowing laugh, their place in the world reaffirmed, then settled back in their silk pajamas and forgot all about the "atrocious" Asian products before the tea had grown tepid in its China cup.

What none of them seemed to realize, and history has all but forgotten, is that the judges were not the first Europeans to quaff Chinese *schnick*. And on the far side of the world, their fellow compatriots had already developed a sincere fondness for it.

The first confirmed international baijiu craze was in the early nineteenth century. And the reason nobody seems to remember it occurred may be because those who partook of it did not call what they drank baijiu. The episode is un-Googleable, functionally invisible to today's armchair researcher.

In precolonial China, European trade was confined to a tiny enclave in Canton, modern-day Guangzhou. While docking there, foreign sailors had their first taste of a drink called *samshu*, which translates roughly to "thrice fired" in Cantonese. Initially, samshu referred to *sam ching chau*, a triple-distilled rice baijiu, but, as colonial British government analyst Frank Browne notes, the term became "loosely applied so as to include any spirit of Chinese production."

There were foreigners who pooh-poohed samshu. In 1885 chemist Charles E. Munsell wrote, "It is not agreeable to the taste of Caucasians, as it tastes and smells like spoiled Jamaican rum." And in 1912 U.S. scientist J. H. Holland wrote that samshu "possesses a peculiar pungent and disagreeable odour, which makes it unsuitable for certain purposes," leaving readers to speculate what those purposes might be. The *Times of London*'s Shanghai correspondent J. O. P. Bland also complained of samshu's "fantastic medley of stinks."

Sailing folk, though, vary little from one culture to another, and it was in their bellies that baijiu found a warm reception. In 1836 Dr. Charles Toogood Downing of the Royal College of Surgeons traveled with the British navy to China, where samshu had become so popular that the admiral of the fleet ordered officers "to guard as much as possible against the introduction of sam-shu among the crews, as it is 'found to be poison to the human frame.'"

As recounted in *The Stranger in China*, Downing believes that baijiu, though pungent, is far from dangerous. The problem was that disreputable samshu peddlers spiked their wares with insalubrious ingredients. Faced with either death and dishonor or long months of sobriety, however, British sailors made the predictable choice. They drank.

Britain's finest proved some of the most capable smugglers in the Seven Seas. They got around the prohibition by lowering a bucket on a rope over the ship's side to a waiting samshu seller on a sampan skiff. The seller collected the payment, replaced it with liquor, and sailed away. The transaction was conducted in absolute silence. Another popular technique had local "tea" salespeople board the ship to peddle their wares, secreting bladders of samshu beneath billowy gowns to literally skirt the ban. Then there was the old switcheroo, whereby sailors sneaked a few barrels of samshu aboard at port while pretending to collect ballast.

On shore leave in Canton, sailors frequented the watering holes that crowded the aptly named Hog Lane. Samshu shops were decorated in the foreign style and featured the "Christian" name of their Chinese proprietors: "Good Tom, Jack, or Jemmy." The Chinese, Downing said, "drench [sailors] with their abominable samshu, feeling no drawback from the strings of conscience; as after all, if their customers die from it, it is nothing but the death of so many Fan-quis [foreign devils], and Fan-quis without money, too, which makes them much more intolerable."

Hopped up on adulterated rotgut and moved to an "absurdly frantic" state, the sailors fell prey to pickpockets and other riffraff. But the worst bit of mischief was the work of the drunken devils themselves. Well-lubricated seamen could turn violent at the slightest provocation and turn a samshu shop inside out. Downing witnessed one such incident on Hog Lane: "One man was singing a vulgar song, but was interrupted by receiving from one of his companions a blow on the face, which was aimed at a passing Chinaman. This accident created a general uproar, in which, very quickly, both natives and foreigners were engaged, and was not terminated until many wounds and bruises were inflicted, and the drunken men laid upon the ground."

Most samshu-fueled brawls ended with scrapes and bruises, but sometimes the wounds festered. In 1839 the British government failed to punish the perpetrators of a drunken rampage in Kowloon that left one Chinese dead, and the incident became a proximate cause of the First Opium War and by extension the rise of British colonialism in the Far East.

As is often the case, war only led to more drinking and bad behavior. *Tait's Edinburgh Magazine* recounts with disgust the actions of British invaders: "Great quantities of a liquor called Samshu were found in [Zhoushan Island], and the soldiers got so completely intoxicated that they had to be carried into the ships by whole companies, and almost regiments, in a state of insensibility." After painting a grim description of the murder and pillage that followed, the writer lamented, "This is the cost at which the bauble called military glory is obtained!"

Amid the drunken chaos and against all odds, the Chinese remained gracious hosts. The Chinese imprisoned the crew of the *Kite*—shipwrecked at Zhoushan in 1840—but remained sensitive to the men's thirst. As crewman John Lee Scott wrote of their yuletide in bondage, the prisoners "prevailed on the old jailer to allow us to have some samshu, a liquor very like gin, and obtained from rice. We made a better Christmas of it than I had expected, and after our dinner we called our jailer in, and drank his health." So touched was the jailer that he brought his charges a fresh haunch of goat and allowed them "as much samshu [as] they liked."

Sober minds occasionally prevailed. Maj. Gen. Hugh Gough, commander of the expeditionary force, wrote that his men at Hong Kong maintained their dignity in the face of liquid temptation. Upon finding a cache of the "pernicious liquid," his regiment smashed the jars to pieces "without the occurrence of a single case of intoxication." It is unlikely that the villagers appreciated this rare triumph of Anglican temperance.

In more peaceful times, long after European spirits were available in China, the Royal Navy still championed baijiu's virtues. In the early 1870s Jr. Cdr. Robert Hastings Harris, who later rose to the rank of admiral, passed through Hong Kong, where a wealthy Cantonese merchant feted him and a fellow officer. As recounted in *From Naval Cadet to Admiral*, the dishes included bird's nest soup, shark's fin, duck and rat baked in oil, and a dog plate that Harris deemed "exceedingly palatable and digestible." We may infer from this that Harris was either daring diner for his times or that the Royal Navy's cuisine prepared one for the worst.

Forced to use chopsticks, the habit of which they were "of course, not expert," Harris and his comrade worked their way through sixteen courses and washed everything down with samshu. After a short break, he was informed that sixteen more courses were on the way. "This was a mild shock," he wrote, "but we faced it manfully and survived." He noted with curiosity that a Chinese woman stood behind each man, eating sunflower seeds and occasionally taking small sips of samshu from a bowl before treating their respective guests to the remainder. Harris was quick to assure readers "the behaviour of these damsels was propriety itself." Harris concludes his account thusly:

> Comparing notes with my brother officer the next day, I found that, like myself, he was none the worse for the festive Chinese banquet, or the large amount of "samshu" that had been swallowed. We concluded that it must have been very good liquor, and also drew the further moral that it is a safe and good practice not to partake of more than one beverage at a big dinner. We had certainly not expected to feel so fit after putting such a big tax upon our digestive organs, seeing that we were thoroughly "stodged" at the end of the second feed.

With samshu, we see not only a drink Europeans found appealing, but one for which drinkers would risk fatal injury, larceny, and court martial—a drink so powerful it could both start wars and bridge cultural chasms.

We are left with a seeming contradiction: the agents of colonialism were Chinese alcohol's most ardent supporters. Maybe it was because an imperial British sailor would drink anything put in front of him. Given what we know of them, this seems plausible. Perhaps it was because of all the early foreigners to indulge in Chinese spirits, these were the most immersed in Chinese culture, regardless of their station.

Somewhere along the way everything changed. The drink, and the visitors' passion for it, vanished. What replaced it was an enmity that far outshined any initial fondness. Maybe it is simply a matter of chronology. As European colonialism later became fully entrenched in the Middle Kingdom, it became easier for foreigners to dismiss the Chinese, along with their customs and products.

It is a story as old as Yellow Peril or *The Insidious Dr. Fu-Manchu*. When outsiders encountered a challenging or unfamiliar aspect of Chinese culture, they reacted with revulsion, hostility, and distrust. Rather than seek understanding, they concocted elaborate fantasies shaped to fit their worst fears.

Even as they set up their enclaves in Canton and Shanghai and elsewhere, reducing Chinese to second-class status in their own country, Western colonialists justified their actions on the pretext of bestowing civilization on savages. Never mind that the Chinese already had a civilization, one that was much older, and arguably more sophisticated, than the Europeans'. In the eyes of the West, the Han people were irreligious heathens, inscrutable villains, and, according to the widely circulated myth of the age, cannibals who delighted in the flesh of infants.

Is it any wonder then that the Western world now takes such a dim view of baijiu? Few non-Chinese have heard of it, and many of those who have despise it, just as I once had.

What gives thoughtful observers pause is an apparent disconnect. How can a drink, consumed for centuries by the world's most populous nation, become the world's best-selling liquor and yet still remain functionally invisible abroad?

If it were any good, the skeptic argues, why aren't *we* drinking it? It must be inferior—exotic, gross, perhaps even toxic—unworthy of consideration alongside the other great world spirits. Mention baijiu where China expatriates congregate, and they say much the same thing.

"I had to drink loads of it at the wedding last week. It was just *vile*."

"I've tried *all* kinds of baijiu. Never found a good one."

They call it "jet fuel," "paint stripper," and, as the *Urban Dictionary* eloquently puts it, "Pure distilled evil in liquid form." But how much of what the Western world thinks about baijiu comes from the character of the drink and how much from the character of the drinker?

"Mr. Ah Sing keeps a general grocery and provision store at No. 13 Wang street. He lavished his hospitality upon our party in the friendliest way," wrote Mark Twain in *Roughing It*, of a visit to a Chinese enclave in Virginia City, Nevada, around 1864. "He had various kinds of colored and colorless wines and brandies, with unpronounceable names, imported from China in little crockery jugs, and which he offered to us in dainty little miniature wash-basins of porcelain." Twain refused Ah Sing's offer of sausage for fear it would contain minced meat of mouse, but in drinking the "brandies" he became the first documented American to consume and favorably review baijiu. He was also one of the earliest to note something less savory: anti-Chinese prejudice.

Twain says that by the early 1870s Chinese immigrants in the region were often falsely accused and convicted of crimes committed by whites. At the time of writing he had just received news of a Chinese man who was stoned to death in San Francisco while locals passively watched. By then the number of Chinese immigrants living in the U.S. West had eclipsed a hundred thousand. In the Idaho Territory Chinese accounted for more than a quarter of the entire population. The immigrants were first attracted by the California gold rush and spurred on by the construction of the transcontinental railroad. After the final spike was driven in 1869, these communities gravitated toward the cities.

Though the Chinese were relatively peaceful and law-abiding, the white working class saw them as a threat. Many of the Chinese had fled crushing poverty, famine, and civil unrest at home—which had laid the groundwork for and been exacerbated by European colonialism—and they gladly did the same work as white laborers for lower wages. They even endured de facto ghettoization, segregated from their white peers. As thanks, they were accused of immorality and unwillingness to conform to the laws and customs of their adopted homeland.

Speaking before the U.S. Congress in 1876, San Francisco spokesperson Frank M. Pixley, described the Chinese as a "perpetual, unchanging, and unchangeable alien element . . . demoralizing and dangerous to the community within which it exists."

The laborers' fear congealed into racism. White Americans began harassing, attacking, and in many cases lynching Chinese Americans across the West Coast. The murderers were seldom tried and almost never convicted, as was the case with the 1887 massacre of thirty-four Chinese miners in Hells Canyon, Oregon. Twain believed anti-Chinese animus emanated from the lower classes of society. "Only the scum of the population do it—they and their children," he writes. "They, and naturally and consistently, the policemen and politicians, likewise, for these are the dust-licking pimps and slaves of the scum, there as well as elsewhere in America."

Lacking the linguistic ability or legal standing to defend themselves, many Chinese immigrants fled to the East Coast, Midwest, and elsewhere. Several discriminatory anti-Chinese laws appeared, culminating in the 1882 Chinese Exclusion Act, which effectively barred Chinese immigration to the United States and rendered settled Chinese Americans ineligible for citizenship. In 1892 the Geary Act extended the earlier law and added a provision requiring Chinese Americans to carry photo identification on them at all times. A decade after that Congress extended the law indefinitely.

The Chinese American population, which was estimated to have stood at over a hundred thousand in 1880, dropped to under sixty thousand by 1920. In roughly the same period, the number of Chinese employed in restaurants surged from the low hundreds to more than eleven thousand, and the number of Chinese restaurants in New York City grew from about five to more than a hundred. The Chinese Americans likewise cornered the market on laundries on both coasts.

Their move from manual labor into the service industry was motivated less by opportunity than by racist fears. American thinking regarding Chinese employment is best summed up by the 1902 pamphlet by pioneering U.S. labor activist Samuel Gompers: "Some Reasons for Chinese Exclusion: Meat Versus Rice, American Manhood Versus Asiatic Coolieism—Which Shall Survive?" As Jennifer 8. Lee explains in *The Fortune Cookie Chronicles*, "Cleaning and cooking were both women's work. They were not threatening to white laborers."

During the era of systematized Chinese exclusion from U.S. society, Chinese food nonetheless became integral to U.S. life. In the span of less than a century Chinese food grew to become one of the largest and most popular subgenres of U.S. cuisine, but always at a distance.

"The way Chinese flavors were introduced to the U.S. they didn't become American—we still refer to it as 'Chinese food'—but it is a completely American phenomenon, and the flavors are totally familiar," says food historian Ken Albala. "Everyone knows it and almost everyone loves it, but it became its own unique thing, and it became identifiable as a separate cuisine in the U.S., because the Chinese people didn't hold mainstream jobs. They didn't assimilate into the culture."

The story of U.S. Chinese food, ubiquitous yet exotic, holds the key to baijiu's international future. But, more than just a roadmap, it is also a cautionary tale. In Chinese food's U.S. journey we see how culture, taste, class, and politics conspire to shape the way we think about what we consume.

In February 1848 the *American Eagle* sailed from Canton to San Francisco. It was the first ship to transport Chinese immigrants to the United States. By the end of the next year, a local newspaper reported around three hundred Chinese congregating at a "Canton" restaurant on Jackson Street, in the heart of what would become the world's most famous Chinatown. The Cantonese—particularly those from Canton, modern-day Guangzhou, and nearby Toisan County—constituted the overwhelming majority of Chinese immigrants to the United States over the next century. They brought with them their culture, their language, their medicine (snake wine and so forth), and, notably, their food.

Soon Californians of all races sought out Chinese restaurants, then called "chow chows," drawn in by the triangular yellow silk flags flying outside their doors. In 1851 William Shaw, an English miner, wrote, "the best eating houses of San Francisco are kept by Celestials and conducted in Chinese fashion." He said the dishes were "exceedingly palatable" but cautioned readers that he was "not curious enough to enquire as to the ingredients." So since the earliest days, we see that despite Chinese food's obvious appeal to domestic diners, it was still regarded with trepidation.

For some Californians distrust of the Chinese proved too powerful to overcome. In an 1868 San Francisco magazine, Noah Brooks said of the Chinese, "Few western palates can endure even the most delicate of their dishes," while other contemporaneous writers penned diatribes against the evils of tofu. This unsavory reputation of Chinese cuisine followed the Chinese wherever they went in the United States. In 1883 The *New York Times* ran an investigative feature on the question of whether the Chinese put rats in their food.

Wong Chin Foo, a prominent Chinese American journalist—"a

stand-up, kick-ass guy who took the whites on," according to biographer Scott Seligman—offered a five hundred dollar reward to anyone that could supply evidence of the practice, but none took up his challenge. Writing for the *Brooklyn Daily Eagle* the following year, Wong said it was a "fiction" that Chinese liked to eat rats, mice, cats, and dogs: "Poor people in China, at times, will eat these, just as starving do in every land, but they are not recognized articles of diet in the great restaurants."

More than a decade later, in Louis Beck's *New York's Chinatown*, writer Lucien Adkins describes taking a friend to a chop suey house. When the dish arrives, the friend "is certain it has rats in it, for the popular superstition that the Chinese eat rats is in-bred." The friend tears the dish apart with his fork before venturing a bite. In the end he not only declares Chinese cuisine rodent-free but becomes so addicted to it he muses about whether it was laced with "dope." Even when inspected and savored, it seems, Americans were unwilling to accept that Chinese food was unadulterated.

The Chinese were hardly the only immigrant group that was, along with its food, bedeviled by prejudice. Like the Chinese, Italian immigrants in the United States lived in communities segregated from the Anglo-Saxon majority, who accused them of being unwilling to assimilate and a threat to the prevailing legal order.

In the latter half of the nineteenth century, Americans got their first taste of Italian food and responded with a panic that is nearly impossible to imagine in retrospect. Most Americans in those days believed tomatoes—so dear to Italian cooking—were unhealthy. One study claimed they were carcinogenic. Garlic was out. Americans believed overly spicy foods led to a breakdown of the nervous system, even alcoholism. The mixing of meats, grains, and vegetables in a pasta sauce would allegedly impede digestion.

The Italian kitchen was seen as unhygienic, a principal cause for the recent immigrants' lowly public standing. If only the Italian Americans would clean up their act and start eating right, it was argued in earnest, they could move out of the slums and become contributing members of society. Even as late as 1955 James Beard jumped on the dogpile. The critic whose name has become synonymous with elite food journalism famously remarked that the food found on French trains "better than all the food of Italy."

But something critical set the Chinese and the Italians apart. While the Exclusion Act diminished the Chinese population from about a hundred thousand to sixty thousand from 1880 to 1920, more than four million Italian immigrants arrived in the United States. By the twenties Italian food had carved out a clear advantage. Italian recipes began to appear in popular homemaking magazines and cookbooks. Campbell's, Heinz, and Kraft all started selling mass-produced and near-tasteless "Italian" spaghettis, and fashionable Italian restaurants popped up in urban areas around the country. Italian is now one of the most cherished cuisines in the U.S. canon, shedding its earlier connotations with poverty and embedding itself within the world of fine dining.

Chinese restaurants also proliferated by the twenties, in part due to an immigration loophole for restaurant workers and in part due to something called chop suey, a thoroughly U.S. "Chinese" dish of mixed-meat sauce over rice that first appeared around the turn of the century. But Chinese food was unable to shake its reputation as an exotic curiosity, cheap and dirty.

This was for many its chief appeal. Chinese food's affordability allowed other recent immigrants the opportunity to dine out. Many Chinese restaurants observed late hours or worked on Christian holidays, forever earning them a place in the hearts of Jewish America.

Many of my happiest early food-related memories were with my Jewish family in Kansas City at Bo Ling's restaurant. I would order the same thing every time, sweet and sour chicken with egg drop soup. In China the sweet and sour preparation is seldom neon pink and usually reserved for pork, which is no less delicious but less likely to find an audience with Semitics. The family style of serving, obligatory in the Sandhaus clan, pushed me out of my pickiness into a world of flavors I would only later appreciate.

Eventually Chinese food became a cherished mainstay not just for American Jews, but for Americans more broadly. For the gentile high society, Chinatown and its restaurants were an escapist wonderland where one went slumming. It was dirty good fun, but above all it was dirty, and this reputation has haunted it ever since.

It is much easier to craft a false narrative than to correct one. Even as Chinese American cuisine transitioned from its chop suey phase to General Tso and beyond, it has stubbornly retained a connotation of otherness and inferiority.

This is seen clearly in the mythology surrounding monosodium glutamate (MSG), a saltlike seasoning invented in 1908 by a Japanese scientist attempting to replicate the umami flavor of his wife's soup. It is an additive so delicious the Chinese call it *weijing*, literally "essence of flavor." Yet in my country it has a different reputation.

In 1968 a physician's letter to the *New England Medical Journal* alleged that MSG caused "numbness at the back of the neck, gradually radiating . . . general weakness and palpitations," a condition later dubbed "Chinese restaurant syndrome." Several subsequent letters acknowledged similar symptoms after ingesting Chinese food, and before long there was widespread anti-MSG feeling in the United States.

Many subsequent medical studies have proved that MSG is harmless, but some Chinese restaurants still feel compelled to advertise "No MSG," and many customers complain that they suffer from the syndrome. Yet in clinical trials when those same diners are served food loaded with MSG and told it contains none, they exhibit no symptoms.

This may be an example of the *nocebo* effect—the placebo effect's inverse—where suggestion of an adverse reaction results in a real reaction, and the sufferer is inclined to reject contradictory data. As Dartmouth professor Brendan Nyhan told Anna Maria Barry-Jester of *FiveThirty-Eight*, "People who felt bad after eating Chinese food in the past may have blamed MSG . . . and thus resist information they encounter later about its actual effects."

The effects of food-borne prejudice are well documented. A 2015 study on food safety violations in five major U.S. cities showed significantly higher numbers of inspections and violations for certain ethnic restaurants, with Asian and Latin American restaurants topping the list. Researchers noted that in certain instances the type and number of violations accurately predicted the ethnicity of the restaurant. The report also noted that diners trust Asian cuisine the least of any category. But they also suggested the high number of violations may be related to differences in equipment, cultural and linguistic differences, and non-Western food preparation techniques.

It is worth pausing to remember that Chinese and Latin Americans, particularly those from Mexico, are among the two oldest ethnic groups in the United States yet remain popular targets of xenophobic U.S. political rhetoric. Their food has also been part of the U.S. culinary landscape longer than most, and, as Jennifer 8. Lee argues, dishes like General Tso's chicken and the burrito are more indigenous than foreign. Yet these dishes are permanently classified as part of a foreign, *other* cuisine.

Many Eastern cooking methods, while hygienic, result in lower scores from inspectors. A negative feedback loop is formed: inspectors are predisposed to find fault with Asian chefs and penalize them for using perfectly safe techniques, which prompt follow-up visits and additional violations that run up the numbers against them.

Yet failing grades are poor predictors of danger. A 2004 study by the Centers for Disease Control and Prevention showed no correlation between food inspection scores and incidences of food poisoning. While many diners report Asian foods causing illness, it is often a case of mis-attribution. The most common food-borne illnesses—salmonella, *E. coli*, and so on—cause symptoms one to eight days after initial contact with contaminated food. Diners tend to believe their last meal made them sick, but the exposure usually occurred much earlier than they suspect. What we think and feel about what we eat, even how our body reacts to it, appears to derive in part from socially constructed ideas. And the data bears it out.

Krishnendu Ray is chair of food studies at New York University. He emigrated from India as a graduate student in 1988. Though he had little culinary experience at the time, he found cooking allowed him to bridge the space between heady intellectualism and daily life, and it also proved the most reliable way to obtain Indian food. The intersection of food and immigration became a focus of his research. Very early on he discovered that "immigrant men and women have disproportionately cooked, cleaned and picked up after Americans," but Americans have responded very differently to different immigrant groups' cuisines.

In *The Ethnic Restaurateur* Ray argues that perceptions of immigrant cooking are more deeply tied to that group's economic and social standing than to any intrinsic quality of its cooking. "Nothing devalues a cuisine more than proximity to subordinate others," he writes. "Poor, mobile people are rarely accorded cultural capital." To chart the cultural trajectory of various global cuisines, Ray examines their respective popularity, as reflected in media coverage from the *New York Times, Los Angeles Times,* and *Chicago Tribune* from the 1880s to 2010. He also assesses their prestige and social value by examining the number of times their restaurants appear and their relative prices in Michelin, Zagat, and Menupages guides. What emerges is a "hierarchy of taste," in which the economic success of a specific ethnic group, actual or perceived, is reflected in the cultural value a society places on that group's food.

Ray's study indicates that Chinese food has always been among the three most-discussed cuisines in the United States during the survey period. Its popularity dipped notably in the second half of the twentieth century but is once more on the rise. Jennifer 8. Lee notes that as of 2007 there were about forty-three thousand Chinese restaurants in the United States—more than the combined number of McDonald's, Burger King, and KFC restaurants.

Yet in terms of prestige, Chinese cuisine hovers near the bottom of Ray's index, with almost half of the surveyed restaurants in New York categorized as inexpensive. Chinese is notable among low-prestige categories for also containing a substantial number of "expensive" and "very expensive" restaurants. Its reputation straddles two poles: "fine dining" and "slumming." Overall, between 1984 and 2014 Chinese cuisine was never ranked higher than tenth (of sixteen) on Zagat's price index.

The only food more consistently popular than Chinese in New York during the same period was Italian, and its price never dropped lower than fifth-most expensive. In about a century Italian Americans, once viewed in the same light as other detested minority groups, had carved out a place for themselves. They counted among their numbers beloved athletes, musicians, actors, and politicians. They started being seen as white by the U.S. mainstream and began displaying the mainstream's racist attitudes toward nonwhites. This, Ray argues, established the distance between Italian Americans and other immigrant groups and created the impetus for elevating their cuisine.

Given this history, we might infer that it should be easiest for the cuisine of white Europeans to be most readily accorded prestige. But it's not just about race; it's about money and class: the prices of Japanese and Korean food have both jumped dramatically since the 1990s, when Japan's and South Korea's soaring economies became major international news. As the public began to associate wealth with these countries, it afforded their cuisines more cultural capital.

So the two factors that offer Chinese cuisine the chance at escaping the U.S. culinary doldrums are China's increasing economic might and the further integration of ethnic Chinese into the U.S. mainstream. The former is already a reality, and there are reasons to feel optimistic about the latter.

Chinese Americans' growth and political power was severely stunted by the Chinese Exclusion Act and subsequent discriminatory measures. The number of ethnically Chinese Americans, which surpassed a hundred thousand in the early 1880s, again reached that number only after the act's repeal in 1943, and it was not until the 1965 Immigration and Nationality Act that more than a *hundred* Chinese per year could legally enter the country. Not until the 1990s did the community's population crack a million.

Today in the United States there are an estimated 3.3 to 4.6 million ethnic Chinese, and there is evidence that a shift is already underway. "I can see a slow change emerging," Krishnendu Ray tells me at, of all places, an Italian bistro. "There are about twenty interesting, upper end of the market to upper end of the midmarket domain of Chinese restaurants. And the clientele is now young professionals with money, who are also opinion makers. . . . Eventually these economies have to move up the chain, just because someone is going to beat them on cheap labor. That's happened in China already," he says. "So the kind of people they are sending out is going to change, the poor compared to the professional, and the kind of stuff they are going to send out into the world is going to change, as more capital value-added products. Not the cheap toys, not the textiles, not the plastics, the next level."

I ask him how soon he thinks Chinese food can escape U.S. culinary purgatory.

"My sense is in the next twenty years, unless something goes seriously wrong with China," he says. "Then all bets are off."

I cannot help but think that Chinese alcohol is viewed through the same lens as its food. In the online comments for a single 2015 *New York Times* article about baijiu, the liquor was compared to jet fuel, kerosene, poison, nail polish remover, drain cleaner, Burgundy cheeses, and salty garbage water. Other readers commented that baijiu's introduction into New York City was a left-wing plot to hoodwink gullible hipsters. Some went so far as to doubt that the Chinese even liked baijiu. Comments sections are a dark corner of the internet, but the attitude was representative of most English-language writing about baijiu at the time. "I read an agenda in some comments here," concluded one reader, "informed by griefs [*sic*] which go far beyond food and drinks."

For many, baijiu is an acquired taste, but it is still indicative of a taste shared by more than a billion people. To imply that Chinese intentionally produce and consume a drink they find repellent is as absurd as it is condescending. It assumes that Chinese distillers are either inept or malevolent and that Chinese drinkers are too stubborn or stupid to try the available alternatives.

As has been noted in previous chapters, social pressure influences drinking habits in China. But it is not the primary motivator. In 2015 market research firm Mintel surveyed thousands of Chinese drinkers and less than 20 percent of them said that they drank baijiu only when they felt compelled. To my mind the opinions of the hundreds of millions of people who enjoy baijiu should not be given less weight than the opinions of their foreign peers.

This discussion is not intended to shame baijiu critics into line but to highlight the ways in which their judgment is rendered more harshly than it might be in a cultural vacuum. When I first encountered baijiu, I was as dismissive as any of the *Times'* readers and made the same sport of belittling it. I can't say I did this entirely because I was raised in the relatively homogenous U.S. Midwest, but I can't rule that possibility out.

There are also larger historical trends to consider. During the early years of Chinese immigration to the United States, many contemporaneous German and Irish immigrants established taverns, pubs, and saloons—then solidly masculine realms. Those jobs were out of reach to the Chinese, thereby barring baijiu's most obvious pathway to mainstream drinkers.

Luckily, in China alcohol is traditionally served in restaurants, and this could have served as the vector for baijiu's introduction into the United States. Indeed, for a time it seems to have been heading in that direction. An 1888 article in the *National Tribune* about restaurants in New York's Chinatown notes, "The Chinaman always takes spirits with his meals, pouring rice whisky into a tiny cup from a pewter pot." That same year in New York's *Sun*, Wong Chin Foo describes plans for a soon-to-be-opened upscale Chinese eatery: "All the heavy dishes are accompanied by wines or other distilled liquors, of which there are several very good ones." He singles out Ung Gwai Loo, an infused baijiu, "resembling our best of brandies, but having a richer if not a pleasanter taste."

Unfortunately, the exact moment that Chinese food began to gain (devalued) currency in the U.S. mainstream coincided with the rise of the U.S. temperance movement, culminating with the Prohibition from 1920 to 1933. The Chinese restaurant lost any connection to alcohol in the United States.

Yet had there never been a Chinese Exclusion Act or the anti-Chinese sentiment that spawned it, history may still not have provided a different outcome for baijiu in the United States.

Most Chinese immigrants to the United States, now and in the past, originate from the southeastern coastal region, which has always preferred lighter wines to spirits. The funkier fermented flavors associated with more complex styles of baijiu are largely absent from U.S. Chinese food. It is also unlikely that the baijiu industry—fragmented and immature until the late twentieth century—could have made significant inroads overseas at an earlier time, particularly not during the height of the Cold War. Vodka rose to prominence at this time, but the Smirnoff recipe that propelled it was smuggled out of Russia decades earlier, and baijiu exports from the People's Republic were impossible before the 1980s.

The comparison with Italian cuisine also has limitations: Americans today might enjoy Campari, but few have interest in the more traditional Italian spirit grappa, a drink with unmistakable similarities to certain styles of baijiu.

A nearer analog might be between baijiu and agave-based Mexican spirits like tequila and mescal, which, despite once-fearsome reputations, have risen to prominence in international drinking circles. My hope is that baijiu can carve out a similar path for itself.

We cannot know what might have been—repression is a story of squandered opportunities—but we may soon discover what is possible.

In a 2017 interview with *Nikkei Asian Review*, Xiamen University professor Zhuang Guotu estimates that there are already sixty million ethnic Chinese living outside of China, a number that would place it in the midtwenties on a list of most-populous nations. The group's collective wealth is an estimated $2.5 trillion. He predicts that in the next twenty years the Chinese American population will reach ten million. U.S. tastes will inevitably evolve with the country's demographics. In fact, the transition is well underway. Asian cuisine is one of the fastest-growing U.S. restaurant categories. A more sophisticated market is emerging, in which patrons can experience regional Chinese dishes, and Chinese fine dining is no longer a contradiction of terms.

"Most Americans will not think about Chinese food and drinks culture as sophisticated until the long run," says Ray. "But in the short run there will be these niches where this foodie-omnivorousness connoisseurship, knowledge of Chinese food and especially drinks, because it is so uninvestigated and uninterrogated, is going to become important. In this case in the next five years. Not commonly, not for most people, but for people who seek and find kind of a quirky knowledge about drinks. Because knowledge about these things is so rare, in the Western world at least."

One day the United States' aversion to baijiu may seem as quaint as its past aversion to garlic and tomatoes. Until that day the gospel of baijiu remains an article of faith. Those of us possessed of enough optimism to preach it must employ whatever tactics are necessary to advance the cause, no matter how distasteful the rest of the world might find it.

19 A Seat at the Bar

"This horrible drink is the delight of the Chinese, especially of those of the North, who swallow it like water," wrote missionary Évariste Huc of baijiu in *The Chinese Empire*. "One can hardly imagine what pleasure the Chinese find in imbibing these burning drinks, which are absolutely like liquid fire, and, moreover, very ill tasted." His sentiment was typical, but his methods were not.

Abbé Huc, as his readers knew him, set off from Canton in the early 1840s, about the same time the city's foreign drug peddlers kicked off the First Opium War. Huc had made a thorough study of China's languages and, to seem less alien in regions that had never encountered a white man, he adopted native dress. He traveled north to Beijing and then west across the length of China into Tibet before he returned to Canton in 1846.

Though very much a product of his times, he was uncharacteristically thoughtful and open-minded in certain respects. He also had a mischievous streak.

On the subject of the locally produced rice wine, Huc noted that, while foreigners widely distrusted it, they were "always disposed to judge *a priori* of Chinese productions," and he decided to test their conviction. He presented a few bottles of "exceptional quality" Chinese wine to an English oenophile for consideration. The man, Huc says, "not only found it excellent, but discovered that it was the produce of some celebrated vintage in Spain."

Letting the mistake stand, Huc allowed the experiment to run its course. The connoisseur served the huangjiu as a dessert wine to a number of British dinner guests, who found in it "the true flavour and *bouquet* of Spanish wines."

In laying bare Western prejudice toward Chinese alcohol, Huc hit on the greatest obstacle to its worldwide acceptance. Though no fan of Eastern libations himself, his experiment hinted at a possible path forward for baijiu. In changing the context of an exotic drink and making it appear more familiar, the inbuilt resistance to it breaks down.

This is what Nir Eyal, author of *Hooked: How to Build Habit-Forming Products*, calls the "California Roll Rule." Until the 1970s almost nobody in the United States consumed sushi. Then along came the California roll, which took an unfamiliar concept (eating raw fish) and reconstituted it with familiar parts (avocado, cucumber, sesame seeds, and crab meat). The standard nori seaweed wrap (unfamiliar) was hidden beneath a rice exterior (familiar). "The lesson of the California Roll is simple," writes Eyal on the *Nir and Far* blog, "*people don't want something truly new; they want the familiar done differently.*"

This naturally raises questions about authenticity. How much can you change a thing before it becomes something else? Again we have an instructive model in U.S. Chinese food, where for more than a hundred years restaurateurs have adapted their cuisine to suit the needs of their diners. Food and drink have never existed in a vacuum. I tend to agree with Jennifer 8. Lee, who writes in *The Fortune Cookie Chronicles*, "'Authenticity' is a concept that food snobs propagate, not one that reflects how people really cook and eat on a daily basis. Improvisation and adaptation have defined cuisine throughout history."

If baijiu is to find a Western audience, if it is to go mainstream in North

America, Europe, and elsewhere, someone has to take on the thankless task of clearing a path. The first to arrive would have not just to find an audience but to cultivate it. They would have to create a context for introducing something new into an unwelcoming environment. They would have to move from strange to strangely familiar.

This will take creativity and dedication, but conventional wisdom suggests that it can be done. And there is no shortage of interested parties vying to be first—it is just a question of which approach will work.

It was a cloudless summer's night in 2015, eighth day of the eighth month. I led a contingent across Houston Street in Manhattan. With me was a group of friends, some of whom I knew from college, others from Buenos Aires, where I lived at the time. We stopped in front of a hat shop, below which hung a hand-painted wooden sign with two Chinese characters reading, *jiu guan.* Bar.

Down an iron staircase and past the threshold was a dark narrow hall. To the right was a wall of exposed brick, to the left a long wooden bar lit by Edison bulbs and capped with a DJ's booth. Behind the bar was the most impressive assortment of baijiu I'd seen in the Western Hemisphere: not just the usual suspects but lesser-known brands— Xifengjiu, Hengshui Laobaigan, and the like—and row after row of homemade herbal infusions. This was Lumos, the United States' first full-service baijiu bar.

Head bartender Orson Salicetti was a close-talking Venezuelan with a well-groomed beard and hair pulled back in a tight ponytail. He left Caracas when he was eighteen, bouncing between Europe and the United States, studying food service and bartending before establishing himself in the New York scene. He met Lumos co-founder Qifan Li through a mutual friend, and they bonded over baijiu, which Qifan thought a novel way of presenting traditional Chinese culture to new audiences.

For Orson the challenge and potential of crafting modern cocktails with an obscure Asian liquor proved irresistible. "Baijiu is a high-proof spirit, so that is the first challenge," he had told me when Lumos first opened its doors. "You need to be familiar and comfortable with the aroma and taste to balance it in a cocktail without sacrificing them."

In a cocktail baijiu is loud and uncooperative. It refuses to play nicely with the other ingredients, shrugging off any attempt to bury its pungent flavors. It has to be cajoled into sharing the cup, where it will never play anything less than a leading role.

The first time I had a baijiu cocktail was on December 31, 2006, just a few months after I arrived in China. A couple of colleagues had invited the rest of us to a bar that offered all-you-can-drink classic cocktails on an English teacher's budget. The joke was on us: all the base liquors had been swapped out with the cheapest baijiu available. The result was revolting.

When I began playing with baijiu in Chengdu years later, I conducted my own amateur mixological experiments. Never did I achieve the intended outcome, just more disappointment and a drink down the drain.

It wasn't until I met Paul Mathew that I began to change my mind. It was in Beijing while I was still working my way around mainland China, chasing those three hundred shots. I'd just visited an erguotou factory with a notably soggy lunch, and I was in a state that Paul euphemistically recalls as "overserved." Paul is a fellow diplomatic "trailing spouse," though a far more accomplished one. He made a name for himself in the London drinks scene, and in Beijing he quickly established himself as the city's premier bartender.

In baijiu he saw untapped potential, a variety of flavors he couldn't find elsewhere in the liquid pharmacopeia. But there was a problem of audience. As a rule, foreigners avoided drinking baijiu, and the Chinese, who drank it neat, would never dream of mixing with it. In the cocktail bar neither audience could get past its respective baggage.

I had no such pretensions. When I stepped into the bar where the lanky Brit practiced his alchemy, I slapped a bottle of erguotou light-aroma baijiu and a crisp red hundred-yuan note on the bar. I told him the bill was his if he could turn the contents of the bottle into a drinkable cocktail.

Paul nodded and calmly set about his work, becoming a blur of activity.

A splash of lemon juice. A dash of syrup. Digging deep into the toolkit, he produced a fresh passion fruit. He shaved ice and rattled the shaker like a jackhammer. From above a pile of spent implements in the sink, he slid a saucer full of bright-yellow liquid across the bar and awaited my response. It was crisp and elegant with a citrus tang. Superb. He had done the seemingly impossible in taming baijiu's fire. Paul now keeps bottles of baijiu handy at both of his London cocktail bars, The Hide and Demon, Wise and Partners.

Back in New York in Lumos's cavernous back room, Salicetti recommended the Sesame Colada, an icy yellow concoction sprinkled with black sesame seeds and served in a porcelain teacup. The fruity strong-aroma base leaped from the glass, but the sesame nuttiness brought it back down to earth. Delicious, but the next creation I sampled—a silky smooth almond cocktail—was far better. Every so often Orson or his brother would appear with a tray of thimble-sized shots of infused baijiu: basil, dill, Sichuan peppercorn. As with the cocktails, the shots got better with each fresh round.

Yet I could not help but notice that, aside from the small crowd I had brought with me, the room was empty. Other patrons would occasionally come in, sit down, and pore over the menu. Only one group stayed to order drinks, and it left after a single round. We cut out after our second round, before the burlesque show began for an audience that presumably consisted of the servers and maybe the doorman.

A charitable reading would suggest that the bar was ahead of the curve, a good concept still finding its groove. A less charitable reading would have us measuring it for a coffin. Indeed, in the time since my visit the bar went under. It reopened as a restaurant in the Lower East Side in the spring of 2018 and again closed shortly thereafter.

But Lumos was only the beginning of the baijiu cocktail story in the United States. By the time the bar shuttered, there were already dozens of bars and restaurants serving baijiu cocktails throughout the United States, mostly in New York, Los Angeles, and San Francisco but also in Seattle, Portland, Boston, and elsewhere.

And in any case Lumos was not the first baijiu cocktail bar. A year before it opened, a group of entrepreneurs beat Lumos to the punch, opening the world's first baijiu-themed bar in Beijing: Capital Spirits. Bill Isler—the aforementioned bovine baby maker—was its head bartender. Two Germans, spirits entrepreneur Matthias Heger and international development worker Johannes Braun; and U.S. publics relations specialist Simon Dang were his partners. For years it remained a popular watering hole for locals and expats because it took the time to educate consumers and tailor its offerings to their tastes.

A baijiu bar later opened in Liverpool and another in Buenos Aires. From Hong Kong to Toronto, Boston to Seattle—the list of cities where one can find baijiu cocktails gets longer each year. Baijiu had started attracting international media attention as well, and not just from *People's Daily* or other Chinese publications. The *New York Times* and the *Wall Street Journal* ran stories, so did *Vogue, Playboy,* and *Bon Appétit* and popular foodie blogs like *Serious Eats* and *Eater.*

What had drawn me to Lumos that night was the celebration of the first annual World Baijiu Day, organized by Jim Boyce. Jim had attended the Shanghai Baijiu Blitz and taken up the zealot's charge. He had lined up twenty events in more than fifteen cities on three continents. The number of events has grown steadily, and at the time of this writing World Baijiu Day recently celebrated its fifth anniversary. "As with any new trend we have to exercise patience," Lumos's Salicetti told me. "It took time for people to like pisco, mezcal, cachaça [spirits] that were not popular years ago in the West and are now strong in the cocktail scene."

When I started the baijiu beat, I arrived in Chengdu hot on the heels of the multinational liquor conglomerations. In 2007 Sichuanese distilleries formed partnerships with the United Kingdom's Diageo, Sweden's Vin and Spirit (later bought out by Pernod Ricard), and France's Louis Vuitton Möet Hennessy (LVMH)—three of the world's largest spirits corporations. Of the first two efforts, led respectively by Kenneth Macpherson and Johan "Danger" Simonsson, I have already spoken. Of the third, the less said the better.

LVMH purchased a controlling stake in a second-tier distillery called Wenjun from Jiannanchun, shortly after the latter distillery went public. It had been a bargain for the French company, which had made a fortune selling cognac to the Chinese and thought it could add to the pile with baijiu. Unfortunately, baijiu is sold in hotels and restaurants, whereas Western spirits are sold in bars, nightclubs, and KTVs. There is little overlap between the two markets.

Wenjun was also in disrepair at the time of purchase. As Charlie Benson notes in *Drinks Business*, Wenjun had "never been recognised as a serious baijiu brand," and consumers opted for better-known brands at the price point. It appears LVMH had failed to predict these hurdles, and the project stalled out of the gate. An industry insider who wished to remain anonymous alleged that LVMH has mostly achieved sales of Wenjun by strong-arming Hennessy distributors into purchasing it with cognac orders. It tidied up the books and circumvents the need to find customers, but Wenjun baijiu just gathered dust in warehouses. After a decade of continually declining sales, LVMH quietly sold its stake back to Jiannanchun in 2017.

When the foreign firms got in the game, there was widely held optimism that baijiu was on the cusp of rapid expansion abroad. Their executives actively encouraged this speculation. "Yeah, sure, it's a bit challenging to some palates," Macpherson said of baijiu when we first spoke. "This thing about its taste is a bit of myth, because who liked their first Scotch, who liked their first tequila, who likes their first whatever? We've got that high-quality spirit, but it's a distinctive taste. The key thing is: Find a global spirits category that hasn't got a distinctive taste? They all do." The plan was to start with baijiu in China, he told me, but always with an aim to develop the category overseas.

This ambition was never realized. All three early players had underestimated the difficulty of breaking into a highly competitive market controlled by established state-run players. Protectionist economic policy forbade purchase of key national brands, and the government rebuffed Jack Daniel's owner Brown-Forman's attempts to purchase various baijiu distilleries in the late nineties. This effectively left foreign players to fight for the scraps when forming joint ventures. Only Diageo's Shui Jing Fang developed a foothold, and when government decree collapsed the industry in 2012, expansion was far from its mind.

More inroads were made overseas by private entrepreneurs. In 2013 Houston-based businessman Matt Trusch began selling a product called Byejoe. His approach was to address "proof, pungency, purity, and price," the alliterative hurdles he believed stood in the way of baijiu's wider acceptance. He started by importing light-aroma baijiu, which he refiltered and watered down to eighty proof (about the same as vodka). In selecting a light-aroma baijiu, Trusch believed he could create a less assertive and more mixable product for the U.S. bar scene. His product launched in Texas and Florida, and it won a handful of spirits awards in its early years on the market.

Another company employing the tweak-and-repackage model was HKB, or Hong Kong Baijiu, started by Frenchman Charles Lanthier. HKB is a strong-aroma baijiu distilled in Sichuan and touched up by an Italian grappa distiller. By the end of its first year on the market, the baijiu was sold in more than a hundred venues in the United States and Europe. (In the interest of transparency, I must note that I assisted Lanthier in finding his Sichuanese baijiu supplier.)

Other early entrants in the international baijiu market, like David Zhou's Confucius Wisdom in metropolitan Washington DC and the Lu brothers' Taizi in Christchurch, New Zealand, stand out. But the most intriguing of the bunch may be Vinn in Wilsonville, Oregon. A small craft distillery, Vinn started off with two types of mijiu made with black and brown rice, respectively, as well as a rice-based vodka and baijiu. They have since added a rice whiskey to their portfolio.

I met co-founder Michelle Ly in 2013 at the distillery's garage-turned-tasting room in Portland's Distillery Row. While we sampled her products, she shared her family's uniquely American story.

When Michelle was born, her family lived along the coast of Vietnam, just south of rice baijiu country in Guangxi Province. In the lead-up to the 1979 Sino-Vietnamese War, the government forcibly uprooted the Lys' ethnically Chinese village.

"We didn't know why we were being deported. All we know is that the whole village—like twelve hundred of us—were all pushed out," she told me. "We were given the choice of leaving with the possessions we could carry and push as they herded us along the way." Those who stayed behind could take their chances and in the end had to leave with only the clothes on their back. "I remember how any time we heard airplanes or anything, we ducked and hid."

When the Lys arrived in China, the locals asked Michelle's father, Phan, why he was so much darker than the rest of the family, and he told them he was a fisherman. This helped him get a job and make the connections necessary for his family's escape. "One person introduced him to another person; they had dinner, got him drunk on baijiu, and offered to sail him out on a fishing boat and take him out to Hong Kong." After fifty-seven days at sea, the Lys arrived in Macau and then Hong Kong, which accepted them as refugees. A short time later a church in Wilsonville sponsored the family's immigration. They were lucky. Not many families got to come over together, and much of Michelle's extended family still lives in South China.

Along this roundabout path the Ly family baijiu recipe, passed down at least seven generations, made its way to the United States. After twenty-five years in the restaurant business making "Chinese food for white people," Phan retired and began experimenting with mijiu and baijiu. His children decided to help him pursue his passion by founding a distillery in 2009. Phan wanted to call it "Five Siblings," but they talked him down to Vinn—the siblings' shared middle name, meaning infinite or eternal. Phan passed away in 2012, not long after my first conversation with Michelle, but Vinn, the United States' first homegrown baijiu distillery, has endured.

Big and small, this initial wave of businesses collectively represented the first serious attempt to market baijiu to a mainstream Western audience. Other entrepreneurs would soon join the fray. All of them saw a future for baijiu, a place for Chinese spirits on international bar shelves—between the tequila and the Jägermeister, I suspect—and have invested their time and resources to get it there a little faster.

Yet those who could most easily promote baijiu abroad—the state-owned megadistilleries—remained passive observers. They had the deepest pockets and the widest breadth of knowledge, and they could mobilize enormous resources at the snap of a finger. They also had the most to gain from baijiu's success. But to outside observers they appeared indifferent.

That was about to change.

As I walked toward the Holiday Inn, a gang of grinning, eight-foot-tall baijiu bottles barred my path. Their eyes bulged and their mouths were frozen in maniacal glee. Blocking my retreat was a battalion of green-uniformed soldiers: Red Guards, the youthful instruments of Maoist terror during the Great Proletarian Cultural Revolution. They squatted on the ground smoking cigarettes. One waved at me and offered a timid "hello." The gold characters on his armband read, "China Fine Alcohol Sales Network."

It was my worst alcohol-induced nightmare made real. It was Tangjiuhui.

Each March Chengdu shakes off its collective Chinese New Year hangover and travels to a sprawling convention center. An unlikely pairing of candy (*tang*) and alcohol (*jiu*), it is the seminal annual alcohol-industry conference (*hui*). Outside the convention hall is lunacy. The mile from the subway to the fair center is a swell of humanity pushing in both directions. To reach or escape the fair, visitors must run a gauntlet of vendors selling baijiu—real and counterfeit—from suitcases and trunks. Among the wares is a colorful assortment of bottles, some in the shape of red Communist stars; others fashioned into the shape of grenades and mortar shells. Off-key wails radiate from impromptu pay-by-the-song karaoke stations. Children eat skewered caramelized fruits and sausages, both the same fire-engine red. The crowd density is suffocating, even by China's supersized standards.

Not long before I left Chengdu, I attended my second Tangjiuhui, this time to scout baijiu suppliers for a consulting client. During a meeting with a potential supplier, the distiller cut me off and pointed to an older

Chinese woman at the next table. "Do you know who that is?" he asked me. "That's Madame Wu Xiaoping."

Wu Xiaoping is as close as anyone comes to celebrity in the baijiu world. She is a master among master blenders, and master blender is the most revered position at any distillery. The baijiu-production process depends on so many natural variables of climate and season that each batch that pours from the still has a slightly different quality. The master blender must take all the disparate parts and create a unified whole that not only balances flavor but remains true to the identity of the house brand. It is difficult work that requires an exceptional nose and palate.

Madame Wu is the talent behind Hunan's now infamous Jiuguijiu brand, LVMH's Wenjun, and Luzhou Laojiao's National Cellar 1573, the drink that made me fall in love with baijiu. The man asked if I would like to meet her, and I told him "Of course." The man got up and whispered something in her ear.

She glanced in my direction with eyes narrowed. She then picked up her chair and turned it ninety degrees to show me her backside.

The manager returned and said, "I believe Madame Wu is busy. This might not be the best time." Apparently not. There's no accounting for taste.

In another room I traded business cards with a distiller from Zhengzhou, not far from where I had met Auntie and Uncle. He was representing Du Kang, the baijiu named for sorghum wine's legendary inventor and the brand with which Uncle had plied me. I said I was looking for a baijiu that could be sold to foreigners.

"You want to sell baijiu to foreigners?" he said. A confused expression crossed his face. "But foreigners don't like baijiu." It was a sentiment I had heard countless times before and one widely held throughout China. The popular mythology envisions the westerner a pink-faced, red-haired barbarian averse to spicy foods and fragrant drinks. There is little point in attempting to sell quality Chinese products to this dim-witted outsiders, as they would be unable to recognize the drink's value and unlikely to possess the patience required to learn. The stereotype no doubt contains a kernel of truth and has been reinforced by China's large and growing expatriate population, which revels in poking fun at its host country's perceived foibles and has few kind words for baijiu.

Sell baijiu overseas? Chinese distilleries had the means and opportunity to export baijiu starting in the eighties, but few thought it worth the bother. The distilleries that did export focused exclusively on the immigrant community and Chinese businessmen. In the decades of uninterrupted growth that followed, it seemed even more pointless. By 2011, with the rise of ganbei culture and state-subsidized binging, industry sales' growth hit around 40 percent a year. Distilleries were essentially printing money. What could be gained by heading into choppy waters when it was nothing but smooth sailing at home?

But then came the plasticizer scandal and Xi Jinping's antiextravagance measures in 2012. In a matter of months the domestic market cratered, bottoming out in 2014. The industry outlook was bleak. Distilleries had to do something they had never done before: find new customers.

The old customers were *really* old. Most young adults I encountered in my time in China had no fondness for heavy drinking. If pressed, some admitted they enjoyed the occasional beer or wine, but mostly they foreswore baijiu. It was too old-fashioned, what their fathers and grandfathers drank.

China is unique among drinking nations in that alcohol consumption there generally peaks in middle age rather than early adulthood. As baijiu sousings are a mark of professional success and rank, recent college graduates tend to partake in them with far less frequency then their elders. "When the next generation comes of age, they will get used to drinking baijiu," baijiu historian Yang Chen once told me. "Before I was twenty-eight, I didn't drink baijiu, either."

A few decades ago the absence of young baijiu drinkers would not have posed an existential threat to the industry, because earlier generations were not widely exposed to foreign alternatives. In 2010 China's *Sweet Wine News* published an article titled, "Baijiu, Are You Fashionable Yet?" It cited a survey of drinkers aged twenty-five to thirty in which 95 percent of respondents said they preferred foreign spirits to baijiu. "Simply put," the author concluded, "the traditional Chinese liquor industry is getting old."

Surveys consistently show that young Chinese eschew baijiu for foreign alcoholic beverages. This generation is wealthier and more cosmopolitan than their parents. Many of the country's elite attend prestigious foreign universities, and many more are developing an appetite for U.S. and European entertainment. When they go out for a night on the town, it is not to a smoke-filled banquet hall but to the venues favored by their global peers: bars and nightclubs and, of course, karaoke parlors. They drink alcohol in the places beyond baijiu's domain.

Wealthy Chinese are also turning away from drink. In 2012 the Hurun research firm published a report on luxury consumers that indicated personal health is a leading motive behind the shift. The report noted a "clear rise" in high net-worth individuals who neither drink nor smoke. Respondents who said they did not drink rose from 19 percent in 2010 to 25 percent in 2011, an increase of more than 30 percent in a single year. And in 2016 Euromonitor noted a 3 percent drop in alcohol consumption throughout the country. This trend is significant in a hierarchical society where consumers take cues from those with more status. In the internet age popular preferences rapidly disseminate to all corners of the country. If China's elites are drawing a line between alcohol consumption and poor health, the rest of the nation cannot be far behind.

One of the few demographic groups that actually drinks more these days is women. "That women are drinking today isn't anything particularly novel. It's just society moving a step forward," wrote one young female professional in *Guangzhou Daily*. "It's also an embodiment of women's elevated position in society."

Traditional Chinese society afforded women little respect. On the Confucian social ladder, women occupy a low rung, somewhere between children and foreigners. In ancient China women were denied education, married off by their parents, and immobilized by foot binding. Save the rare instance that an empress ascended China's throne, women had no place in political and professional life. For most of the nation's history, there was no seat at the liquor table for women. They were simply there to facilitate and serve male drinkers.

There were some exceptions, especially among the aristocracy. During the Tang dynasty courtly women painted their cheeks red to give the impression of tipsiness, and the most famous beauty of the era, imperial concubine Yang Guifei, drank to great excess. William of Rubruck complained of men and women drinking together in the Yuan court, and the celebrated Song poet Li Qingzhao often wrote about her love of drinking.

Most women, however, were not afforded such freedom. Their social standing in classical China was perhaps best enunciated in an odious passage from the Confucian *Classic of Poetry*:

'Tis also fated that daughters shall be born;
Plain cotton wrappers shall by them be worn;
With broken tiles for toys the girls may play.
Of knowing right from wrong small power have they.
To furnish food and wine is woman's part,
And cause no sorrow to their parent's heart.

The People's Republic codified female emancipation, but centuries-old gender roles have proved harder to break down. Women may now drink with men, but they are outnumbered by a wide margin. Most Chinese women do not describe themselves as drinkers—only 15 percent say they regularly drink, according to Alex Yichong Li's 2011 study in *Addiction*. Women face less social pressure than men to overindulge, so they tend to drink for pleasure with like-minded peers. When they drink, most prefer low-alcohol drinks. Despite the fact that men out-drink women more than three to one in China, the U.S. Department of Agriculture estimates that women account for 40 percent of China's red wine consumption.

Baijiu, neither particularly healthy nor fashionable, is less popular with women, who consume it almost exclusively in a professional context. Women's alcohol-consumption patterns mirror what is popular in larger society, which is to say, what is international.

The slow creep of Western influence has been an enduring source of anxiety in the People's Republic. Though Western liquor accounts for only a small fraction of the contemporary mainland liquor market, its popularity is growing much faster than that of baijiu. Beer is already the most widely consumed alcoholic beverage in the country. The market research firm Mintel notes that Chinese consumers are far more likely to view grape wine and Western spirits as premium products than Chinese spirits. In the wake of the government's anticorruption campaign, lower prices have made premium baijiu more accessible to consumers in second-tier markets, which may further reinforce these perceptions. If these trends continue, baijiu could be eclipsed in a single generation.

The future of the national drink depends on the industry's willingness to adapt to the times. Baijiu producers have to find ways to attract younger and more diverse customers. To survive they may need to reposition their products for nontraditional venues—bars, clubs, and KTVs—where the Chinese drinkers of tomorrow can be found. This means breaking the long-standing taboo on using baijiu in cocktails and using baijiu in new and creative ways.

Distilleries have responded with speed. In the years since the official baijiu market collapsed, most major distilleries have begun selling lower-proof flavored baijius with packaging aimed at younger consumers. One of the most popular low-end brands in recent years is a Chongqing baijiu called Jiangxiaobai, sold in hip flasks emblazoned with a youthful cartoonish man. Ready-to-drink mixed drinks—think Smirnoff Ice and Bacardi Breezers—are also pouring out of baijiu distilleries.

In 2014 Brown-Forman—the U.S. spirits conglomerate shut out of the baijiu industry in the nineties—signed a cooperation deal with Wuliangye to create flavored drinks for nightclubs. The next year the government rescinded the foreign-capital restrictions that had blocked the company's earlier efforts. The government also began drafting more stringent quality standards to allay consumer health concerns. These are encouraging signs, but they do little to address baijiu's perception vis-à-vis international spirits.

Ironically, the best tactic Chinese distilleries can employ to fight back this foreign incursion may be to establish an overseas presence. If young Chinese prefer drinking international spirits, baijiu must carve out a place for itself in the global spirits canon. It must itself become an international drink.

In the aftermath of the baijiu industry's great reckoning, distilleries have stopped stating as fact that foreigners do not like baijiu and begun asking *how* foreigners might begin to start liking baijiu. In the past, distilleries were content to simply off-load their products to foreign importers for sale into Asian specialty stores and Chinatown markets. Now they have begun selling their products directly into mainstream foreign markets. By 2016 some of the nation's largest distilleries—Red Star, Kweichow Moutai, and Yanghe among them—hungrily eyed the Western market, and a new wave of foreign investors prepared to join the fray.

The domestic baijiu industry began to stabilize in 2015 and has made up much of the lost ground in the time since. The recovery was accomplished through a combination of price slashing, asset dumping, and increased investment in online sales channels. According to the research firm Brand Finance's *Alcoholic Beverages 2017* report, the baijiu industry accounted for almost 40 percent of total global spirits value that year. But the future course had already been set. At the time of this writing, the global baijiu movement is bounding forward, gathering ever-greater momentum. I too have been swept up in the moment.

No longer just an observer, I decided to join forces with the team behind the Capital Spirits bar in Beijing. Working with Luzhou Laojiao—the Sichuanese distillery whose drinks won me over to baijiu so many years ago—we launched our own baijiu, Ming River, aimed at the international market. Already it is sold in many parts of the United States and Europe, and plans are underway for further expansion in the coming years.

Many of the earlier baijiu brands that attempted to get into the international market tried to filter the drink to make it more palatable to Western drinkers. Our approach is slightly different. Working with input from some of New York's best bartenders, we created a unique blend of the same style of baijiu Luzhou Laojiao sells in China. The only adjustments we have made are to the packaging, using a name and a design we think better suited to a Western cocktail bar.

We also want to make the product more familiar to our audience.

When we head into a new market, I fly there ahead of time and hold classes about baijiu for bartenders and consumers, where they can learn what it is and where it comes from. Always I pour a range of drinks, not just my own, so that attendees can see the range of complex flavors that can be found in Chinese spirits. In short, we are attempting to change the context, not the drink. We are starting with the bars and restaurants, where a baijiu cocktail might provide the "strangely familiar" element.

Will it work? Can baijiu overcome centuries of prejudice and finally be embraced by the wider world? It's impossible to say at this stage.

But in a certain sense Chinese alcohol has already succeeded. Born nine thousand years ago, it was the world's first proper drink—the common ancestor from which all of our glasses are filled. It was the diversity of China and the interplay between neighboring civilizations that gave it its infinite complexity. And if not for the wine still, which may have first traveled to China with a caravan from a faraway land, there would be no baijiu at all.

Baijiu has always been an international drink. There is much of it in the liquors of the world and vice versa. Recognizing it is only a matter of perspective.

Afterword

WHY WE DRINK

ALL THAT JADE

ULRIC NIJS—*Bar-Face, Germany*

Muddle *five pieces* of **chopped celery** in a cocktail shaker. Add an *ounce* of **light-aroma baijiu**, *two-thirds of an ounce* of **Fino sherry**, *one-third of an ounce* of **Poire Williams**, *two-thirds of an ounce* of **lemon juice**, a *half ounce* of **simple syrup**, and *two dashes* of **celery bitters**. Shake over ice. Fine strain into a rocks glass and garnish with a celery knot.

Late in the first century the Han dynasty philologist Xu Shen compiled a dictionary that traced the etymologies of almost ten thousand Chinese characters. In his entry for the alcoholic beverage *jiu*, Xu suggests the character derives from another homophonous word, meaning "to accomplish." He writes, "It is the means whereby the good and evil in human nature are achieved. . . . It also means *zao* [to make] and is the means whereby good and bad fortune are made to arise."

The ancient Chinese believed that drink was a divine gift that imbued those who used it with tremendous power. In the hands of the righteous, alcohol had the ability to elevate humanity, but if abused it could bring nations to ruin. It was a cipher that illuminated a drinker's inner life.

I have come to agree with the ancients. One can learn a great deal about a place through its drinks. One can also learn much about oneself.

Years have passed since I left China, but it remains with me. I've since lived in Buenos Aires, Jerusalem, and Washington DC. Wherever I go, I find myself drawn back to China. I jump on every invitation to visit, no matter how long the commute. When I read newspapers, I always look for the latest dispatch from the Middle Kingdom.

As a Kansan I am cursed to go through life repeatedly told, "There's no place like home." In truth, there are many places like Kansas—Iowa and Nebraska come to mind—but there's nowhere else like China. I miss its cacophony, the sound of ancient values screeching against modern realities. I miss the tug and pull of insular thought and outward gazes. Most of all, I miss the long meals over a hot pot, when the room is humming and the steam fogs my glasses, when I don't know when the next toast will land and I don't care, because I know I am among friends. I miss it all.

With baijiu it is much the same. There's just nothing else like it.

My experiences with alcohol in China revealed much more about the place than I might have otherwise encountered. Once liberated from their inhibitions, my drinking companions showed me more of who they were. In sharing with me their beliefs and ambitions, they demonstrated a generosity of spirit I have rarely encountered elsewhere. You discover remarkable things at the bottom of a bottle.

I don't know whether liquor has unlocked any grand mystery of the Far East, but it has provided a lens with which to better understand life there, past and present.

And as much as alcohol is a lens, it is also a mirror. In examining my initial reaction to baijiu and how my tastes evolved, I better understand how I view the world and what I had been conditioned to believe about it. If we accept the maxim that societies are judged on the basis of how they treat their weakest among them, let me add a permutation: a society's openness must be judged on how it responds to the most inaccessible aspects of another culture. If a place can be appreciated only within a narrow comfort zone, is it truly appreciated? I have my doubts.

Of course, it's easy for me to say to this—I speak with the zeal of a convert—but I take comfort in the knowledge that I am not especially tolerant or remarkable. I suffer from the usual foibles and pretensions. If I could obtain a better understanding of China through drink, anyone can. And that's not just the booze talking.

My goal in telling this story was to present a more nuanced portrait of China. And so I remind the reader what I said at the outset: this a book about Chinese alcohol, which is to say it is a book about China. If I've done my job, my meaning should by now be clear.

The quest for understanding is a lifelong pursuit. The goal often feels elusive, and perhaps it is beyond reach. In any case I find the journey endlessly rewarding. After years of sipping and savoring baijiu, I also have come to agree with the Daoists: there is wisdom to be found in strong drink and good conversation. But wisdom may be found else-where. No alcohol is required. The point is not the drink but what the drink reveals. And the soberest of minds can comprehend anything discussed in these pages.

But if a glass of baijiu hastens the path to enlightenment, who am I to disagree with the ancients?

APPENDIX

ABOUT THE RECIPES

PAPER CRANE
DAVID PUTNEY—*Capital Spirits, Beijing*

Shake *equal parts* of **strong-aroma baijiu**, **Aperol**, **Amaro Montenegro**, and **lemon juice**. Double strain over ice.

Each of the cocktail recipes was included with the permission and cooperation of its creator. I have reformatted recipes for consistency. The specific brand of baijiu used was also replaced with its more general baijiu category, so readers with limited access to certain ingredients might more easily prepare them. All recipes requiring a strong-aroma baijiu were originally made with Ming River Sichuan Baijiu. **Runaway Horse** was prepared with Kinmen Kaoliang 58. **Elixir of Life** used Kweichow Moutai Feitian as the sauce-aroma baijiu. **All That Jade** was prepared using Xinghuacun Qinghua 20.

Runaway Horse was created by Jesse Shapell, beverage director at Win Son in Brooklyn, New York. Win Son was created by Josh Ku and Trigg Brown to highlight contemporary Taiwanese American flavors and uses the popular Taiwanese light-aroma baijiu Kinmen Kaoliang as its house pour. Shapell created Runaway Horse to kick off this book and has my eternal gratitude for it. The drink is a brambly berry riff on the Aviation cocktail. It is an excellent patio aperitif that pairs well with Win Son's marinated cucumbers and stinky tofu.

Sichuan Sour was the happy result of a Ming River cocktail development session with Shannon Mustipher, who runs the bar program at Glady's in New York. She is also the author of *Tiki: Modern Tropical Cocktails.*

Monkey Writes a Poem first appeared on the cocktail menu of Kings Co Imperial on the Lower East Side. New York–based drinks consultant Justin Lane Briggs was an early adopter of baijiu as a cocktail ingredient. This drink is named after the eponymous poem by Joshua Ip, reprinted here with the author's permission.

> oh poets and your oft-rotating heads,
> you stage your revolutions, rock and sway,
> and still return to what is known and read:
> someone's already written that, that way,
> no matter how you slant or skew the blurbs,
> scrabble to make a new thing, or adapt
> an old one, nouns are nouns and verbs are verbs—
> there are only so many rhymes for crap.
>
> old monkey's got you covered, here, behold
> my typewriter: vintage, art deco, old,
> already I've got hipster cred to start.
> now add my hundred thousand monkey minions:
> we'll bang out random doggerel by the millions
> but once each thousand keystrokes break your heart.

Elixir of Life was also crafted to appear in this book by the man who made me my first great baijiu cocktail, Paul Mathew. It is unique cocktail that combines baijiu styles, inspired by the quest of China's ancient Daoist alchemists, who sought to balance disparate elements to create a potion granting immortality. Mathew is the owner of Demon, Wise and Partners, the Arbitrager, and The Hide in London.

Yellow Drink No. 1 is the creation of Don Lee, co-owner (with David Arnold) of Existing Conditions, in Manhattan. Lee is an innovative mixologist who draws on a scientific background and a superb understanding of flavors when crafting his cocktails. In the same development session, he also perfected another Yellow Drink, two Red Drinks, and the Dr. BJ (Dr. Pepper, baijiu, and Angostura bitters).

All That Jade was created by Ulric Nijs, founder of Bar-Face drinks consultancy in Germany. Ulric has developed drinks for many of the world's leading baijiu producers, including the best sauce-aroma baijiu cocktail I have ever tried, the Nei Caifu Sour. This particular drink accentuates the grassy notes of Fenjiu-style light-aroma baijiu with celery.

Paper Crane was created by David Putney, former owner of Beijing's Capital Spirits baijiu bar. Putney has worked tirelessly for many years to promote the baijiu category broadly and baijiu cocktails specifically—he credibly claims to have poured more baijiu for China expats than any other living bartender. This recipe is a riff on Sam Ross's Paper Plane cocktail (itself a riff on the Last Word).

For additional notes on these recipes and other baijiu cocktails, please check out www.drinkbaijiu.com.

NOTES

vi "O wine, who gave to thee thy subtle power?": Herbert Giles, *Chinese Poetry in English Verse* (Shanghai: Kelly and Walsh, 1898), 81.

13 "The road to Sichuan is hard": In the original poem Li Bai refers to Sichuan by one of its ancient names, "Shu."

42 "How many great men were forgotten": Quoted in Li Zhengping, *Chinese Wine* (Cambridge: Cambridge University Press, 2011), 126.

45 "There are many monkeys in Huangshan": Quoted in H. T. Huang, *Science and Civilisation in China*, vol. 6, *Biology and Biological Technology*, pt. 5, *Fermentations and Food Science* (Cambridge: Cambridge University Press, 2000), 245.

47 "Our ancestors first planted rice": Translated from Xu Ganrong and Bao Tongfa, *Grandiose Survey of Chinese Alcoholic Drinks and Beverages*, Jiangnan University, 1998, www.sytu.edu.cn/zhgjiu/jmain.htm (site discontinued). The original Chinese versions of this wonderful resource can still be accessed using the Wayback Machine on archive.org.

49 "Of the various kinds of ceremonies": James G. Bridgman and Samuel W. Williams, eds, *Chinese Repository* 17 (1848): 175.

50 "the ruler and his three ministers": James Legge, trans., *The Sacred Books of China*, pt. 4, *The Li Ki* (Oxford: Clarendon, 1885), 242.

50 "Roast crane is next served": Quoted in H. T. Huang, *Science and Civilisation in China*, vol. 6, *Biology and Biological Technology*, pt. 5, *Fermentations and Food Science* (Cambridge: Cambridge University Press, 2000), 95.

54 "What can dispel the sorrow?": Cao Cao, "Short Song Style," *Wikisource*, last modified April 7, 2014, https://en.wikisource.org/wiki/Translation:Short_Song_Style.

54 "It's mostly just empty talk": Translated from Xu Ganrong and Bao Tongfa, *Grandiose Survey of Chinese Alcoholic Drinks and Beverages*, Jiangnan University, 1998, www.sytu.edu.cn/zhgjiu/jmain.htm (site discontinued).

54 "Yu used government; Jie used disorder": Sarah Allen, *The Heir and the Sage,* rev. ed. (Albany: State University of New York Press, 2016), 85.

54 "They were reckless, arrogant, and profligate": Translated from Liu Xiang, *Exemplary Women of Early China,* trans. Anne Behnke Kinney (New York: Columbia University Press, 2014), 136.

55 "a pool of wine and a forest of hanging meats": Translated from Xu Ganrong and Bao Tongfa, *Grandiose Survey of Chinese Alcoholic Drinks and Beverages,* Jiangnan University, 1998, www.sytu.edu.cn/zhgjiu/jmain.htm (site discontinued).

56 "beyond the power of even the sages": Quoted in James Samuelson, *The History of Drink* (London: Trübner, 1880), 20.

61 "Later generations disliked the lightness of li": Translated from Xu Ganrong and Bao Tongfa, *Grandiose Survey of Chinese Alcoholic Drinks and Beverages,* Jiangnan University, 1998, www.sytu.edu.cn/zhgjiu/jmain.htm (site discontinued).

64 "If when a guest has drunk too much": Helen Waddell, trans., *Lyrics from the Chinese* (New York: Houghton Mifflin, 1913), 26.

66 "The Heavens created Liu Ling": Translated from Xu Ganrong and Bao Tongfa, *Grandiose Survey of Chinese Alcoholic Drinks and Beverages,* Jiangnan University, 1998, www.sytu.edu.cn/zhgjiu/jmain.htm (site discontinued).

67 "He travels without wheels or tracks": Quoted in Livia Kohn, *Introducing Daoism* (New York: Routledge, 2009), 46.

67 "They laugh at one another, drunk and sober": This and subsequent Tao Yuanming excerpts are from James Robert, Hightower, trans., *The Poetry of T'ao Ch'ien* (Oxford: Clarendon, 1970).

69 "a hundred poems per gallon of wine": From Du Fu's "Eight Immortals of the Wine Glass." Translated from Peng Ding Qiu, *Quan Tangshi, Shang* (Shanghai: Shanghai Guji Chubanshe, 1986), 511.

69–70 "A cup of wine, under the flowering trees": Arthur Waley, trans., *More Translations from the Chinese* (New York: Knopf, 1919), 27.

70 "tossed in his saddle like a ship at sea": This and subsequent poet descriptions are from Du Fu's "Eight Immortals of the Wine Glass." Translated from Peng Ding Qiu, *Quan Tangshi, Shang* (Shanghai: Shanghai Guji Chubanshe, 1986), 511.

71 "Our drinking is different": Quoted in Pieter Eijkhoff, *Wine in China,* October 15, 2000, www.eykhoff.nl/Wine%20in%20China.pdf, 15.

73 "When the wise man drinks he remains wise": Quoted in Peter Kupfer, "Amber Shine and Black Dragon Pearls: The History of Chinese Wine Culture," *Sino-Platonic Papers* 278 (June 2018): 20.

75 "the color of rainwater": Quoted in Iain Gately, *Drink: A Cultural History of Alcohol* (New York: Gotham Books, 2008), 72.

76 "Spirits were not made in ancient times": Li Shizhen, *Bencao Gangmu* (Compendium of materia medica), (Nanjing, 1596). https://zh.wikisource.org/zh -hans/%E6%9C%AC%E8%8D%89%E7%B6%B1%E7%9B%AE/%E7%A9%80 %E4%B9%8B%E5%9B%9B.

77 "After acquainting myself with the burnt wine": Translated from Xu Ganrong and Bao Tongfa, *Grandiose Survey of Chinese Alcoholic Drinks and Beverages,* Jiangnan University, 1998, www.sytu.edu.cn/zhgjiu/jmain.htm (site discontinued).

77 "When the wine catches fire": Quoted in H. T. Huang, *Science and Civilisation in China,* vol. 6, *Biology and Biological Technology,* pt. 5, *Fermentations and Food Science* (Cambridge: Cambridge University Press, 2000), 206.

77 "Sweet and pungent in flavour": Quoted in H. T. Huang, *Science and Civilisation in China,* vol. 6, *Biology and Biological Technology,* pt. 5, *Fermentations and Food Science* (Cambridge: Cambridge University Press, 2000), 227.

78 "In winter they make a capital drink": William Woodville Rockhill, ed. and trans. *The Journey of William of Rubruck to the Eastern Parts of the World, 1253–55* (London: Hakluyt Society, 1900), 62.

78 "Master William of Paris": William Woodville Rockhill, ed. and trans. *The Journey of William of Rubruck to the Eastern Parts of the World, 1253–55* (London: Hakluyt Society, 1900), 208.

78 "I could not discern any difference": William Woodville Rockhill, ed. and trans. *The Journey of William of Rubruck to the Eastern Parts of the World, 1253–55* (London: Hakluyt Society, 1900), 166.

79 "The grain can be hulled and eaten": Quoted in Wayne C. Smith and Richard A. Frederiksen, eds., *Sorghum: Origin, History, Technology, and Production* (New York: Wiley and Sons, 2000), 63.

115 "He tested the properties of the hundred plants": Quoted in H. T. Huang, *Science and Civilisation in China,* vol. 6, *Biology and Biological Technology,* pt. 5, *Fermentations and Food Science* (Cambridge: Cambridge University Press, 2000), 134.

116 "By imbibing the wines and decoctions": Quoted in H. T. Huang, *Science and Civilisation in China,* vol. 6, *Biology and Biological Technology,* pt. 5, *Fermentations and Food Science* (Cambridge: Cambridge University Press, 2000), 233.

117 "The wine of rice is the best suited": Quoted in John Dudgeon, *The Beverages of the Chinese* (Tianjin: Tientsin, 1895), 21–22.

117 "Of all the medicines": Translated from Xu Ganrong and Bao Tongfa, *Grandiose Survey of Chinese Alcoholic Drinks and Beverages,* Jiangnan University, 1998, www.sytu.edu.cn/zhgjiu/jmain.htm (site discontinued).

161 "If you drink too much": This and other Hu Sihui excerpts *are* from John Dudgeon, *The Beverages of the Chinese* (Tianjin: Tientsin, 1895), 24–26.

174 **"with regards to negative news"**: *China Digital Times*, "Ministry of Truth: Less Bad Reporting on Liquor," December 19, 2012, https://chinadigitaltimes .net/2012/12/ministry-of-truth-less-bad-reporting-on-liquor.

197 **"Corruption is the biggest danger"**: Quoted in Robert Cookson, "Wen Drink Warning Hits Moutai Shares," *Financial Times*, March 27, 2012.

198 **"The Revolution is not a dinner party"**: Quoted in Chen Guidi and Wu Chuntao, *Will the Boat Sink the Water?*, trans. Zhu Hong (New York: Public Affairs, 2006), 184.

199 **"purchased with public funds"**: Translated from Li Xiaomin, "Shenzhen Shi-wei Shuji: Meiyou Gongkuan Xiaofei Maotai Bu Hui Name Gui" (Shenzhen Party secretary: If public funds weren't spent on Moutai, it wouldn't be so expensive), *Nanfang Ribao* (Southern daily), January 10, 2012.

199 **"The price of Moutai keeps soaring"**: Quoted in Song Shengxia, "Hard Drinking," *Global Times*, February 2, 2012.

253 **"traditional Chinese liquor industry"**: Quoted in *Jing Daily*, "Will Baijiu Ever Become Fashionable?," May 25, 2010, https://jingdaily.com/will-baijiu-ever -become-fashionable.

255 **"'Tis also fated that daughters shall be born"**: Clement Francis Romilly Allen, trans., *The Book of Chinese Poetry* (London: Kegan Paul, Trench, Trübner, 1891).

259 **"to accomplish"**: Adapted from Roel Sterckx, "Alcohol and Historiography in Early China," *Global Food History* 1 (2015), 13–32.

BIBLIOGRAPHY

Agence France-Presse. "Four Die in China after Drinking Toxic Alcohol." March 25, 2009.

———. "Tough Sell: Baijiu, China's Potent Tipple, Looks Abroad." *MSN Money*, June 17, 2019. https://www.msn.com/en-us/money/news/tough-sell-baijiu -chinas-potent-tipple-looks-abroad/ar-AACZtKU

Allen, Clement Francis Romilly, trans. *The Book of Chinese Poetry*. London: Kegan Paul, Trench, Trübner, 1891.

Allen, Sarah. *The Heir and the Sage*. Rev. ed. Albany: State University of New York Press, 2016.

Ang, Kristiano. "Is the World Ready for Baijiu?" *Wall Street Journal*, August 12, 2011. http://blogs.wsj.com/scene/2011/08/12/is-the-world-ready-for-baijiu.

Appelbaum, Binyamin. "Beer Drinking and What It Says about China's Economy." *New York Times*, April 23, 2011. http://economix.blogs.nytimes.com/2011/04 /23/beer-drinking-and-what-it-says-about-chinas-economy.

Aristotle. *Meteorology*. Translated by Erwin Wentworth Webster. Adelaide: University of Adelaide, 2012.

Asia Sentinel. "China Tries to Crack Down on Fake Moutai." March 29, 2012. www .asiasentinel.com/society/china-tries-to-crack-down-on-fake-moutai/.

Associated Press. "Third Chinese Official Dies from Excessive Drinking." *Guardian*, November 9, 2009.

Baker, Neal. "Diageo 'Shelves' £240M Chinese Scheme." *Drinks Business*, July 2, 2015. www.thedrinksbusiness.com/2015/07/diageo-shelves-240m-chinese-scheme.

Balazovic, Todd, and Li Aoxue. "A Growing Problem: China's Battle of the Bulge." *China Daily*, August 4, 2011.

Ball, James Dyer. *Things Chinese*. Hong Kong: Kelly and Walsh, 1903.

Barry-Jester, Anna Maria. "How MSG Got a Bad Rap: Flawed Science and Xenophobia." *FiveThirtyEight*, January 8, 2016. https://fivethirtyeight.com/features /how-msg-got-a-bad-rap-flawed-science-and-xenophobia.

Bazzano, Lydia, Gu Dongfeng, Kristi Reynolds, Wu Xiqui, Chen Chiung-Shiuan, Duan Xiufang, Chen Jing, Rachel Wildman, Michael Klag, and Jiang He. "Alcohol Consumption and Risk of Stroke among Chinese Men." *Annals of Neurology* 62, no. 6 (2007): 569–78.

Beck, Louis Joseph. *New York's Chinatown*. New York: Bohemia, 1898.

Becker, Jasper. *The Chinese*. New York: Oxford University Press, 2000.

Beech, Hannah. "China's Anti-corruption Toolkit: No Flowers, Expensive Booze or 'Empty Talk.'" *Time*, December 26, 2012.

Benitez, Mary Ann. "Mystery Wine Is 'All Fake.'" *Standard*, November 18, 2011.

Benson, Charlie. "Baijiu: Acquiring the Taste." *Drinks Business*, September 24, 2011. www.thedrinksbusiness.com/2011/09/baijiu-acquiring-the-taste.

Bishop, Bill. "Xi Jiu, a Baijiu Bet on Xi Jinping." *Sinocism*, June 3, 2012. http://sinocism.com/?p=5036.

Bittman, Mark, and Andrew Kligerman. "Why Europeans Drank Beer and Asians Drank Tea." *New York Times*, July 11, 2008. http://dinersjournal.blogs.nytimes.com/2008/07/11/why-europeans-drank-beer-and-asians-drank-tea.

Bland, John Otway Percy. *Houseboat Days in China*. London: Arnold, 1909.

Bloomberg. "Moutai Profit Growth Slows Amid Xi Austerity Push." April 17, 2013.

Booth, Robert. "Bordeaux Vintners Raise Their Glasses to China's Wine Buffs." *Guardian*, April 2, 2010.

Botsman, Rachel. *Who Can You Trust?* Penguin: New York, 2017.

Bouckley, Ben. "'Shui Jing Fang Appears to Be Broken, from the Outside': Analyst Tells Diageo Boss." *Beverage Daily*, August 1, 2014. www.beveragedaily.com/Manufacturers/Shui-Jing-Fang-seems-broken-from-the-outside-Analyst-tells-Diageo.

Boyce, Jim. "China Wine Press: Baijiu, Smugglers, China vs Britain, Wine Auctions." *Grape Wall of China*, January 15, 2012. www.grapewallofchina.com/2012/01/15/china-wine-press-baijiu-smugglers-china-vs-britain-wine-auctions.

Brand Finance. *Alcoholic Beverages 2017*. March 2017. https://brandfinance.com/images/upload/brand_finance_alcoholic_beverages_2017_locked.pdf.

Branigan, Tania. "Chinese Drink-Driving Campaign Hits Slow Lane after Tough Start." *Guardian*, May 18, 2011.

———. "Chinese Policeman's Binge-Drinking Death Highlights Danger of Ganbei Culture." *Guardian*, December 14, 2009.

———. "Chinese to Become Biggest Spenders as Record Numbers Head Overseas." *Guardian*, August 17, 2012.

———. "The Rise of Binge Drinking in China." *Guardian*, August 22, 2011.

Bridgman, Elijah Coleman, ed. *Chinese Repository* 10 (1841): 544.

Bridgman, James G., and Samuel W. Williams, eds. *Chinese Repository* 17 (1848): 175.

British Broadcasting Corporation. "China's Economic Miracle." October 24, 2012. www.bbc.co.uk/news/world-asia-china-20069627.

Brooks, Noah. "Restaurant Life in San Francisco." *Overland Monthly* 1, no. 5 (1868): 465–73.

Browne, Frank. "Samshu." *Pharmaceutical Journal* 61 (October 29, 1898): 460–61.

Burkitt, Laurie. "Awarded Abroad, China's National Liquor Takes Hit at Home." *Wall Street Journal*, March 28, 2012. http://blogs.wsj.com/chinarealtime/2012/03/28/awarded-abroad-chinas-national-liquor-takes-hit-at-home.

———. "Chinese Liquor Makers Take Hit." *Wall Street Journal*, November 21, 2012.

Burrows, Dan. "China's Diabetes Epidemic Boosts Big Pharma." *InvestorPlace*, November 6, 2012. http://investorplace.com/2012/11/chinas-diabetes-epidemic-boosts-big-pharma.

Business Wire. "Launch of New Flavors and Varieties Will Significantly Propel the Demand for Specialty Spirits through 2020, Says Technavio." April 14, 2016. www.businesswire.com/news/home/20160414005050/en/Launch-New-Flavors-Varieties-Significantly-Propel-Demand.

Cao Cao. "Short Song Style." *Wikisource*. Last modified April 7, 2014. https://en.wikisource.org/wiki/Translation:Short_Song_Style.

CapitalVue. "China Spirits Makers Face Tough Times." June 13, 2012. www.capitalvue.com/home/CE-news/inset/@10063/post/10902154 (site discontinued).

Cassel, Susie Lan. *The Chinese in America*. Walnut Creek: AltaMira, 2002.

Chang, Iris. *The Chinese in America: A Narrative History*. New York: Penguin, 2004.

Changzhang Jingli Ribao (Factory manager daily). "Sichuan Dazao 'Zhongguo Baijiu Jinsanjiao' Chengxiao Xianzhu" (Sichuan creates "Golden Triangle of Chinese Baijiu" with impressive results). October 8, 2012.

Cheng Hui G., Deng Fei, Xiong Wei, and Michael R. Phillips. "Prevalence of Alcohol Use Disorders in Mainland China: A Systematic Review." *Addiction* 110, no. 5 (2015): 761–74.

Cheng Juetang, ed. *Zhongguo Yaojiu Peifang Daquan* (A collection of Chinese medicinal alcohol recipes). 2nd. ed. Beijing: People's Military Medical, 2003.

Chen Guidi and Wu Chuntao. *Will the Boat Sink the Water?* Translated by Zhu Hong. New York: Public Affairs, 2006.

Chen Hong. "Drinking Death in 'Line of Duty.'" *China Daily*, December 15, 2009.

China Daily. "Breaking Out of the Bottle." July 20, 2014.

———. "Chinese Alcohol, Chinese Spirits." October 27, 2010.

———. "Chinese Liquor Producers Feel Hangover." July 18, 2013.

———. "Moutai Chairman Refutes Fake Liquor Reports." April 16, 2012.

———. "Urbanization Could Cost 24 Trillion Yuan." September 23, 2010.

China Digital Times. "Ministry of Truth: Less Bad Reporting on Liquor." December 19, 2012. https://chinadigitaltimes.net/2012/12/ministry-of-truth-less-bad-reporting-on-liquor.

China Economic Review. "Pouring a Big One." May 1, 2008.

China Intellectual Property. "158,400 Bottles of Fake Maotai Wine Destroyed." October 13, 2011. www.chinaipmagazine.com/en/news-show.asp?id=3702.

Chinese Phrase Book. Washington DC: United States War Department, 1943.

Chinoy, Mike. *Assignment: China; "The Week That Changed the World."* Los Angeles: University of Southern California, U.S.-China Institute, 2012. DVD.

Choi, Charles Q. "Beer Lubricated the Rise of Civilization, Study Suggests." *Live Science,* November 5, 2010. www.livescience.com/10221-beer-lubricated-rise -civilization-study-suggests.html.

Chow, Jason. "Lost in Translation: The Lingo for Tasting Wine." *Wall Street Journal,* March 20, 2013.

Clark, Sierra Burnett. "A Liquid Spirit: Materiality and Meaning in the Making of Quality American Whiskey." PhD diss., New York University, 2014.

Cochrane, Johanne, Hanhui Chen, Katherine M. Conigrave, and Wei Hao. "Alcohol Use in China." *Alcohol and Alcoholism* 38, no. 6 (2003): 537–42.

Consumer Trends: Wine, Beer and Spirits in China. Ottawa: Agriculture and Agri-food Canada, International Markets Bureau, 2010.

Cookson, Robert. "Wen Drink Warning Hits Moutai Shares." *Financial Times,* March 27, 2012.

Cooper, Arthur R. V., trans. *Li Po and Tu Fu.* New York: Penguin, 1973.

Craughwell, Thomas J. *The Rise and Fall of the Second Largest Empire in History: How Genghis Khan's Mongols Almost Conquered the World.* Beverly MA: Fair Winds, 2010.

Criswell, Colin N. *The Taipans: Hong Kong's Merchant Princes.* Oxford: Oxford University Press, 1981.

Crummy, Martin. "Top 10 Wine Consuming Countries." *Drinks Business,* April 24, 2012. www.thedrinksbusiness.com/2012/04/wine-consuming-countries-2014.

Cui Jia. "Ganbei Culture Killing Officials." *China Daily,* July 20, 2009.

Curry, Andrew. "A 9,000-Year Love Affair." *National Geographic,* February 2017.

Davidson, James Wheeler. *The Island of Formosa: Historical View from 1430 to 1900.* New York: Macmillan, 1903.

Davis, Albert Richard, ed. *The Penguin Book of Chinese Verse.* New York: Penguin, 1970.

Des Voeux, William. *My Colonial Service.* London: Murray, 1903.

Diamond, Jared M. *Guns, Germs, and Steel.* New York: Norton, 1999.

Dicke, William. "Chinese Herb Remedy Curbs Alcohol Desire." *New York Times,* November 2, 1993.

Dickie, Mure, and Jones, Adam. "LVMH Soaks Up Wenjun Stake." *Financial Times,* May 17, 2007.

Dikshith, T.S.S., and Prakash V. Diwan. *Industrial Guide to Chemical and Drug Safety.* Hoboken: Wiley and Sons, 2003.

Doolittle, Justus. *Social Life of the Chinese.* Vol. 2. New York: Harper and Brothers, 1865.

Doubek, James. "China Removes Presidential Term Limits, Enabling Xi Jinping to Rule Indefinitely." National Public Radio. March 11, 2018. www.npr.org /sections/thetwo-way/2018/03/11/592694991/china-removes-presidential -term-limits-enabling-xi-jinping-to-rule-indefinitely.

Downing, Charles Toogood. *The Stranger in China, or The Fan-Qui's Visit to the Celestial Empire, in 1836–7.* Vol. 1. Philadelphia: Lea and Blanchard, 1838.

Drinks International. "Chinese Whispers on Baijiu." August 27, 2008. http://drinksint .com/news/archivestory.php/aid/414/Chinese_whispers_on_baijiu.html.

Dudgeon, John. *The Beverages of the Chinese.* Tianjin: Tientsin, 1895.

Duggan, Oliver. "How China's 'Anti-extravagance' Laws Left Diageo's Glass Half Empty." *Telegraph,* July 31, 2014.

Duncan, Maxim. "Wine from the Gobi Desert Aims at Booming Market." Reuters, May 29, 2012. www.reuters.com/article/uk-china-desert-wine/wine-from-the -gobi-desert-aims-at-booming-market-idUSLNE84S00Q20120529.

Dylan, Abram. "The East Is Drunk: Hammered and Sickled in China." *Awl,* June 19, 2012. www.theawl.com/2012/06/the-east-is-drunk-hammered-and-sickled -in-china/.

Ebrey, Patricia Buckley, ed. *Chinese Civilization: A Sourcebook.* New York: Free Press, 1993.

ECNS. "Wine Fraud More Mature, More Profitable." November 8, 2011. www.ecns .cn/in-depth/2011/11-08/3667.shtml.

Eijkhoff, Pieter. *Wine in China.* October 15, 2000. www.eykhoff.nl/Wine%20in %20China.pdf.

Elder, Bryce. "Diageo under Spotlight over Moët Venture." *Financial Times,* July 12, 2012.

Ember, Melvin, Carol R. Ember, and Ian A. Skoggard. *Encyclopedia of Diasporas: Immigrant and Refugee Cultures around the World.* New York: Springer, 2005.

Emler, Ron. "Companies Coy over Chinese Gains." *Drinks Business,* November 4, 2011. www.thedrinksbusiness.com/2011/11/companies-coy-over-chinese-gains.

Evans, Judith. "Fiery Chinese Drink Challenges West." Agence France-Presse, October 19, 2011.

Eyal, Nir. "People Don't Want Something Truly New, They Want the Familiar Done Differently." *Nir and Far,* June 2015. www.nirandfar.com/2015/06/california -role-rule.html.

Fairbank, John King, and Merle Goldman. *China: A New History.* Cambridge: Belknap Press of Harvard University Press, 2006.

Feng Qunxing. "Zhongguoren Ai Mai Shenme Jiu? Jingdong Gongbu Baijiu Xiaoshou Bang, Wuliangye Maotai Yanghe Pai Qian San" (What kind of alcohol do Chinese love buying? Jingdong publishes baijiu sales report: Wuliangye, Moutai, and Yanghe are the top three). *Southern Metropolis Daily,* March 19, 2018.

Ferdman, Roberto A. "Asian Food: The Fastest Growing Food in the World." *Washington Post*, February 3, 2015.

Fisher, Max. "How China Stays Stable Despite 500 Protests Every Day." *Atlantic*, January 5, 2012.

Flora, Liz. "China's Millionaires Prefer Apple and Chanel as Luxury Gift Spending Rebounds." *Jing Daily*, January 18, 2016. https://jingdaily.com/chinas -millionaires-prefer-apple-and-chanel-as-luxury-gift-spending-rebounds.

Ford, Peter. "China's Challenge with Corruption." *Christian Science Monitor*, November 23, 2012.

Foster, Charles A. "A Visit to Nanking, China." *Science and Industry* 5, no. 8 (1900): 425–27.

Fu Jianwei. *Intoxicated in the Land of Wine*. Translated by Orientaltrans. Beijing: China Publishing Group, 2009.

Fuyumi Takeuchi. "Luxury Chinese Spirits Maker Recovering from 2012 Pummeling." *Nikkei Asian Review*, October 5, 2014.

Gaber, Cynthia. "Snake Oil Salesmen Were on to Something." *Scientific American*, November 1, 2007.

Gao Qihui. "90% of Hubei Civil Servants Have Medical Conditions." *China Daily*, November 14, 2011.

Gargan, Edward A. "China's Heady and Heralded Yellow Wine from Shaoxing." *New York Times*, August 31, 1988.

Gately, Iain. *Drink: A Cultural History of Alcohol*. New York: Gotham Books, 2008.

Gifford, Rob. *China Road: A Journey into the Future of a Rising Power*. New York: Random House, 2007.

Giles, Herbert A. *Chinese Poetry in English Verse*. Shanghai: Kelly and Walsh, 1898.

———. *A History of Chinese Literature*. New York: Grove, 1923.

Glaser, Gabrielle. "The Irrationality of Alcoholics Anonymous." *Atlantic*, April 2015.

Global Times. "Big Fat Deal." April 4, 2016.

———. "Fake Wine Stuns Nation, Six Wrongdoers Detained." December 27, 2010.

———. "Maotai's Lower US Prices Irk Some." January 7, 2011.

———. "Officials Gorge Themselves on the Public Purse." November 15, 2011.

———. "Plasticizer Scandals Dull French Cognac Luster." March 3, 2012.

———. "When Moutai Met the World." April 26, 2011.

Godoy, Maria. "Lo Mein Loophole: How U.S. Immigration Law Fueled a Chinese Restaurant Boom." National Public Radio. February 22, 2016. www .npr.org/sections/thesalt/2016/02/22/467113401/lo-mein-loophole-how -u-s-immigration-law-fueled-a-chinese-restaurant-boom.

———. "Why Hunting Down 'Authentic Ethnic Food' Is a Loaded Proposition." National Public Radio. April 9, 2016. www.npr.org/sections/thesalt/2016/04/09 /472568085/why-hunting-down-authentic-ethnic-food-is-a-loaded-proposition.

Goh, Meow Hui. *Sight and Sound: Poetry and Courtier Culture in the Yongming Era.* Stanford: Stanford University Press, 2010.

Guangzhou Daily. "Nuren He Jiu" (Women drink alcohol). July 17, 2008.

Hancock, Tom. "Beijing Presses World's Most Valuable Liquor Company on Prices." *Financial Times,* February 17, 2018.

———. "China's Moutai Overtakes Diageo to Become Most-Valuable Liquor Company." *Financial Times,* April 9, 2017.

———. "Desk Time, Poor Diet and Drink Weigh on China's Civil Servants." *Financial Times,* March 14, 2017.

Hanson, David J. *Preventing Alcohol Abuse: Alcohol, Culture, and Control.* Westport: Praeger, 1995.

Harris, Kimberly J., Kevin S. Murphy, Robin B. DiPietro, and Gretchen L. Rivera. "Food Safety Inspections Results: A Comparison of Ethnic-Operated Restaurants to Non-ethnic-Operated Restaurants." *International Journal of Hospitality Management* 46 (April 2015): 190–99.

Harris, Sir Robert Hastings. *From Naval Cadet to Admiral.* New York: Cassell, 1913.

Hayden, Brian. "The Proof Is in the Pudding: Feasting and the Origins of Domestication." *Current Anthropology* 50 (October 2009): 597–601, 708–9.

Hazelwood, Lucie A., Jean-Marc Daran, Antonius J. A. van Maris, Jack T. Pronk, and J. Richard Dickinson. "The Ehrlich Pathway for Fusel Alcohol Production: A Century of Research on *Saccharomyces cerevisiae* Metabolism." *Applied and Environmental Microbiology* 74, no. 8 (2008): 2259–66.

Heath, Nicholas. "Chinese Mayor Sacked after Official Dies from Alcohol Poisoning." Reuters, June 27, 2015. www.reuters.com/article/us-china-corruption -hunan-idUSKBN0P707S20150627.

He Chunmei. "Message in a Bottle for Spirits Maker Moutai." *ChinaFile,* May 18, 2012. www.chinafile.com/reporting-opinion/caixin-media/message-bottle -spirits-maker-moutai.

Hermoso, Jose Luis. *China.* London: IWSR, 2011.

Hightower, James Robert, trans. *The Poetry of T'ao Ch'ien.* Oxford: Clarendon, 1970.

Ho, Soleil. "Craving the Other." *Bitch,* February 18, 2016. www.bitchmedia.org /article/craving-the-other-0.

Holland, J. H. *The Bulletin of Miscellaneous Information.* London: Darling and Son, 1912.

Hopkins, Katy. "International Students Continue to Flock to U.S. Colleges, Grad Schools." *U.S. News and World Report,* November 12, 2012.

Hori, Hisako, Wataru Fujii, Yutaka Hatanaka, and Yoshihide Suwa. "Effects of Fusel Oil on Animal Hangover Models." *Alcoholism: Clinical and Experimental Research* 27, S1 (2003): 37S–41S.

Hornsey, Ian Spencer. *A History of Beer and Brewing.* Cornwall: Royal Society of Chemistry, 2003.

Huang, H. T. *Science and Civilisation in China.* Vol. 6, *Biology and Biological Technology.* Pt. 5, *Fermentations and Food Science.* Cambridge: Cambridge University Press, 2000.

Huang, Michelle. "International and China Retail Market Trends." Presentation at Asian Wine and Spirits: The Silk Route First Conference and Competition, Beijing, October 10, 2016.

Huang Faxin, David Tiande Cai, and Wai-Kit Nip. "Chinese Wines: Jiu." In *Handbook of Food Science, Technology, and Engineering,* vol. 4, edited by Y. H. Hui, 1–52. New York: Taylor and Francis, 2005.

Huang Shusheng. *Lun Jiu* (On alcohol). Beijing: Zhongguo Shidai Jingji Chuban She, 2012.

Huang Zhiling. "Expo of Chinese Liquor Golden Triangle Held in Luzhou." *China Daily,* March 26, 2012.

———. "Steering Alcoholics on the Road to Recovery." *China Daily,* July 7, 2010.

Huc, Évariste Régis. *The Chinese Empire.* London: Longman, Brown, Green, Longmans, and Roberts, 1859.

Hu Haiyan. "Raising Their Spirits." *China Daily,* September 30, 2011.

Hurun Report. "Top Ten Gifts for the Chinese Luxury Consumer 2012." January 11, 2012.

INSEAD. "Sichuan Wenjun Spirits Sales Company's Allan Hong on LVMH's Entry into the Chinese Liquor Market." YouTube video, 5:45. Posted August 26, 2012. www.youtube.com/watch?v=6oPp42Gpahw.

International Herald Tribune. "Holding Up Half the Sky." March 6, 2012.

Ip, Joshua. *Sonnets from the Singlish.* Singapore: Math Paper, 2012.

Ives, Mike. "China: A Domestic Wine Industry Starts to Take Root." *Los Angeles Times,* January 15, 2012.

The IWSR Baijiu Report. London: IWSR, 2011.

Jacobs, Andrew. "Elite in China Face Austerity under Xi's Rule." *New York Times,* March 27, 2013.

———. "Maotai Journal." *New York Times,* February 13, 2011.

Jenkins, Lucy. "Millennials 'New Hope' for Baijiu Market." *Drinks Business,* April 1, 2016. www.thedrinksbusiness.com/2016/04/millennials-new-hope-for-baijiu-market.

Jia Huajie. "Jiannanchun Dongshizhang Qiao Tianming Qubao Houshen" (Jiannanchun chairman Qiao Tianming on bail pending trial). *Caixin,* January 17, 2017. http://companies.caixin.com/2017-01-17/101044747.html.

———. "Jiannanchun Dongshizhang Qiao Tianming Shilian" (Jiannanchun chairman Qiao Tianming missing). *Caixin,* March 1, 2016. http://companies.caixin.com/2016-03-01/100914498.html.

Jing Daily. "Baijiu's Boom Times Continue as 1930s Vintage Sells for $409,000 in Beijing." July 1, 2011. https://jingdaily.com/baijius-boom-times-continue-as-1930s-vintage-sells-for-409000-in-beijing/.

————. "China's Booze Collectors to Duke It Out for $160K Vintage Moutai." May 30, 2012. https://jingdaily.com/chinas-wealthy-collectors-to-fight-for-vintage-moutai-in-beijing.

————. "Cognac Demand Surges in China, but Whisky Makers Won't Go Down Easily." February 21, 2012. https://jingdaily.com/cognac-demand-surges-in-china-but-whisky-makers-wont-go-down-easy.

————. "Ganbei! Demand for High-End Spirits Buoys Chinese Producers." October 30, 2012. https://jingdaily.com/ganbei-demand-for-high-end-spirits-buoys-chinese-producers.

————. "More Bad News for Baijiu as Bottle Prices Drop." May 3, 2013. https://jingdaily.com/more-bad-news-for-baijiu-as-bottle-prices-drop.

————. "More Chinese Drinkers Turning to Imported Spirits, but Baijiu Still King." May 4, 2012. https://jingdaily.com/chinese-drinkers-turning-to-imported-spirits-but-baijiu-still-king.

————. "Will Baijiu Ever Become Fashionable?" May 25, 2010. https://jingdaily.com/will-baijiu-ever-become-fashionable.

Jinrong Jie (China finance world). "Jingdong Jia Maotai Shijian Fajiao Maotai Yi Zanting Dui Jingdong Ziying Gonghuo" (Jingdong fake Moutai incident ferments, Moutai suspends supply to Jingdong). May 25, 2018. http://money.jrj.com.cn/2018/05/25081524588924.shtml.

Jin Xiaoyan. "Jiannanchun Zaidu Zhangduo Wenjun Jiu Zhong Duo Gaoduan Shichang Shengsuan?" (Jiannanchun once more Helming Wenjun Jiu: What are its chances of recapturing the high-end market?) *Huaxia Shibao*, January 20, 2017. http://finance.sina.com.cn/roll/2017-01-20/doc-ifxzunxf1629281.shtml.

Johnson, Ian. "Q. and A.: John Osburg on the Angst Found among China's Newly Rich." *New York Times*, December 16, 2014. https://sinosphere.blogs.nytimes.com/2014/12/16/q-and-a-john-osburg-on-the-angst-found-among-chinas-newly-rich.

Jourdan, Adam. "China Gift Crackdown Hits Watches, Booze but Foreign Brands Hold On." Reuters, January 15, 2013. www.reuters.com/article/china-luxury-gifts/china-gift-crackdown-hits-watches-booze-but-foreign-brands-hold-on-idUSL4N0AK2B820130115.

Just-drinks. "China: Moët Hennessy Takes Control of Wen Jun Distillery." May 17, 2007. www.just-drinks.com/news/mo%C3%ABt-hennessy-takes-control-of-wen-jun-distillery_id90320.aspx.

Kan, Michael. "Did a Thirst for Beer Spark Civilization?" *Independent*, January 15, 2010.

Keeling, Tommy. *The IWSR Baijiu Report*. London: IWSR, 2016.

Knapp, Ronald G. *China's Old Dwellings*. Honolulu: University of Hawai'i Press, 2000.

Kohler, Heinz. *Caution: Snake Oil!* Minneapolis: Mill City, 2010.

Kohn, Livia. *Introducing Daoism*. New York: Routledge, 2009.

Kuo, Lily. "China Just Seized $14.5 Billion from Almost Everyone Close to Its Ex-security Chief." *Quartz*, March 31, 2014. http://qz.com/193646/china-just-seized-14-billion-from-almost-everyone-close-to-chinas-ex-security-chief.

Kupfer, Peter. "Amber Shine and Black Dragon Pearls: The History of Chinese Wine Culture." *Sino-Platonic Papers* 278 (June 2018): 1–47.

Lee, Jennifer 8. *The Fortune Cookie Chronicles*. New York: Twelve, 2009.

Legge, James, trans. *The Sacred Books of China*. Pt. 4, *The Li Ki*. Oxford: Clarendon, 1885.

Lendler, Ian. *Alcoholica Esoterica*. New York: Penguin, 2005.

Liao Yuqun. *Traditional Chinese Medicine*. Singapore: Cambridge University Press, 2010.

Li Er. "Zhiming Weiji: Jiugui Jiu Su Hua Ji Chaobiao 260%." (Deadly crisis: Jiugui Jiu plasticizer levels exceed the norm by 260%.) *21st Century Business Herald*, November 19, 2012. www.21cbh.com/HTML/2012-11-19/4NNTQxXzU2NTA4Ng.html (site discontinued).

Life Times. "More than Just Sulphates: China's Counterfeit Wine Pandemic." Translated by eChinacities.com. November 25, 2011. www.echinacities.com/china-media/more-than-just-sulphates-china-s-counterfeit-wine-pandemic.html.

Lin, Liza, and Yang Yuling. "China's Luxury Liquor Wants to Go Mass Market." *Bloomberg*, April 8, 2015.

Li Shizhen. *Bencao Gangmu* (Compendium of materia medica). Nanjing, 1596. https://zh.wikisource.org/zh-hans/%E6%9C%AC%E8%8D%89%E7%B6%B1%E7%9B%AE/%E7%A9%80%E4%B9%8B%E5%9B%9B.

Liu, Cecily, and Zhang Haizhou. "Toast of the Town." *China Daily European Weekly*, June 1, 2012.

Liu Jie. "Drinking to the Spirit of Globalization." *China Daily*, June 4, 2012.

Liu Li and Che Li. "Suhuaji Cheng Baijiu Ye Qianguize Zhuanjia Huyu Buyao Mixin Gaoduan Jiu" (Plasticizer becomes the unwritten rule of the baijiu industry: Experts warn against blind trust in high-end alcohol). *Zhongguo Guangbo Wang* (China radio network), November 27, 2012.

Liu Xiang. *Exemplary Women of Early China*. Translated by Anne Behnke Kinney. New York: Columbia University Press, 2014.

Li Xiang and Zhang Han. "Liquor Purchase Case Points to Culture of Corporate Corruption." *Global Times*, April 27, 2011.

Li Xiaobing, ed. *China at War: An Encyclopedia*. Santa Barbara: ABC-CLIO, 2012.

Li Xiaomin. "Shenzhen Shiwei Shuji: Meiyou Gongkuan Xiaofei Maotai Bu Hui Name Gui." (Shenzhen Party secretary: If public funds weren't spent on Moutai, it wouldn't be so expensive). *Nanfang Ribao* (Southern daily), January 10, 2012.

Li Yichong, Alex, Yong Jiang, Mei Zhang, Peng Yin, Fan Wu, and Wenhua Zhao. "Drinking Behaviours among Men and Women in China: The 2007 China Chronic Disease and Risk Factor Surveillance." *Addiction* 106, no. 11 (2011): 1946–56.

Li Yuyang. "Changsha 10 Tian 103 Ren Jiujing Zongdu Changjia Qijiang Yinjiu You-zhuo Dian" (Ten days, 103 alcohol poisonings in Changsha: Ease up on forced drinking during the long holiday). *Changsha Evening News*, October 5, 2010.

Li Zhengping. *Chinese Wine*. Cambridge: Cambridge University Press, 2011.

Los Angeles Times. "Moonshine Liquor Kills 33 in China." May 28, 1987.

Lucas, Louise. "Diageo's Hopes Rise over Baijiu Move." *Financial Times*, March 2, 2011.

Lu Chang and Kelly Dawson. "Drying Up the New Scene." *China Daily*, July 5, 2010.

Lu Xun. *Diary of a Madman, and Other Stories*. Translated by William A. Lyell. Honolulu: University of Hawai'i Press, 1990.

Luxury Insider. "Bai Jiu Fervor: LVMH Launches Wenjun in HK." October 21, 2011. www.luxury-insider.com/luxury-news/2011/10/bai-jiu-fervor-lvmh-launches -wenjun-in-hk.

Lu Yiyi. "Publicizing the 'Three Publics': China Lets Transparency Genie Out of the Bottle." *Wall Street Journal*, July 28, 2011. http://blogs.wsj.com/chinarealtime /2011/07/28/publicizing-the-three-publics-china-lets-transparency-genie-out -of-the-bottle.

MacMillan, Margaret. "Don't Drink the Mao-Tai." *Washingtonian*, February 1, 2007.

———. *Nixon and Mao: The Week That Changed the World*. New York: Random House, 2007.

Magistad, Mary Kay. "China's Hakka People." *PRI's The World*, April 9, 2007.

Ma Jun. "Zhongguo Xian You Yu 4000 Wan Shi Jiu Zhe 'Jiugui' Huzhu Xiaoguo Xianzhu" (China currently has forty million alcoholics, mutual support shows significant results"). *Zhongguo Xinwen Zhoukan* (China news week), June 3, 2010.

Marshall, S. J. *The Mandate of Heaven*. New York: Routledge, 2001.

Master, Farah. "As Beijing Clamps Down on Gift-Giving, Luxury Goods Losing Their Appeal." *New York Times*, September 24, 2012.

Martin, Laura C. *Tea: The Drink That Changed the World*. Tokyo: Tuttle, 2007.

McCraw, David. *Du Fu's Laments from the South*. Honolulu: University of Hawai'i Press, 1992.

McDonald, Mark. "One Chinese Liquor Brand Is the Life of the Party." *International Herald Tribune*, July 3, 2012. http://rendezvous.blogs.nytimes.com/2012/07 /03/one-chinese-liquor-brand-is-the-life-of-the-party.

McGovern, Patrick E. "Conspicuous Consumption: Ancient Feasting and Drinking." *Copia* 6 (February 2003): 15–21.

———. "Searching for the Beginnings of Winemaking." *Expedition* 41 (1999): 4–5.

———. *Uncorking the Past: The Quest for Wine, Beer, and Other Alcoholic Beverages*. Berkeley: University of California Press, 2009.

McGovern, Patrick E., Zhang Juzhong, Tang Jigen, Zhang Zhiqing, Gretchen R. Hall, Robert A. Moreau, Alberto Nunez, et al. "Fermented Beverages of

Pre- and Proto-historic China." *Proceedings of the National Academy of Sciences USA* 101, no. 51 (2004): 17593–98.

McGovern, Patrick E., Anne P. Underhill, Fang Hui, Luan Fengshi, Gretchen R. Hall, Yu Haiguang, Wang Chen-Shan, Cai Fengshu, Zhao Zhijun, and Gary M. Feinman. "Chemical Identification and Cultural Implications of a Mixed Fermented Beverage from Late Prehistoric China." *Asian Perspectives* 44 (2004): 249–75.

McMahon, Dinny. "Forget Stocks: Chinese Turn Bullish on Booze and Caterpillar Fungus." *Wall Street Journal*, January 30, 2012.

Medhurst, Walter Henry. "An Inquiry into the Proper Mode of Rendering the Word God in Translating the Sacred Scriptures into the Chinese Language." *Chinese Repository* 17, no. 4 (1848): 161–87.

Mintel. *On-Trade Alcoholic Drinks: China, June 2015.* London: Mintel Group, 2015.

"A 'Moonshine' Still in China." *World's Advance* 30, no. 4 (1915): 442.

Moore, Victoria. "Let's Raise a Glass to China's Wine." *Telegraph*, September 8, 2011.

Moreira, Peter. *Hemingway on the China Front: His WWII Spy Mission with Martha Gellhorn.* Washington DC: Potomac, 2006.

Morris, Eric A. "Get into My Car: The Congested Future of Worldwide Auto Ownership." *Freakanomics*, April 25, 2011. www.freakonomics.com/2011/04/25/get-into-my-car-the-congested-future-of-worldwide-auto-ownership.

Munsell, Charles E. "Analysis of Sam-Shu, a Chinese Liquor." *Journal of the American Chemical Society* 7 (1885): 243.

National Tribune. "Chinese Restaurants." October 4, 1888.

Osnos, Evan. "Did a Chinese Oil Executive Consume $243,604 in Booze?" *New Yorker*, May 5, 2011.

———. "Pardon Me, Would You Have Any Pabst Blue Ribbon?" *New Yorker*, July 19, 2010.

Palmer, James. "The Bro Code." *ChinaFile*, February 4, 2015. www.chinafile.com/reporting-opinion/postcard/bro-code.

Pang Xiao-Na, Han Bei-Zhong, Huang Xiao-Ning, Zhang Xin, Hou Lin-Feng, Cao Ming, Gao Li-Juan, Hu Guang-Hui, and Chen Jing-Yu. "Effect of the Environment Microbiota on the Flavour of Light-Flavour Baijiu during Spontaneous Fermentation." *Scientific Reports* 8, no. 3396 (2018): 1–11.

Park, J. P. *Art by the Book: Painting Manuals and the Leisure Life in Late Ming China.* Seattle: University of Washington Press, 2012.

Parkinson, Rhonda. "The Legend of the Historic Liquor 'Du Kang.'" *Spruce Eats*, February 4, 2019. www.thespruceeats.com/historic-liquor-du-kang-694735.

Paskin, Becky. "Diageo's Sales 'Severely Impacted' as China Bites." *Spirits Business*, July 31, 2014. www.thespiritsbusiness.com/2014/07/diageos-sales-severely-impacted-as-china-bites.

Peng Ding Qiu. *Quan Tangshi, Shang.* Shanghai: Shanghai Guji Chubanshe, 1986.

People's Daily. "How Did the Ancient Chinese Distill Spirits?" September 29, 2006.

Perlez, Jane. "Waste Project Is Abandoned Following Protests in China." *New York Times,* July 29, 2012.

Pew Research Center. "Asians Projected to Become the Largest Immigrant Group, Surpassing Hispanics." September 23, 2015. www.pewhispanic.org/2015/09/28 /modern-immigration-wave-brings-59-million-to-u-s-driving-population-growth -and-change-through-2065/ph_2015-09-28_immigration-through-2065-05.

Phillips, Tom. "Chinese General Caught with 'Pure Gold' Statue of Chairman Mao." *Telegraph,* January 14, 2014.

Pinsker, Joe. "The Future Is Expensive Chinese Food." *Atlantic,* July 13, 2016.

Polo, Marco. *The Travels of Marco Polo.* Translated by William Marsden. New York: Barnes and Noble, 2005.

Qian Guilin. "Don't Be Taken In by 'Aged' Liquor." *Global Times,* July 4, 2013.

Qu Yunxu and Wang Chen. "End of Baijiu Binge Means Party Is Over for Producers, Dealers." *Caixin,* February 21, 2013. www.caixinglobal.com/2013-02-21 /101014694.html.

Rainey, Lee Dian. *Confucius and Confucianism: The Essentials.* Malaysia: Wiley and Sons, 2010.

Ralph, Talia. "China's Elaborate Military Banquets Banned." *Global Post,* December 22, 2012. www.pri.org/stories/2012-12-22/chinas-elaborate-military-banquets -banned.

Ray, Krishnendu. *The Ethnic Restaurateur.* New York: Bloomsbury, 2016.

Reuters. "Cognac Sales Hit Record as Demand Soars in China." January 14, 2012. www.reuters.com/article/us-france-cognac/cognac-sales-hit-record-as-demand -soars-in-china-idUSTRE80D0KF20120114.

Risen, Clay. "Baijiu, the National Drink of China, Heads West." *New York Times,* December 29, 2015.

———. "Is This the Best-Selling Liquor in the World?" *Atlantic,* April 15, 2009.

Roberts, Kevin R., Junehee Kwon, Carol W. Shanklin, Pei Liu and Wen-Shen Yen. "Food Safety Practices Lacking in Independent Ethnic Restaurants." *Journal of Culinary Science and Technology* 9, no. 1 (2011): 1–16.

Rockhill, William Woodville, ed. and trans. *The Journey of William of Rubruck to the Eastern Parts of the World, 1253–55.* London: Hakluyt Society, 1900.

Roland, Denise. "Diageo Seals 'Milestone' China Acquisition." *Telegraph,* July 23, 2013.

Ruan, Victoria. "China to Ban Public Purchases of 'High-End' Alcohol." *Bloomberg Businessweek,* March 27, 2012.

Ruwitch, John. "China Cancels Waste Project after Protests Turn Violent." Reuters, July 28, 2012. www.reuters.com/article/us-china-environment-protest/china -cancels-waste-project-after-protests-turn-violent-idUSBRE86R02Y20120728.

Sala, George Augustus. *Paris Herself Again in 1878–9*. London: Vizetelly, 1884.

Samuelson, James. *The History of Drink*. London: Trübner, 1880.

Sauer, Abe. "Faux Bordeaux and Copycat Wine Spoil China's 'Homegrown' Brand Drive." *BrandChannel*, March 15, 2012. www.brandchannel.com/home/post /2012/03/15/China-Counterfeit-Wine-031512.aspx.

Schmitt, Patrick. "China Austerity Drive to Impact until 2017." *Drinks Business*, January 5, 2015. www.thedrinksbusiness.com/2015/01/china-austerity-drive -to-impact-until-2017.

Scott, John Lee. *Narrative of a Recent Imprisonment in China after the Wreck of the Kite*. London: Dalton, 1841.

Seligman, Scott D. "Everything but Rats and Puppies." *Cleaver Quarterly*, Summer 2014.

———. *The First Chinese American: The Remarkable Life of Wong Chin Foo*. Hong Kong: Hong Kong University Press, 2013.

Semple, Kirk, and Jeffrey E. Singer. "Illegal Sale of Rice Wine Thrives in Chinese Enclaves." *New York Times*, July 19, 2011.

Shanghai Daily. "Chateau Lafite Often Not What It Seems." December 5, 2011.

———. "TV Exposes Bogus Wine Scandal." December 25, 2010.

———. "Will Investors at Last Drown Their Sorrows over Baijiu?" June 21, 2012.

Shaw, Lucy. "French Wine Campaign to Tap Chinese Market." *Drinks Business*, May 9, 2012. www.thedrinksbusiness.com/2012/05/french-wine-campaign -to-tap-chinese-market.

Shaw, William. *Golden Dreams and Waking Realities*. London: Smith, Elder, 1851.

Shen, Andrew. "Reality Check: The Chinese Government Spends as Much on Alcohol as National Defense." *Business Insider*, November 16, 2011. www .businessinsider.com/china-spends-three-times-more-on-drinking-than -national-defense-2011-11.

Shen Hong. "Shenzhen Party Chief: Corruption to Blame for Pricey Moutai." *Wall Street Journal*, January 11, 2012. http://blogs.wsj.com/chinarealtime/2012 /01/11/shenzhen-party-chief-corruption-to-blame-for-chinaspricey-moutai.

Shi Nai'an. *The Water Margin*, Vol. 1. Translated by J. H. Jackson. Shanghai: Commercial Press, 1937.

Shunsuke Tabeta. "Xi's Secret Economic Weapon: Overseas Chinese." *Nikkei Asian Review*, April 3, 2017.

Simmons, Andrew. "Gastronomic Bigotry." *Slate*, June 6, 2014. www.slate.com/articles /life/food/2014/06/ethnic_restaurants_and_food_poisoning_the_subtle _racism_of_saying_chinese.html.

Smith, Craig S. "Aggressive Little Wines? China's Acquiring a Taste." *New York Times*, March 13, 2000.

Smith, Wayne C., and Richard A. Frederiksen, eds. *Sorghum: Origin, History, Technology, and Production*. New York: Wiley and Sons, 2000.

Song Shengxia. "Hard Drinking." *Global Times*, February 2, 2012.

Sonne, Paul, and James T. Areddy. "Diageo to Acquire Chinese Brand." *Wall Street Journal*, March 1, 2010.

Sonne, Paul, and Laurie Burkitt. "China Approves Diageo Baijiu Bid." *Wall Street Journal*, June 27, 2011.

South China Morning Post. "China Investigates Former Moutai Liquor Executive over Suspected Corruption: Watchdog." March 25, 2016.

———. "Two Firms Investigated over Viagra in Liquor." August 2, 2015.

Steger, Isabella. "Baijiu All Around as Diageo Wins Bid Approval." *Wall Street Journal*, June 28, 2011. http://blogs.wsj.com/exchange/2011/06/28/baijiu-all -around-as-diageo-wins-bid-approval.

Sterckx, Roel. "Alcohol and Historiography in Early China." *Global Food History* 1 (2015): 13–32.

Stevens, William K. "Does Civilization Owe a Debt to Beer?" *New York Times*, March 24, 1987.

Sun, Ben B. *Gain Report*. Global Agricultural Information Network. U.S. Department of Agriculture Foreign Agricultural Service. August 19, 2009. https://gain.fas .usda.gov/Recent%20GAIN%20Publications/National%20Wine%20Market _Shanghai%20ATO_China%20-%20Peoples%20Republic%20of_8-19-2009.pdf.

Sun Li. "Getting a Handle on Rural China's Baijiu Culture," *China Daily*, October 20, 2011.

Sun Xia, Li Xianyun, and Fei Lipeng. "A Cross-Sectional Survey of the Awareness of Common Mental Disorders among Urban and Rural Residents in Northern China." *Chinese Mental Health Journal* 10 (2009): 729–33, 741.

Tait, William. *Tait's Edinburgh Magazine* 8 (1841): 65–66.

Tam, Ruth. "How It Feels When White People Shame Your Culture's Food—Then Make It Trendy." *Washington Post*, August 31, 2015.

Tan, Clement, and John Ruwitch. "China's Downturn-Proof Booze Makers Hit Government Wall." Reuters, August 10, 2012. www.reuters.com/article /us-china-liquor/chinas-downturn-proof-booze-makers-hit-government-wall -idUSBRE8781DL20120810.

Tang Yi-Lang, Wei Hao, and Lorenzo Leggio. "Treatments for Alcohol-Related Disorders in China: A Developing Story." *Alcohol and Alcoholism* 47, no. 5 (2012): 563–70.

Tan Huileng. "China's Drinking Habits Are Changing, and That's a Big Opportunity for Beverage Makers." CNBC, December 28, 2017. www.cnbc.com/2017 /12/28/beverage-makers-chinese-are-drinking-craft-beer-wine-baijiu.html.

Telegraph. "Protesters Clash with Police in China over Pollution from Paper Factory." July 28, 2012.

Temple, Robert. *The Genius of China*. New York: Simon and Schuster, 1986.

Tian Xiaofei. *Tao Yuanming and Manuscript Culture*. Seattle: University of Washington Press, 2005.

Tsang, Patricia. *Optimal Healing*. San Francisco: Balance for Health, 2008.

Twain, Mark. *Roughing It*. Hartford CT: American, 1872.

United States Army. *Pocket Guide to China*. Washington DC: U.S. War and Navy Departments, 1942.

Uretsky, Elanah. *Occupational Hazards: Sex, Business, and HIV in Post-Mao China*. Stanford: Stanford University Press, 2016.

U.S. Congress, Senate. Joint Special Committee to Investigate Chinese Immigration. *Report of the Joint Special Committee to Investigate Chinese Immigration*. February 27, 1877. 44th Cong., 2d Sess. (1877), 31.

Valkeinen, Jutta. "Maotai: The Spirit of China." *Radio86*. Streaming audio. September 27, 2006. http://gbtimes.com/lifestyle/maotai-spirit-china (site discontinued).

Waddell, Helen, trans. *Lyrics from the Chinese*. New York: Houghton Mifflin, 1913.

Wadley, Greg, and Angus Martin. "The Origins of Agriculture: A Biological Perspective and a New Hypothesis." *Australian Biologist* 6 (June 1993): 96–105.

Waldmeir, Patti. "Beijing's Top Tipple Heads Downmarket after Communist Crackdown." *Financial Times*, November 22, 2013.

———. "Diageo: The Long View on Baijiu." *Financial Times*, March 21, 2012.

Waley, Arthur, trans. *A Hundred and Seventy Chinese Poems*. New York: Knopf, 1919.

———, trans. *More Translations from the Chinese*. New York: Knopf, 1919.

Wan, William. "China's New Leaders Focus on Fighting Corruption." *Washington Post*, December 28, 2012.

Wang, Natalie. "Chinese Official Failed to Impress Xi with RMB 99 Baijiu." *Drinks Business*, October 25, 2017. www.thedrinksbusiness.com/2017/10/chinese-official-failed-to-impress-xi-with-rmb-99-baijiu.

Wang Hongyi. "Ganbei Culture 'Kills' Anhui Village Leader." *China Daily*, November 9, 2009.

Wang Kai, ed. *Lifeweek* 675 (March 26, 2012).

Wang Ying. "Liquor Firms Hung Over from Luxury Dinner Ban." *China Daily*, December 25, 2012.

Want China Times. "Fake Chinese Liquor Makers Go Upmarket with Improved Packaging." December 14, 2012. www.wantchinatimes.com/news-subclass-cnt.aspx?id=20111214000008&cid=1103 (site discontinued).

———. "Kweichow Moutai Outshines Apple in Rewarding Shareholders." June 19, 2012. www.wantchinatimes.com/news-subclass-cnt.aspx?id=20120619000064&cid=1102 (site discontinued).

———. "LVMH Rebrands Chinese Wenjun Liquor." March 25, 2012. www.wantchinatimes.com/news-subclass-cnt.aspx?id=20120325000008&cid=1206 (site discontinued).

Watson, Burton. *Chinese Lyricism: Shih Poetry from the Second to the Twelfth Century.* New York: Columbia University Press, 1971.

Weiner, Tim. "Word for Word/Kissinger Transcripts: Sex, Spooks and the Hereafter; Private Banter with Brezhnev and Mao." *New York Times,* January 10, 1999.

Wheeler, Carolynne. "Less Lavish Banquets? China Feels Squeeze of Anti-consumption Campaign." *Globe and Mail,* March 25, 2013.

Will, George F. "Survival of the Sudsiest." *Washington Post,* July 10, 2008.

Wong Chin Foo. "Chinese Cooking." *Biddeford Daily Journal,* August 1, 1885.

———. "Chinese Cooking." *Brooklyn Daily Eagle,* July 6, 1884.

———. "The Chinese Cuisine." *Washington Post,* July 13, 1884.

———. "Chinese Food for New Yorkers." *Sun,* March 19, 1888.

Wood, Janice. "Chinese Herb May Curb Binge Drinking." *PsychCentral,* May 17, 2012. http://psychcentral.com/news/2012/05/18/chinese-herb-may-curb-binge-drinking/38861.html.

World Health Organization. *Global Status Report on Alcohol and Health.* Geneva: WHO Press, 2011.

Wuhan Wanbao. "Hubei Jiucheng Gongwuyuan Shenti You Yang Jiujing Gan Yi Bei Shiwei Zhiyebing" (90 Percent of Hubei Officials Suffer from Alcohol-Related Liver Disease, Seen as Occupational Hazard). November 14, 2011.

Xiang Yu-Tao, Xin Ma, Lu Jin-Yan, Cai Zhuo-Ji, Li Shu-Ran, Xiang Ying-Qiang, Guo Hong-Li, et al. "Alcohol-Related Disorders in Beijing, China: Prevalence, Socio-demographic Correlates, and Unmet Need for Treatment." *Alcoholism Clinical and Experimental Research* 33, no. 6 (2009): 1111–18.

Xie Yu. "Ban Moutai at Official Banquets, Says Deputy." *China Daily,* January 17, 2012.

———. "Gan Bei to Top Baijiu Stocks Even as Outlook Dims for Traditional Chinese Alcoholic Drinks." *South China Morning Post,* February 1, 2016.

Xinhua. "'Bordeaux of Chinese Liquor' Promoted in Britain." May 24, 2012.

———. "China's Drunk Driving Cases Drop 40 Pct Following New Law." May 23, 2012.

———. "China's Motor Vehicles Top 233 Mln." July 17, 2012.

———. "Posthumous Award Removed from Official Who Died after Night." *China Daily,* March 13, 2008.

Xu Ganrong and Bao Tongfa. *Grandiose Survey of Chinese Alcoholic Drinks and Beverages.* Jiangnan University. 1998. www.sytu.edu.cn/zhgjiu/jmain.htm (site discontinued).

Xu Junqian. "Liquor Maker to Join Online Sales Market." *China Daily,* October 21, 2015.

Xu Yuanzhong, trans. *300 Tang Poems.* Beijing: China Translation Export, 1987.

Yan, Alice. "Drinks Group Fights Back in Row on Toxic Chemical." *South China Morning Post,* November 21, 2012.

Yang, Mayfair Mei-hui. *Gifts, Favors, and Banquets.* Ithaca: Cornell University Press, 1994.

Yang Chen, ed. *Luzhou Laojiao: Zhongguo Rongyao* (Luzhou Laojiao: China's pride). Chengdu: Qiyuan Zhiban, 2010.

Yang Xianyi and Gladys Yang, trans. *Poetry and Prose of the Tang and Song*. Beijing: Panda Books, 1984.

Yao Feng, Yi Bin, Shen Caihong, Tao Fei, Liu Yumin, Lin Zhixin, and Xu Ping. "Chemical Analysis of the Chinese Liquor Luzhoulaojiao by Comprehensive Two-Dimensional Gas Chromatography/Time-of-Flight Mass Spectrometry." *Scientific Reports* 5, no. 9553 (2015): 1–6.

Yardley, Jim. "Got a Mint, Comrade? Chinese Ban Liquid Lunch." *New York Times*, March 8, 2008.

———. "In China, a Patriotic Death Reeks of Alcohol." *New York Times*, March 14, 2008.

Yeo, Kenneth. "Bright Prospects Seen for China's Wine Industry." *China Daily*, December 1, 2011.

Yong Kwek Ping. *Due Diligence in China*. Singapore: Wiley and Sons, 2013.

Yuan Lijun. *Reconceiving Women's Equality in China*. Lanham: Lexington Books, 2005.

Yu Renqui. "Chop Suey: From Chinese Food to Chinese American Food." In *Chinese America: History and Perspectives, 1987*, 87–100. San Francisco: Chinese Historical Society of America, 1987.

Zhang Feng. "'No Trouble Brewing,' Beer Industry Insists." *China Daily*, July 14, 2005.

Zhang Liping and Li You. "Brewing Trouble." *Sixth Tone*, February 2018. http://interaction.sixthtone.com/feature/2018/brewing-trouble-maotai/index.html.

Zhang Qin and Lucy Carmody. *Food Safety in China*. London: Responsible Research, 2009.

Zhang Shidong. "China's Distillers Say Ganbei as Banquets and Parties Resume." *South China Morning Post*, April 28, 2017.

Zhang Wenxue and Xie Ming, eds. *Zhongguo Jiu Ji Jiu Wenhua Gailun* (Introduction to Chinese alcohol and drinking culture). Chengdu: Sichuan University Press, 2010.

Zhang Yi, He Yue, and Zhou Changqing. "Nation's Oldest Brewery Unearthed in Northeast China." *Xinhua*, May 14, 2012.

Zhao Enuo. "350,000 Chinese Students to Study Abroad in 2011." *People's Daily*, December 19, 2011.

Zheng Yangwen. *The Social Life of Opium in China*. Singapore: Cambridge University Press, 2005.

Zhou Huiying and Ma Zhenhua. "Learning to Refuse Toasts in the Season of Ganbei." *China Daily*, January 26, 2012.

Zhou Xin and Koh Gui Qing. "China Liquor Maker Jacks Up Prices by 30 Pct." Reuters, August 31, 2011. https://uk.reuters.com/article/idUKL4E7JV07820110831.

INDEX

addiction. *See* alcoholism

adulterated alcohol. *See* product safety

agriculture, 21, 46–49, 79–80, 83, 115, 170, 184

alcohol, counterfeit. *See* counterfeit alcohol

alcohol consumption in China, demographic changes, 83–85, 91, 182–87, 253–57

alcohol dehydrogenase deficiency, 56–57, 184, 187

alcohol dependency. *See* alcoholism

alcoholism, 178–79, 183–86, 190–95, 232

alcohol poisoning, 161–62, 165–67, 171–77, 179–81, 189–91, 206

alcohol prohibition: in China, 53, 55–67, 61, 68, 131, 180; in the United States, 171, 239

alcohol tolerance, 57, 82, 101, 148–49, 153, 182–86

alcohol use disorder. *See* alcoholism

anti-Chinese sentiment. *See* prejudice

anti-corruption campaign, 197–208, 256

anti-graft campaign. *See* anti-corruption campaign

ape wine, 45–46

Asian flush. *See* alcohol dehydrogenase deficiency

authenticity, 243

baijiu: chemical analysis of, 172–74, 217–9; classification of, 213–17; cocktails, 5, 33, 221, 244–47, 256–58, 263–65; definition of, xi, 2, 33, 52, 80; exports, 177, 240, 252–53, 256–58; origins of, 74–84; serving, 151–53, 159; taste of, 213–19, 223–24, 228, 238–41

baijiu industry, 5–6, 21–24, 86–88, 90–91, 98, 140–41, 169–77 , 186, 197–208, 247–53, 256–58

baojianjiu. See medicinal alcohol

Batu Khan, 78

Beard, James, 232–33

beer, xi, 26, 38, 39, 44, 46–49, 51–52, 56, 59, 61, 75, 86, 126, 164, 171–72, 253, 256

"beer-before-bread" theory, 45–48

Beijing, 6–7, 23, 73, 76, 81, 85–88, 95, 194, 220–21, 242, 245, 247

Bi Gan, 55, 148–49

binge drinking, 54–55, 65–67, 69–71, 81–82, 179–95, 197

Book of Odes, 50–51, 54, 64, 255

Book of Rites, 49, 64, 183

Boyce, Jim, 212, 247